THE CLIMBER'S BEDSIDE BOOK

by the same author

*

ROCK AND ROPE
MODERN MOUNTAINEERING
BLUE REMEMBERED HILLS

*

NUMBER TWO-NINETY
GENTLEMAN JOHNNY
THE SEA OFFICER
WOLFE COMMANDS YOU
HIS WAS THE FIRE
THE ADMIRAL'S FANCY

*

INDESTRUCTIBLE JONES
MIDSHIPMAN QUINN
QUINN OF THE 'FURY'
MIDSHIPMAN QUINN WINS THROUGH
QUINN AT TRAFALGAR
THE FLYING ENSIGN
BYRD OF THE 95TH

The Climber's Bedside Book

SHOWELL STYLES

FABER AND FABER
24 Russell Square
London

*First published in 1968
by Faber and Faber Limited
24 Russell Square London WC1
Printed in Great Britain by
Latimer Trend & Co Ltd Plymouth
All rights reserved*

SBN 571 08196 7

© *Showell Styles 1968*

FOREWORD

Eric Shipton was the first to observe that bedsores are the occupational disease of the Himalayan mountaineer. Jack Longland, on the 1933 Everest Expedition, 'went to considerable trouble to see that the expedition was well equipped with a travelling library'. The climber who has not at some time luxuriated in book and blankets while the snowstorm shook the Alpine hut, or while the rain lashed his tent in British hills, does not exist. Thus, although the term 'climber' does not usually connote studious inaction, the words *climber*, *bedside*, and *book* united in the title of this volume are not as unrelated as they might seem.

What does the mountaineer look for in the book at his bedside? It depends, of course, on the mountaineer and the bedside. Remote from his beloved mountains, he will like to recall the glories and discomforts and rewards—*Bedsides* less snug than his present one, *Dawns* that repaid the night of unease with a splendid ascent. Some like to read themselves to sleep with a chuckle; for them the humour of the game, or the account of a climb whereon there was no shadow of storm or tragedy, leads to *Pleasant Dreams*. Some, relatives of the Fat Boy in *Pickwick*, prefer to make their flesh creep with tales of *The Supernatural* or with one of those terrible stories which are the *Nightmares* of mountaineering record. Others, perhaps engaging in drowsy argument between sleeping-bag and sleeping-bag, will want to confirm a fact of mountaineering history—the height of a great peak or the deeds and dates of a famous climber.

FOREWORD

In *The Climber's Bedside Book* I have tried to supply these varied needs. The two reference sections are arranged alphabetically: information about fifty of the famous climbers of the past is to be found under the heading *Soaring Spirits*, a hundred peaks of special fame or interest are listed under *The Mountains Wait*. For the rest, I have drawn true mountaineering stories from the records of many great climbers but have not hesitated to include two or three sketches from my own mountain experience. And if any sceptic should object that those encounters with the Supernatural could not possibly be called 'true', I would answer that they were all certainly true for the persons who experienced them.

CONTENTS

Foreword	*page* 5
The Climber's Bedside	
The First Mountain Tent	13
Mr. Kennedy at Boval	18
Above the White Spider	24
Alpine Hut	31
The Ice-Cave on Kommunizma	36
At Camp 4W	41
Pleasant Dreams	
The Dream of Mr. Smith	49
Prisoner's Dream	55
The Gully that Was	61
Dream of a Virgin	68
The Conquest of Mac	73
The Dream of Eternity	80
The Supernatural	
The Grey Man	87
Geister on the Matterhorn	92
'I have to go on'	97
Yeti	101
The Horns of Elfland	105
Soaring Spirits	
Fifty Names famous in Mountaineering History	111

CONTENTS

NIGHTMARE
- The Prophecy of Doctor Hamel — 157
- The Survivor — 163
- The Cold Hell — 170
- No Way Back — 178

DAWN
- With the Goal Forgot — 191
- The West Face — 197
- High Table — 204
- Dawn on Everest — 209

THE MOUNTAINS WAIT
- One hundred notable mountains — 217

BIBLIOGRAPHY — 250

INDEX — 252

TEXT ILLUSTRATIONS

1. Diagram of the Eigerwand   *page* 26
2. Craig y Cae, Cader Idris, from Llyn y Cae   62
3. A fragment of music   108
4. The Brenva Face of Mont Blanc   193

THE CLIMBER'S BEDSIDE

The guardian stars their watches keep,
 The mountain walls their ward extend,
Where Nature holds in quiet sleep
 Her own interpreter and friend.
                    D. W. FRESHFIELD

THE FIRST MOUNTAIN TENT

Edward Whymper was barely twenty-one years old when he made his first attempt on the unclimbed Matterhorn. At the time of the successful and tragic first ascent of that mountain he was only twenty-five. These facts, often unrealized by climbers familiar with the most dramatic episode in mountaineering history, go some way towards explaining the youthful imprudences and bravados which stand out from the classic pages of *Scrambles Amongst the Alps;* the solitary explorations, the angry misunderstanding with Carrel, that frenzied hurling-down of boulders from the conquered summit. In his twentieth year, the year of his first visit to the Alps on a sketching tour, he contrived to serve what must be the shortest Alpine apprenticeship on record. Always unaccompanied, he wandered and scrambled on glaciers, rock-faces, and snowslopes, experiencing—naturally enough—a number of hairbreadth escapes. The next year, with only these few weeks of novitiate behind him, he set out with Reynaud, Macdonald and two local porters to climb Mont Pelvoux in the Dauphiné, then thought to be unclimbed and even unclimbable. They succeeded—it was in fact the second ascent—but were overtaken by night on the descent and had to bivouac at 10,500 feet.

'It would be difficult to select a more destestable locality for a night out of doors. There was not shelter of any kind, and it was too steep to promenade. Loose rubbly stones covered the ground, and had to be moved before we could sit with any comfort. Reynaud . . . at last settled down to a deep dramatic despair, and wrung his hands with frantic gesture,

THE CLIMBER'S BEDSIDE

as he exclaimed "Oh, malheur, malheur! Oh misérables!" '

There was thunder and lightning and a freezing wind. The party got out its reserves of sustenance but failed to extract any comfort therefrom; which was not surprising, seeing that they consisted of 'six and a half cigars, two boxes of vesuvians, one-third of a pint of brandy-and-water, and half a pint of spirits of wine'. It was very probably the misery of this impromptu bivouac that led to the designing of the Whymper tent.

Born in England during the winter of 1861, Whymper's mountain tent was to have an effective and popular lifetime of at least seventy-two years, for Hugh Ruttledge used twelve Whymper tents on the Everest Expedition of 1933. It was a product of unhappy experience with an earlier design suggested by a Mr. Francis Galton and constructed by Whymper for use on that first Matterhorn attempt. 'Deserted' by the two Carrels, Whymper and his gigantic but cowardly guide pitched this tent on the snow of the Col du Lion, below the upper part of the Matterhorn's Italian ridge, but found it useless as a shelter. 'The flaps of the tent would not keep down, the pegs would not stay in, and it exhibited so marked a desire to go to the top of the Dent Blanche that we thought it prudent to take it down and sit upon it.' This tent was of the ridge pattern, made to be used with two alpenstocks as poles. The sides had cords attached for securing to stones and were extended in flaps which were turned in underneath. Whymper, a born engineer and designer (as his often boring descriptions of tunnelling and railway-construction show), perceived that two upright poles and a ridge cord were inefficient supports for a tent to be used in exposed situations above the snowline and devised the first A-frame—the principle used for the high-altitude tents of today. The sewn-in groundsheet, an invariable feature of the modern mountain tent, was also his invention, though he had not the advantage of the strong lightweight fabrics that were to be available a century later.

THE FIRST MOUNTAIN TENT

Most mountaineers are campers nowadays, and Whymper's own description of his brain-child is worth quoting:

'Its base was just under six feet square, and a cross-section perpendicular to its length was an equilateral triangle, the sides of which were six feet long. It was intended to accommodate four persons. It was supported by four ash-poles, six feet and a half long, and one inch and a quarter thick, tapering at the top to an inch and an eighth; these were shod with iron points. The order of proceeding in the construction of the tent was as follows. Holes were drilled through the poles above five inches from their tops, for the insertion of two wrought-iron bolts, three inches long and one quarter of an inch thick. The bolts were then inserted, and the two pairs of poles were set out (and fixed up by a cord) to the proper dimensions. The roof was then put on. This was made of the rough, unbleached calico called forfar, which can be obtained in six-foot widths, and it was continued round for about two feet on each side to the floor. The width of the material was the length of the tent, and seams were thus avoided in the roof. The forfar was sewn round each pole, particular care being taken to avoid wrinkles, and to get the whole perfectly taut. The flooring was next put in and sewn down to the forfar. This was of the ordinary plaid mackintosh, about nine feet square, the surplus three feet being continued up the sides to prevent draughts. One end was then permanently closed by a triangular piece of forfar, which was sewn down to that which was already fixed. The other end was left open, and had two triangular flaps that overlapped each other, and which were fastened up when we were inside by pieces of tape. Lastly, the forfar was nailed down to the poles to prevent the tent getting out of shape. The cord which was used for climbing served for the tent. It was passed over the crossed poles and underneath the ridge of the roof, and the two ends—one fore and the other aft—were easily secured to pieces of rock.'

It would not be difficult to make a Whymper tent from this verbal blueprint, *mutatis mutandis* where the materials are concerned. Nor would it be merely the construction of a useless exhibit. The great ascents of Freshfield and Moore in the Caucasus and of Martin Conway in the Himalaya were all done with the aid of the Whymper tent. If it is bulky compared with more up-to-date models, at least it can accommodate a climbing-party of four; and its very simple design allows it to be erected in two minutes, which is about one-tenth of the time it would take to set up two two-man tents of modern design. Of course it would be heavy; Whymper puts its weight complete at twenty-three pounds without flysheet. And it is doubtful whether the annoyance of toting about a six-and-a-half-foot bundle would be offset nowadays by the convenience noted in the Lonsdale *Mountaineering* of 1935: 'It may be useful to know that the step of a twelve horse-power motor-car will carry two Whymper tents with the poles already in position.' For modern climbers do not hire Swiss porters to carry up their tents.

It was little Luc Meynet, you remember, who carried the famous tent high on the Matterhorn on more than one occasion; Meynet the hunchback of Breuil, 'an ungainly, wobbling figure . . . he seemed to be built on principle with no two parts alike.' Whymper comments (a little brutally, perhaps) that Meynet's deformities were handily arranged for tent-carrying. But the twisted dwarf was a mountaineer too, and it was with him alone—the Carrels having once again deserted the party—that Whymper in July 1862 made his sixth attempt to climb the Matterhorn from the Italian side and reached a height of 13,460 feet, only 1,200 feet below the summit. They pitched the tent at about 13,000 feet on the Col du Lion, where Whymper had camped on his first attempt and where he and Meynet had stood together before.

THE FIRST MOUNTAIN TENT

'It was the first time Meynet had seen the view unclouded. The poor little deformed peasant gazed upon it silently and reverently for a time, and then, unconsciously, fell on one knee in an attitude of adoration, and clasped his hands, exclaiming in ecstasy, "Oh, beautiful mountains!" His actions were as appropriate as his words were natural, and tears bore witness to the reality of his emotion.'

Somehow one feels more affection for Luc Meynet than for the Lion of the Matterhorn himself.

Fortunately perhaps for him, it was not the hunchback of Breuil who carried up the tent three years later, when Whymper's long siege of the mountain ended in triumph and disaster. One of 'old' Peter Taugwalder's two sons bore it up the easy lower part of the Hörnli Ridge from Zermatt to about 11,000 feet, where it was pitched on the stony slopes of the east face above the Furggen Glacier at noon. Michel Croz and 'young' Peter went on to reconnoitre and returned to report 'not a difficulty, not a single difficulty!' The party passed the remainder of that perfect afternoon basking in the sun or sketching, and at sunset gathered at the tent to arrange for the night. The Rev. Charles Hudson, with his young friend Douglas Hadow and Croz the guide, elected to sleep outside under the calm beauty of the stars; unaware that this was to be their last night on earth. Whymper and Lord Francis Douglas shared the tent with old Peter and his sons. 'Long after dusk,' says Whymper with a rare touch of artistry, 'the cliffs above echoed with our laughter and the songs of the guides; for we were happy that night in camp, and feared no evil.'

With the first light of a superlatively calm and clear morning they assembled outside the tent. The youngest of the Taugwalders started down for Zermatt. The remaining seven men began the climb that was to end in success; the climb from which four of them were not to return.

MR. KENNEDY AT BOVAL

It seems incredible that anyone should have been so impercipient as to describe the Victorians and their Age as 'stodgy'. Consider our own era with its grimy ideals of uniformity and security; compare the variety and brilliance, the adventurous individualism, of the mid nineteenth century; and ask where the epithet *stodgy* will stick. Injustice and poverty were part of the Victorian scene along with privilege and riches, but a half-day tour of London or Liverpool will reveal that these things are still with us. For the gentlemen who lived on inherited wealth we have merely substituted the Football Pool winners. And it might well be maintained that the Idle Rich of our own day are less useful members of society (they are certainly less brilliant) than the Idle Rich of the Victorian Era.

Mr. Edward Shirley Kennedy was one of the Idle Rich. He had been left a fortune by his father at the age of sixteen and saw no reason to distribute it among his less fortunate fellow citizens or to undertake any kind of productive labour. Let us not be too censorious. Into a million modern homes there comes each week, with the approval of our rulers, a paper offering a quarter of a million pounds to anyone who will risk a shilling on 'farthing points', and pointing out that 'You Too Could Live A Life of Luxury'. Kennedy could have Lived A Life Of Luxury. Instead, like the majority of privileged Victorians, he seized the opportunity of a life of thought and action. He had the inquiring spirit characteristic of his era. He published his book *Thoughts On Being* when he was thirty-

MR. KENNEDY AT BOVAL

three. His persistent question 'Is it right?' was applied to everything and became something of a jest among his less reflective companions. He lived for a time among thieves and garrotters to study their ways, tramped from London to Brighton, became captain of the London Amateur Sculling Club, and was a pioneer of guideless climbing in the Alps. It was while Kennedy, with his friend the Reverend J. F. Hardy and three companions, was taking part in the first British ascent of the Finsteraarhorn that the formation of the Alpine Club was determined upon.

In July 1861 Kennedy and Hardy started from Kredig's inn at Pontresina for the ascent of Piz Bernina. At 13,304 feet the highest of the Bernina Alps, Piz Bernina had already been climbed once; this was to be the first British ascent. For guide they had the village cobbler, a man of uncommon ability and character named Jenni, with Jenni's brother Fleuri and another local man as his lieutenants. 'I promise, gentlemen,' Jenni had said more than once, 'to provide everything for the great ascent.' And he kept his promise, beginning with the provision of sleeping-quarters at 9,000 feet, high above the slow-creeping ice of the Morteratsch Glacier.

The 'so-called châlet' of Boval was typical of the climber's advanced base in the Golden Age of mountaineering. The Whymper tent had not yet been devised, and though the bivouac among the high rocks was the start for many a historic ascent there was as often as not some rough and solitary hut, the summer shelter of Alpine herdsmen, where a few hours of the night could be spent in rest before setting forth by starlight for the snows. The Boval hut stood close to a huge flat rock on the crest of a precipice overhanging the glacier, its walls of unmortared stones admitting the chill wind and its fir-tree beams imperfectly covered with wooden shingles which rattled in the blast. There was a crude fireplace at one end and at the other a very dirty wooden dais raised three feet above the beaten mud of the floor. Mist was writhing up the crags below it, lightning playing on the pale snowcrests overhead, when the two Englishmen and their guides toiled up to the hut in the evening of a stormy day. They, too, were typical of their kind. Kennedy slim and keen-featured with a downward drooping moustache; Hardy—a burlier figure—sidewhiskered and jovial; both, of course, wearing the inevitable thick tweed jackets and breeches and heavy nailed boots and carrying long ash-poles tipped with iron. Behind them the three sturdy peasants carried the food and equipment, including the coils of hemp rope 'strong enough to moor the *Great Eastern*'. Jenni and his brother had collected wood on the way up, and as soon as they were all inside the hut with the rickety door shut a fire was lit, its pungent smoke instantly penetrating to every corner of the tiny building.

To Kennedy it seemed that he and his four companions completely filled the hut. It was soon apparent that he was mistaken. The two owners of the hut—a shepherd and a goatherd—arrived, tall men in conical hats and long black cloaks dripping with rain, wooden sabots on their feet and short black pipes in their mouths. They came in; the sheep came in; the goats came in. Men and animals were packed tightly together in the smoke-filled space until the closed door flew open under the pressure—an opportunity which was seized by a she-ass and her foal who wished to join the party. Hardy, less patient than his friend, charged resolutely with his alpenstock and drove these last intruders outside, discovering in the act that the rain had stopped and the storm was rolling away to eastward. The climbing-party extricated itself from the hut and established itself in freer quarters on the flat rock to prepare for the evening meal.

From its deep bed below their perch the glacier swept up, past green icefalls and the blue streaks of bergschrunds, to the *névé* under a cirque of splendid snowpeaks. Piz Palu, Piz Zupo,

MR. KENNEDY AT BOVAL

Crast' Aguzza towered high above an amphitheatre of snow and crag, and farther to the right soared the shoulders and ridges of Piz Bernina itself, the summit invisible beyond the giant buttresses that rose behind the hut. Looking outwards from the Boval ledge, they saw the sun sinking redly into the welter of departing storm-clouds, leaving a clear sky where the first pale stars twinkled. The guides had carried out their pine-logs, and now a huge bonfire was lit in the centre of the flat rock. The two herdsmen joined them for the meal of bread and meat and wine; and afterwards, as they sat round the blaze with the red glow on their faces and the blue twilight dropping round them from the glimmer of the high snows, songs English and Bergomasque echoed from the walls of ice and rock.

It was half-past ten before the dying fire and the cold breath from the darkened snowfields drove them into the Boval hut to get what sleep they could. Hardy, casting himself down on the hard dais in the darkness, leapt up again hastily when a high-pitched moan sounded in his ear. A small white bitch, nestling in a corner with three sightless puppies, was protesting against the threat of destruction to her litter. At length the seven men had somehow established themselves in a close-packed row on the creaking planks, with due allowance for the anxious mother, and while the sheep and goats stank and shifted in the darkness and the five peasants snored in chorus Kennedy tried to sleep. He needed sleep, for he was to start at midnight for a great peak by a route that was quite uncharted and probably difficult, where success was doubtful and the only certain thing was that body and mind would be at the full stretch of endeavour for twelve hours at the very least. He had no map to help him, no guidebook with diagram and description, no certificated guide with expert knowledge of mountain-craft. The sturdy Jenni (who had promised to provide everything) had brought along a leathern belt for each of the party, with metal rings attached through which the rope could be passed and the ends held by way of safeguard; this was the measure of rope-tactics in 1861. Much as he needed that couple of hours of restful slumber, Kennedy could only doze and dreamily reflect on past days and nights. 'How many a time had I sought to stretch my limbs upon these uneasy troughs, dignified by the natives with the name of beds!' The snores, the stink, the fiery biting of the inevitable fleas (a concomitant of almost every Alpine climb in those days) kept sleep from him. There would have been little enough for him in any case, for shortly after eleven the guides were astir and preparing breakfast—or, more accurately, a second supper.

The rivulet in which Kennedy and Hardy bathed faces and hands was silver in the clear moonlight, and icy cold. Far overhead the Bernina peaks loomed enormous in the night sky. At ten minutes past midnight they were away, groping down the blackness of a vast boulder-slope to the ice of the glacier; and the Boval hut, with its 'bedside' of sheep and goats, puppies and herdsmen, was one more memory to add to the treasures accumulated by the author of *Thoughts On Being*.

The record of that exciting day's climbing is perpetuated in *Peaks, Passes and Glaciers*. Here we rejoin the victorious mountaineers on the last part of the descent. It is twilight, they are lost in the intricacies of the glacier, and they have been on their feet for nineteen hours performing continuous feats of gymnastics and endurance. It is perfectly plain that there is no onward way through the tilted maze of ice-chasms and snow-bridges. But Jenni has a special reason for haste. 'Wir *mussen* vörwarts!'—and he leaps an obstructing crevasse, cuts steps up a perilous ice-wall, leads the way at last off the glacier. There is a glimmer of torchlight down the darkling hillside, scintillant in reflection on the bottles of wine held aloft by half a dozen men. Jenni beams delightedly. 'These are my friends, come to meet us. Didn't I promise to provide everything?'

After the reviving draught, the short descent through pinewoods to the mountain road. A carriage is waiting—'a gorgeous contrivance, drawn by a white pony'. Kennedy and Hardy climb wearily into the seats of honour, and Jenni produces two huge bunches of artificial flowers tied with white ribbons which he fastens on the Englishmen's hats as they clatter down the winding road to Pontresina. Just outside the village the whole population of Pontresina is waiting, headed by Herr Saratz, the President of the Republic of Ober-Engadin, and his brother. One on either side of the carriage, these notabilities doff hats and present mighty bouquets—of real flowers this time—while the Pontresina band strikes up *God Save the Queen* with more enthusiasm than accuracy. The carriage rolls on towards the bonfire that illuminates the village square and halts amid the plaudits of the crowd. Kennedy and Hardy, bouquet in one hand and flower-decked hat in the other, bow and grin in a state between bewilderment and utter weariness. 'We felt that our triumphal entry was wholly undeserved, and were quite unable to express our sense of the kind feelings that had suggested it.'

But if they were the heroes of the occasion, it was really Jenni's day. He had promised to provide everything; and he had certainly kept his promise.

ABOVE THE WHITE SPIDER

The bulge of green ice was only ten or twelve feet high, one of a hundred thousand such details on the tremendous vertical wall. Like the four gloved and goggled figures who climbed stiffly and with infinite caution up to it, linked now by a single rope, it was utterly lost in the vastness of the face. The Eigerwand, the north face of the Eiger, is a precipice more than a mile high from base to summit and half a mile wide, its sheer facets of rock vertical or overhanging except where the veneer of ice finds hold on a slightly receding angle. On such a wall men feel themselves smaller than ants. Even the watchers at Kleine Scheidegg, peering anxiously through telescopes whenever the grey rainclouds parted for an instant, saw them as tiny figures impossibly small for the hugeness of their undertaking. The clouds closed finally across the mountain, soaking up the flood of twilight like blotting-paper. It was 9 p.m. in the evening of 23rd July 1938; the beginning of the third night the climbers had spent on the Eigerwand.

Andreas Heckmair was in the lead and first over the bulge, chipping immature steps in the smooth ice for the front claws of his crampons. A foot in front of his nose the rock-wall rose vertical, towering into the darkening mists overhead, stretching away on either hand into obscurity. It looked unclimbable and it had never been climbed; Heckmair and his companions were higher than any man had ever been on the North Face, though they were still more than a thousand feet vertically below the summit of the Eiger. Tomorrow that last thousand feet had to be climbed, for retreat down the 5,000 feet that had taken them fifty hazardous hours to climb, though in theory just possible, was unthinkable for men as tired and cold as they were—and one of the party was injured. Heckmair looked desperately for a place, any place, where they could spend the night. There was a ledge running across the wall just above him, an intermittent shelf marked in the dim light by the narrow band of snow that rested on it. At its widest it was as broad as the sole of a climbing-boot. Heckmair called down to the men who clung to the ice below him.

'We bivouac! Come on!'

Ludvig Vörg, his climbing partner and a Bavarian like himself, followed Heckmair. Fritz Kasparek and Heinrich Harrer, the Austrians, joined them. They had climbed as two ropes until the great avalanche pouring down the White Spider had nearly taken them down with it and torn all the skin from the back of Kasparek's hand. Now they were one party, linked for life or death until the Eigerwand was climbed.

Heckmair, flattened like a lizard against the rock-wall, was banging in pitons above the ledge. Not only he and his companions, but also every item of their equipment, had to be tied securely to the face if they were to live through that night and the next day. Looking downwards over his shoulder he could see the grey-green knob of the ice-bulge close under his boot-heels and beyond it nothing but empty space filled with shadowy mist. By leaning outward a little—testing the driven piton to which he had fastened himself with a snaplink—he could just see a white ribbon of ice diving downwards between snow-plastered overhangs into the grey vacancy. That was the 'leg' of the White Spider, up which they had just climbed, escaping death by what Harrer had called 'an outright miracle'. It was something to know that the most dangerous place on the whole 6,000 feet of continuous hazard had been passed, was below them now. But if anything was accidentally dropped (and everything they had with them was vitally necessary to

DIAGRAM OF THE EIGERWAND

GRINDELWALD
3500 FEET
BELOW

F = First Pillar
H = Hinterstoisser
    Traverse
1 = First Icefield
2 = Second Icefield
3 = Third Icefield
R = The Ramp

T = The Traverse
W = The White
    Spider
B = Final Bivouac
E = Exit Cracks
S = Summit Icefield

survival) it would fall straight to the screes a vertical mile below. At ever-increasing speed it would shoot past all the terrible features of their route: down the sprawling ice-trough of the White Spider, that unavoidable avalanche-trap which is the Eigerwand's supreme test of skill and courage; down past the Traverse and the Ramp, to bound over the ice-nose between the Second and Third Icefields; down through thin air past the glassy sheet of the First Icefield and the sheer rock-wall of the Hinterstoisser Traverse, to embed itself deep in one of the gigantic avalanche cones at the bottom. That way they would go too, if their strength or their luck failed.

Heckmair had succeeded in making himself and Vörg reasonably secure to the banged-in pegs. Vörg could manage a sitting posture with a few inches of his rump on the ledge and a sling to hold him in balance, but Heckmair had to adopt a half-crouching stance, supported by his crampons nicked into a plaque of ice below the ledge. His head rested on Vörg's back. There was no room here for Kasparek and Harrer, so they found a point of attachment ten feet away from the others. The ledge below it was too narrow to sit on. They emptied their rucksacks, hanging the contents from carefully driven pitons, and slung the sacks from more pitons so that they could put their feet into them and support themselves. By the time they were ready to face the long night at 12,000 feet above the sea it was quite dark, and the abyss under their feet was a pit of blackness.

Each of these four men was a man in a million—in ten million, perhaps. The strongest, bravest, most athletic human being in the world could not have taken the road they had been following, unless he had served their long apprenticeship. Nor would it have been enough to have mastered the finest details of mountaincraft, to possess nerves of steel and wills of iron. Heckmair and his three comrades had learned by heart everything that had been noted and written about the Eigerwand; they had watched its behaviour in fair weather and foul, studied where the avalanches of snow or stones came pouring down, planned over the months the mechanics of rope and peg that would be needed on the dizzy traverses. They had learned much, too, from the stories of the ten men who had attempted the climb before them; but only two of these stories had they heard at first-hand, for eight of the ten had been killed on the Eigerwand. Above all, they had had to acquire, by hard experience, knowledge of the hidden reserves a man may draw on in emergency. It was this special knowledge that had enabled them to survive the drenching cold of the cascades pouring down from the overhangs, the dozens of small avalanches and the big one that had caught them on the White Spider. Now they were drenched to the skin and chilled to the bone, exhausted and in extreme discomfort; cut off from all hope of retreat, with bad weather the only certainty for the next eighteen hours. Yet they were happy.

Incredibly, in that extraordinary situation, they were happy. 'This sense of peace increased to a conscious glow of happiness,' says Heinrich Harrer in his book *The White Spider*, writing of that night. And he adds that this was one of the rare times when happiness was immediately recognizable, not merely realized in retrospect as it is in the experience of most of us.

Vörg had the one cooking pot and a little stove. Somehow (his writhings and contortions can be guessed at) he brewed coffee, scooping up and melting snow from ledge and cranny. A traversing rope had been slung across betweeen the two pairs of men, and on it the pot was drawn back and forth between them, hanging from a snaplink. Hour after hour Vörg brewed and the pot journeyed until all the coffee was gone. None of the four could eat; drink was all they wanted. And cigarettes—but their cigarettes were a pulpy mass in their soaked clothing. The cold black hours crept on. Heckmair dozed, supported by his comrade's broad back; and Vörg stayed hunched and perfectly still so that their leader could get the rest that might make the difference between life and death for all of them. Harrer and Kasparek had brought a Zdarsky tent-sack, a flimsy envelope of close-woven fabric, and this they managed to pull over both of them as they hung suspended in their rucksack 'stirrups'. Kasparek slept a little in spite of the pain of his flayed hand. Harrer, drifting into a twilight state between waking and sleeping, heard the stealthy unceasing whisper as of a soft brush drawn continuously across their covering, and knew that it was snowing. Far up on the steepness of the summit icefield the tiny flakes would be settling, clinging precariously until by sheer weight of their millions they would slide off and come roaring down as an avalanche. Already the snow-slides were hissing occasionally over the the skin of the sack—small and harmless cascades these, almost instantly discharged as the snow lodged in some fissure high overhead. There was little or no danger of a big avalanche sweeping down on their bivouac-place. They knew (it was Heckmair's reason for staying here instead of going a little higher in search of roomier quarters) that the wall above them was topped by huge overhangs, so that any avalanche pouring from the summit snows to the White Spider—as all avalanches did—must fall outside of them.

Harrer thought about those overhangs, for the hundredth time. They were totally unclimbable and there was no way of getting past them on the right. On the left, soaring up at a very steep diagonal from their present position, there was a hardly perceptible yielding of the general verticality in the form of a long narrow gully. This was to be their route tomorrow—as far, if the gully could be climbed, as the impossible wall of ice-covered rock that closed its upper end. Here their intention was to climb out of the gully by one of the long vertical cracks running up the face on the right, optimistically called the Exit Cracks. It was all, he realized suddenly, still very much in the balance. The worst objective dangers of the North Face might be below them now, but who could say with certainty that the worst difficulties did not still lie ahead? *If* the gully could be climbed—*if* one of the Exit Cracks would 'go'—*if* new powder-snow did not treacherously mask every hold and detail of the unknown route. . . .

The little transparent window in the tent-sack was a square of dark grey, slowly lightening. Harrer, waking his friend, cautiously pulled off the sack. Dawn was a paling of the grey fog that hung in front and beneath, and they looked out on a strange landscape, an Arctic wilderness turned up at right angles and stood on end. Snow was still falling, snow had plastered the vertical rocks and even the overhangs, cemented with ice-glaze. The Bavarians ten feet away appeared to be stuck on to a perpendicular wall of white, for ledge, pitons, ropes and all had disappeared under the coating of snow. The air was calm; but at intervals a gust swept inwards from an avalanche falling from overhead, invisible in the fog, to roar down the ice-limbs of the White Spider.

The four men stirred and shook the snow from stiffened limbs. Vörg started his stove and melted chocolate in condensed milk for breakfast. Heckmair was confident, refreshed after his rest, and the pain of Kasparek's injured hand seemed to have diminished. When they had finished their hurried meal they tied on the rope, all four on the single length, and with Andreas Heckmair in the lead began the final part of the ascent.

It was late in the afternoon of that day, 24th July, when the anxious throng at Kleine Scheidegg saw four ragged figures coming down the slopes at the foot of the easy route up the Eiger and ran to meet them. A boy reached them first. They were stumbling, bumping into each other like drunken men, and stared idiotically when he gasped out his question.

'Have you—have you come off the Face?'

One of them mumbled at him through swollen lips.

'Yes. Off the Face.'

The first ascent of the Eigerwand had been accomplished.

ALPINE HUT

We climbed out of the stuffy little cars of the *Téléférique* at Plan de l'Aiguille, which was as far as the cable railway went in 1947, and started along the stony path in hot sunshine. There were sixteen of us from England, two-thirds of the party—including me—in our first Alpine season, and we shared two guides between us because at that time we were allowed to take only a very little money abroad. We straggled on the path, halting for photography or to exclaim at the views. The precipices of the Aiguille du Midi sprang straight up on the left from the path's edge, on the right the steeps of rubble dropped away to remote pinewoods and the valley of Chamonix. An angry bellow from the guide in the lead set us all closing-up at the double; we hadn't known it, but the frequent stonefalls from the Aiguille du Midi make this path the only really dangerous place on the ordinary way up Mont Blanc.

At the path's end we clambered on to the dirty ice of the Bossons glacier and tied on the rope. There were real *séracs*, genuine crevasses. We swung our brand-new ice axes with enthusiasm and sucked in the chill of the little breeze that blew down from the summit 8,000 feet above.

'Thank God for fresh air!' growled Jack from behind me. 'I nearly passed out in that ruddy cable-car.'

The glacier was easy enough, for the most part a trudge. Two and a half hours of it made the first sight of the Grands Mulets very welcome. Sticking out of the white slope ahead was a crag as big as a cathedral, its crest of dark pinnacles rising with the angle of the glacier. When we had turned its flank we saw the hut, a biggish wooden shanty perched 200 feet up on the crest where there was a flat saddle of rock. For a top rock-climber there was probably more than one way of getting to the hut, but for moderate mountaineers like ourselves the main entrance to the 'hotel' (as it called itself) was good enough. You had to climb a sheer rock-wall by means of smooth footholds, hanging on to a singularly rickety iron handrail attached to the wall by rusty stanchions to haul yourself higher and higher above the glacier directly beneath. At the top there was a narrow gallery of rocks built precariously on the edge of the precipice and running along the front wall of the hut; by this persons with steady heads could reach the door.

Jack filled his lungs with the pure mountain air of 10,000 feet above the sea and surveyed the Grands Mulets Hotel with a critical eye.

'Someone had fun building this,' he observed, 'in the days of the Second Empire.'

The hut was plainly very old; first opened, in fact, in 1853. It was built of wood with overhanging eaves like a large single-storied chalet and looked as if any considerable gale would carry it away. To guard against this, rusty iron wires were stretched across its much-mended roof and anchored to the crags fore and aft. The situation was certainly romantic. Immediately above the hut roof one of the Mulets' fantastic little pinnacles jutted up, and beyond and above that—far beyond and far above—the ragged precipices of the Aiguille de Saussure glowed in the fading sunshine. All around our curious island of rock was the glacier, an arrested white torrent pouring from Mont Blanc itself to divide at the Grands Mulets and join again for the plunge towards the green valley.

The planking of the ancient floor creaked under our boots as we went inside, to be greeted by a mingled smell of soup

ALPINE HUT

and straw bedding. Ours was the first party to arrive that evening and so won the undivided attention of the hut *gardien* and his wife, who supplied us with good soup at 40 francs the bowl and water at 10 francs a litre; since the water supply at the Grands Mulets consisted of snow which had to be melted on a stove whose fuel was carried up from Chamonix, the water charge was fair enough. When we had eaten, Jack and I inspected our sleeping quarters. The *dortoir*, by some past subsidence of the floor, sloped sharply towards its outer wall, in which there was a window, and this general tilt enabled the blue crevasses of the glacier to be viewed as from an aircraft about to dive on them. Round the three inner walls ran a tier of broad shelves like hayracks, with very thin straw palliasses closely ranged on them; another rank of palliasses under the shelves indicated a second layer of sleeping accommodation. The *dortoir* was both stuffy and cold.

Jack slid down the floor to the window and banged lustily at the frame, for some time without result.

'The ruddy thing's *made* to open,' he said between his teeth.

It opened with a suddenness that almost sent him through it and down to the glacier, but the freezing air that poured into the room evidently gave him the keenest satisfaction.

'Can't sleep in a ruddy fug,' he remarked with the conscious rectitude of a public benefactor.

We sought and found the 'water-closet'. Fortunately the twilight lingered although the sun had set, and we could see our footing. You edged along the stone gallery and out on to the unprotected slabs at the verge of a precipice. The precipice was precisely vertical; it had to be. The wooden box, just large enough for a man to crouch in, had the inner three inches of its floor resting on the cliff edge and the rest of it overhanging the glacier 200 feet below. It was held in position (only just, it seemed) by a couple of wires twisted round pegs driven into the rock. To step inside, to look straight down through the round hole in the floor to the diminished crevasse that did duty as a sewer, called for a summoning of faith and a dismissal of imagination. The whole contraption wobbled unnervingly and induced uncomfortable haste.

When we returned to the hut several other parties were arriving in company, all French, all noisily cheerful. There was a deal of coming and going, jesting and singing and drinking, while the silent English smoked their pipes and wrote up their diaries. At nine o'clock we retired to the *dortoir*, for the guides had discerned bad weather on its way and were demanding an early start. The *dortoir* window had been firmly closed.

'Who the heck shut this ruddy thing?' inquired Jack savagely, and banged it open again.

We lay down fully dressed on the hayracks. There were two blankets or pieces of blanket each. The four girls modestly chose to lie on the upper tier apart from the men, but their choice was in vain; before long the men of the French parties invaded us and their semi-privacy was no more. The first thing the Frenchmen did when they had lit a candle was to shut the window. Jack sat up with a muttered oath. I grabbed his arm and told him he'd better wait till they were asleep, and he subsided, muttering further oaths. At last the candle was blown out, the glacier glimmered bluely up through the panes of the closed window, the sighs and rustlings were succeeded by the loud breathing of tired men. Beside me a ghostly figure uprose and skidded down the floor in stockinged feet to the window. There was a creak and a thud, neither very loud, and the figure shuffled back up the slope.

'Done it!' whispered Jack gleefully, pulling the thin blanket over his head.

In five minutes he was snoring heartily. Sleep didn't come so easily to me, and I lay thinking about the men of Mont

ALPINE HUT

Blanc: Balmat and Paccard, who had first gained the summit a hundred and sixty years ago; De Saussure and his long-term scientific observations on the summit; Graham Brown, who made that wonderful 'triptych' of routes on the Brenva Face. It was perishing cold in the *dortoir*. Someone stirred on the upper tier, near the window. The blue glimmer from the glacier was blotted out for thirty seconds. When the shadowy obstruction had vanished the *dortoir* window was closed once again.

Jack snored on and presently I dozed. At 1.30 a.m. we all turned out to climb Mont Blanc.

It was an easy ascent in soft snow, rendered unenjoyable by the dullness of the weather and the tendency of all our party to suffer from mountain-sickness. The most exciting part was the descent, half asleep and in pitchy darkness, of that little cliff below the hut with its slippery footholds and frighteningly insecure handrail.

Jack did not reach the summit. Half-way up the endless snowslopes he collapsed, overcome by a bad attack of mountain-sickness, and had to be shepherded down again.

'But I'd have got up,' he said afterwards, 'if it hadn't been for that ruddy Frog shutting the ruddy window!'

THE ICE-CAVE ON KOMMUNIZMA

In May 1961 Sir John Hunt learned that he and a small British party would be allowed to join a Russian climbing party in an assault on Peak Stalin. By April of next year there was no Peak Stalin. 'The Supreme Soviet of the Tajikistan S.S.R. has decreed that the highest mountain of the Soviet Union shall henceforward be known as Pik Kommunizma.' This Peak of Communism, thus de-Stalinized, has a height of 24,590 feet and though climbed by crack Russian teams in 1933 and 1955 is a very difficult mountain; as with the greater Himalayan peaks, success upon it depends not only on the skill and endurance of the party but also on a special bond of sympathy, stronger than mere comradeship, between its members.

When, after days of gruelling ascent, four members of the British party and six Russian climbers reached the narrow ice-ridge 3,000 feet below the summit the special bond had still not been established. The representatives of the Trades Union Mountaineering Clubs—Spartak—were clearly first-rate mountaineers, the picked men of a population numbering more than two hundred millions, and in the technicalities of climbing there was common ground to be found. But from first to last the Russians failed to comprehend the British attitude towards mountain climbing. All ten of the men on the final ridge of Pik Kommunizma could agree to the proposition 'that mountaineering is a sport'. But whereas Malcolm Slesser and McNaught-Davis, Joe Brown and Graeme Nicol, considered that a sport was primarily something that one enjoyed,

THE ICE-CAVE ON KOMMUNIZMA

the Russians under their leader Tolia Ovchinikov regarded it rather as the fanatical Puritans regarded their religion. It was no laughing matter; certain rules were sacred, an iron discipline essential; failure was shameful. Members of Spartak caught smoking on a mountain were at once sent home by their leader. And when Wilfred Noyce and Robin Smith had lost their lives on Pik Garmo a fortnight earlier Sir John Hunt's suggestion that the expedition should be called off there and then, as would have been done by a British Himalayan expedition, had been so angrily received by the Russian leader that Hunt had agreed—in the interests of international relations—that a small party should stay on to take part in the ascent of Pik Kommunizma.

Slesser, now leader of the remaining British contingent, was very far from enjoying himself as he climbed wearily up the snow-covered ice. He was not so much a climber seeking pleasure in his chosen sport as a kind of capitalist champion, he felt. The Russians were leading, high above on the soaring ridge 22,000 feet above the sea, and if he and his men failed to reach the top in this hazardous game of follow-my-leader the Spartak party would undoubtedly see in the failure the final proof of Western decadence. To make matters worse, the Russians were fit and acclimatized and the British four were not. Indeed, Graeme—the expedition's doctor—had declared that if his three companions had come to see him in his city clinic he would have ordered them into a hospital bed at once. They could keep no food in their stomachs. At intervals they vomited, and Slesser had often to halt the rope, on that ladder of icy steps, to relieve himself. In the emptiness of their bellies malodorous gases formed and were noisily expelled. A fierce wind with a temperature of twenty below zero drove holes in the ragged clouds through which the immense white sea of the Pamirs could be glimpsed rolling to the horizon. In the lead the indomitable Joe Brown hewed a ladder of steps, for the steps left by the Russians in front had been filled in by the incoherent powder snow that drifted like a flood across the slope of ice. The other three reeled and stumbled up behind him, gasping painfully for breath at every step. Slesser, who was carrying the little blue tent which was to be their last camp before the top, was going badly and had to hand over his burden to McNaught-Davis.

Lack of acclimatization was responsible for much of the British party's trouble, but some of it was doubtless due to lack of dedication. The Soviet climbers were only on the mountain at all by special permission of the Central Council of the Union of Sports, granted because they had passed extremely stringent examinations in mountaineering. They had excelled in years of competition climbing. One of them, who held the coveted and supreme Master of Sport certificate, had that year won the two-day rock climbing competition of the Soviet Union. On the first day of this the candidates race in turn up a 165-foot cliff; on the second they are given a photograph of an unknown rock face on which they must choose and mark a route, thereafter climbing that route without the least deviation. To attempt any climb beyond the grade for which the mountaineer holds a certificate is, in Soviet Russia, a punishable crime. In the face of such grim professionalism the British four felt themselves almost culpably amateurish.

The windy afternoon darkened. The Russians on the ridge above were hidden by flying cloud. The endless slope was split here and there by crevasses and broken by little ice walls, and the weary men looked covetously at the frozen ledges where there was room to pitch their tent. But Gippenreiter, on in front, had complained that morning that the two parties were not keeping together properly and they felt bound to go on. The mist hid everything above and below except a few yards of featureless snow, and when a ragged hole blew in the

THE ICE-CAVE ON KOMMUNIZMA

greyness overhead there was nothing to be seen except more of the relentless ridge. The treadmill grind went on.

Suddenly an upright streak showed on the blank whiteness above them. It had a fluttering rag attached—a flag. They crawled up to it, and saw a few feet beyond the flag a hole in the steep bank of snow, two or three feet in diameter. Joe Brown peered into it.

'Funny—there's no one here,' he panted; and then, wriggling farther in, 'Aye, they're here.'

The others writhed after him. They were sick men and the effort of writhing brought them close to collapse. They were in an ice grotto, four feet high at its centre and with a floor area of some four square yards, hewn out by a Russian party who had reached this point earlier in the month. The six Soviet climbers, huddled in one corner, stared at the newcomers in silence for a moment. Gippenreiter's welcome, as reported by Slesser in his book *Red Peak*, was of a qualified warmth.

'You are welcome to stay in the Spartak ice cave. Here, there shall be very strict rules. There must be no spoiling of the air and no smoking. We shall occupy this half, and you that half. If Mac and Joe wish to smoke they must be near the entrance.'

There was warrant enough for the 'strict rules', for in the confined space with its tiny entrance there would be little of the rarefied air for ten men to share; but the chilly manner in which the rules were enunciated did not comfort the exhausted British. It was only too obvious that their arrival was going to make things very unpleasant for the Russians and they could do nothing to prevent it.

Shelter and the cessation of effort revived them more than they had anticipated. Igloos dug out in snow or ice are by no means the refrigerators one would expect, as the Eskimos long ago discovered. Even with a sizeable hole opening to the cold of 23,000 feet, the Spartak cave was comparatively warm. The four British climbers agreed that they must at least try to eat, and Slessor produced the concoction of dried meat and curry which, they had decided, was the only meal they were likely to keep down. On the tiny stove he melted snow and made a thin gruel of the mixture. When they had eaten a little of this they arranged the tent and other equipment on the floor of ice in their allotted half of the cave and lay down.

Outside the wind hissed and whistled, filling in the entrance with the powder snow, as dry and loose as granulated sugar, which had so hampered the ascent. They slept a little, in fitful dozes interrupted by stomach pains, there in the stuffy chill of their burrow high above the world. And the results of Slessor's gruel were as unpleasant as he had feared they would be. Wrathful growlings from the Russians in their corner greeted this involuntary 'spoiling of the air' and heralded a bold sally by Gippenreiter, who donned his climbing equipment and pushed his way outside to hack a second ventilating hole. Sanitary conditions were at once improved, but at the cost of losing all warmth from the ice cave. The temperature dropped to minus $25°$ centigrade.

There was no more sleep after that. In the early morning of next day, with the sky clearing and the wind less violent, the ten men started together for the summit of Kommunizma and reached it. The remaining distance of less than 2,000 feet took the British party almost eight hours to climb, which is less astonishing when one remembers that four slow deep breaths were needed for each upward step. Perhaps there was more of relief than triumph in their arrival on the summit of the highest peak in the U.S.S.R., but there was a strange satisfaction in having succeeded in company with men whose views on life and mountain-climbing diverged so sharply from their own. As the author of *Red Peak* wrote afterwards, 'To bring such vast differences in background and approach together at one time, at this elevated spot, was triumph enough.'

AT CAMP 4W

'Heroic' is not a word mountaineers like to use, or to read, in connexion with their chosen pastime. On the highest mountain in the world, however, the case is altered; climbing Everest can hardly be called a pastime. And if the ascent of Everest was a heroic feat, the idea of traversing Everest was epic in conception and in fulfilment.

On 1st May 1963 two members of the American Expedition to Everest reached the summit by the South Col route used by Hillary and Tenzing of the British Expedition ten years earlier. The American team, led by Norman G. Dyhrenfurth and twenty men strong, planned now to climb the mountain again by a new and quite unknown route up the West Ridge; and not merely to climb to the summit but to cross it and descend by the South Col route, thus traversing the peak. It was a tremendous undertaking on such a mountain. Its final success was as great a triumph as the historic first ascent itself, for to traverse one's peak is a more complete piece of mountaineering than ascent and descent by the same route.

Already, during early April, the climbers had gained a footing on the West Ridge and reconnoitred a route as high as 25,100 feet, where it was proposed to place the fourth camp on this ridge. One more camp would be needed above it, and from Camp 5W (so called to distinguish it from Camp 5 on the South Col route) two men would try for the summit and—if they reached it—go on to descend to the South Col on the other side. After the successful ascent by the original route the climbing teams went down to Base Camp for a rest, but within the week loads were being ferried up the difficult lower reaches of the West Ridge and the camps stocked ready for the traverse attempt. Two days of storm delayed the work and an avalanche swept away the unoccupied tents at one of the dump sites, but the slow work of edging men and gear higher and higher on the enormous flank of the peak—comparable to the work of old-time sappers approaching a beleaguered fortress—went on steadily until Camp 4W was at last established.

The camp site, 4,000 feet below the summit of Everest and 10,000 feet higher than the top of the Matterhorn, was a splendid one. Where the great snow *arête* of the West Ridge soared up to abut against the steepening rock of the final pyramid the snow had been shovelled and smoothed into a flat platform on which one small tent and two larger ones could be pitched. Behind the tents rose the snow-powdered wall of rock, in front the narrow foreground of white ridge dropped away into space with the gleaming summits of a score of great peaks thrusting up into mid air beyond. To the left of the platform, looking outwards, a 4,000-foot precipice fell sheer into the Western Cwm, so that the tent dwellers looked across the Cwm to the savage crest of Nuptse, hardly higher than their position. To the right, across vast slopes swept by avalanches, they looked down on the North Col where so many early Everesters had stood and gazed in vain hope up the North Ridge. Beyond the snowy breach of the North Col they saw the endless brown undulations of Tibet stretching into the haze of distance. Tom Hornbein thought it must be the most beautiful place in the whole Himalaya.

Hornbein was one of the four Americans who occupied Camp 4W on the night of 16th May. On the afternoon of that day he and Willi Unsoeld had climbed up to 26,200 feet in a vain search for a site for Camp 5W. As they descended the

AT CAMP 4W

wind was rising steadily but gustily, each gust stronger than the preceding one, and dark clouds were scudding across the sky. (Hornbein, a doctor of medicine, and Unsoeld, a university professor, were in the event to be the first men to reach the summit of Everest by the West Ridge and the first men to traverse the mountain.) When they came down again to Camp 4W Barry Bishop and Al Auten, with four Sherpas, had reached the camp and were preparing to spend the night with them.

The tents were of nylon with sewn-in groundsheets, slung from external tubular A-frames. The two larger tents had been set up end to end with their circular entrances together for better communication, and their frames lashed together with line. Bishop and Auten and the Sherpas occupied these tents and Hornbein and Unsoeld the smaller one beside them. With nightfall the weather was clearly worsening, but when they had eaten supper the eight men felt cheerful and confident and mocked the rising wind with an exchange of Sherpa songs and American folk music. Then, snug in their sleeping-bags, they fixed the lightweight polyethylene masks over their faces and turned on the low-rate oxygen flow that gave a reasonably restful sleep even at this height of four miles above sea-level.

An hour or two later an observer at Base Camp on the Khumbu Glacier, where the night was almost windless, noticed a constant roar like the noise of a jet plane high above. It was a high storm, one of the tremendous winds that strike the loftier points of earth while the habitable regions of the world are calm. At midnight it had reached its crux.

At midnight, in one of the linked tents at Camp 4W on its lofty platform, Bishop and Auten woke suddenly to find a disturbing movement below their sleeping-bags. The deafening roar of the wind, unceasing, forcing the strong nylon of the tent wall into a rigid curve, had not prevented them from sleeping, but now their bodies were being shaken and lifted. The wind was under the tent floor, heaving it savagely and tossing them from side to side. They sat up hastily and tore off their oxygen masks. There was no time to do more before the heaving motion changed to something more comfortable and a great deal more frightening—the tents had been torn loose from their securing guys and were sliding off the platform. The tent floor tilted, the motion became swifter. Both tents, lashed together, were tobogganing down the slope of the West Ridge.

There was nothing the two men could do about it except to dig their fingers into the fabric of the groundsheet, trying to exert a braking hold on the snow beneath. The yelling Sherpas in their tent were doing the same. It was utterly useless. In a few seconds and a few yards of distance they would be sailing to their deaths in the Western Cwm 4,000 feet below, or—for they could not tell which direction the locked tents were taking—on the Rongbuk Glacier even farther down on the Tibetan side. Hardly had these dreadful alternatives crossed their minds when it seemed that the fatal fall had begun, for they were thrown into the air and hurled against each other. Repeated contact with the hard snow beneath was not reassuring, for they realized that now the tents were no longer sliding but rolling down the mountain.

Over and over went the men, half in and half out of their sleeping-bags. Round them and on them and between them flew all the various things the tent contained—food, stove, climbing equipment, oxygen apparatus. It seemed impossible that the next bounce, the next revolution of that nylon-encased jumble of climbers and flying objects, should not hurl them out into space. And then—it all stopped. The booming roar of the wind went on, the racket of drumming fabric sounded again, but the climbers were stationary and alive in the midst of chaos.

AT CAMP 4W

The tent was a wreck, with its groundsheet overhead and the men sprawled among their belongings on what had been the roof. Yelling above the din of the gale, the Americans ascertained that none of the occupants was seriously hurt. The next step was to find out where they were. It was obvious that this might be only a temporary stop, that the gale might at any moment set them off again on the final stage of the terrible flight. All but one man must stay inside to ballast the wreckage while an inspection was made. Bishop managed to find a torch and Auten crawled outside with it into the tearing wind and driving snow. He saw then that by a miracle the tents had slid down to the one obstacle that could have stopped them, a shallow trough of snow fifty yards down the crest of the ridge. With gusts of a hundred miles an hour forcing him to hands and knees Auten could do little by himself to pin the tents down where they were. He crawled back through the blizzard to the remaining tent above. Even that short distance was a tremendous effort without oxygen.

In their small tent Hornbein and Unsoeld were awake, but had no inkling of what had happened until Auten, breathless and plastered with snow, appeared in the entrance. They put on their windproof parkas at once and crept down through the dark and the storm. It was a long time before they had secured the wrecked tents, lashing ropes to them and leading the ropes back up the slope to belay-points, but the job was done at last. Barry Bishop and the Sherpas huddled under the flapping nylon through the rest of that night while Auten crowded in with the other two.

Next day the small tent collapsed. And, with Camp 4W completely disintegrated, there was nothing for it but to battle a way down through the unabated gale to the comparative security of the lower camps. But three days later, when the storm had passed, Camp 4W was equipped and reoccupied; and within forty-eight hours of that the West

Ridge had been climbed. The traverse of Everest was an accomplished fact.

Hornbein and Unsoeld were only the eleventh and twelfth men to stand on the summit of Everest. But, as James Ramsay Ullman points out in his book *Americans on Everest*, they were the only ones to have reached it by a different route from the original South Col way. And he adds with truth; 'Theirs was one of the great "firsts" of mountainering history.'

PLEASANT DREAMS

Fanatics have their dreams, wherein they weave
A paradise for a sect.
                                KEATS

THE DREAM OF MR. SMITH

Albert Smith, said the Victorian *cognoscenti*, was just the name for him. Mr. Douglas Jerrold said that his initials represented only two-thirds of the truth. He was a cheap wit, a cad, a little vulgarian from Chertsey. His ascent of Mont Blanc was the most impertinent piece of publicity-seeking ever heard of. So they said; and they were wrong. In his way Mr. Albert Smith was a pioneer, the forerunner of the dedicated mountaineers like Gwen Moffat and Chris Bonington who were only to appear, in England, a century after him. For Mr. Smith dreamed of mountains and of one mountain in particular, and followed his dream into the greatest climbing venture of his day.

When he was a small boy someone gave Albert a book called *The Peasants of Chamouni*. In it there was a description of a fatal accident on Mont Blanc, the ascent of which was rarely made and was still the most daring feat to be performed in Europe. The woodcuts of the great mountain and its wild surroundings fired his imagination and touched that special chord of desire which is in the born mountaineer. To climb Mont Blanc—it was an obsession that was to stay with him through youth and middle age; an obsession very rare in those days when there was no Alpine Club, when hardly an Englishman had heard of the Matterhorn and only one in a thousand knew the name of Mont Blanc.

Albert Smith's father was a small country surgeon and his son was intended to follow him. When Albert was sent to Paris to study medicine the thought that he was in the same country as the 'Chamouni' of his dream soon took charge. In the very spirit of the modern 'hard man'—that of the dedicated, antisocial pilgrim—he slung a knapsack on his back and set off across France, tramping, begging lifts on wagons and coaches, drinking in cafés and sleeping in ditches. He reached Chamonix and at last saw Mont Blanc. The mountain had then been climbed fewer than thirty times and the attempt was regarded as rash to the point of lunacy. Murray's Swiss guidebook declared, meaningly, 'Several of those who have made this ascent have been persons of unsound mind.' Smith could not possibly afford the small fortune and the army of guides required for the venture. He gave it out in Chamonix that he was ready to accompany any climbing party up Mont Blanc as a porter, unpaid, but there was no one to take up his offer and he returned disconsolate to London.

The taste of freedom and the Bohemian life had spoiled him for the profession of medicine. He became a journalist and comic writer, struggling at first and then just successful enough to afford other journeys to Chamonix, where he could only gaze at the great mountain and discuss the dangers of its ascent with Chamouniards in the local *bistros*. It was considered impossible to tackle the climb without a small army of assistants, and the cost of an ascent—something like £100—was quite beyond his means. He did not lose his dream, however. And in 1851, when he was 35 years old, he discovered the road to fortune.

Returning from an adventurous journey in the Middle East, Mr. Smith conceived the idea of giving a public entertainment based upon his travels. He concocted a lively lecture, hired a hall, and was soon drawing big audiences, for as speaker and showman he was notably gifted. By the summer of that same year he had enough capital for his purpose. He set out once more for Chamonix, this time determined to climb Mont

THE DREAM OF MR. SMITH

Blanc. 'I found my old knapsack in a store-room', he wrote, 'and I beat out the moths and spiders, and filled it as of old, and on the first of August I left London Bridge in the mail train of the South Eastern Railway, with my Lord Mayor and other distinguished members of the corporation, who were going to the *fêtes* at Paris in honour of the Exhibition, and who, not having a knapsack under their seat, lost all their luggage, as is no doubt chronicled in the City archives.'

Chamonix was already a popular centre, a station on the Grand Tour. Sir Robert Peel was there with a lively party of affluent youngsters escaping from the social barriers of Victorian London. The happy-go-lucky journalist with his quick wit, his flowing brown locks and his magnificent sidewhiskers was welcomed into the circle when his extraordinary intention became known. Three young men who cared more for fun and adventure than for risk joined him: Charles Floyd, Francis Philips, and the Honourable William Sackville-West. They subscribed £60 each towards the cost of the ascent and set about collecting a party. Sixteen 'guides', sturdy local men with some knowledge of the mountain, were to accompany them, with a score of porters to carry the provisions. There was to be no lack of delicacies for Albert Smith and his friends, no sparse mountain diet of beef extract and ship's biscuits. Their list of provisions makes mouth-watering reading:

> 60 bottles of Vin Ordinaire
> 6 bottles of Bordeaux
> 10 bottles of St. George
> 15 bottles of St. Jean
> 3 bottles of Cognac
> 1 bottle of Syrup of Raspberries
> 6 bottles of Lemonade
> 2 bottles of Champagne
> 20 loaves

- 10 small cheeses
- 6 packets of chocolate
- 6 packets of sugar
- 4 packets of prunes
- 4 packets of raisins
- 2 packets of salt
- 4 wax candles
- 6 lemons
- 4 legs of mutton
- 4 shoulders of mutton
- 6 pieces of veal
- 1 piece of beef
- 11 large fowls
- 35 small fowls

Apart from the food, it was no small matter to transport 103 bottles of liquor from Chamonix to the rocks of the Grands Mulets at nearly 10,000 feet above the sea.

The party waited for fine weather and started when it was clear and settled. In 1851 there was only one accepted route up Mont Blanc, by the Bossons glacier and the Grands Mulets to the Grand Plateau and then by a snow corridor across the Mur de la Côte to the summit dome. The original route, ascending from the Grand Plateau to the top, was no longer used since the fatal accident to Dr. Hamel's party in 1820. Both routes are dangerous because of their exposure to avalanche, but Albert Smith and his caravan were lucky. Ill shod and unsuitably clad, with no inkling of the safety a rope could give and no knowledge of that vitally important thing 'the condition of the snow', they encountered nothing untowards. The ascent flowed smoothly, like a pleasant dream.

There was the thrilling passage of the glacier, with the peasants lifting their employers bodily up ice walls; the cheerful bivouac on the fortress-like rocks of the Grands Mulets, where most of the contents of the 103 bottles were absorbed;

THE DREAM OF MR. SMITH

the lantern-lit toil on the vast slopes of snow to the Grand Plateau, the splendour of sunrise, the penultimate excitement of the passage of the Mur de la Côte. 'Should the foot slip, or the baton give way, there is no chance for life—you would glide like lightning from one frozen crag to another and finally be dashed to pieces, hundreds and hundreds of feet below in the horrible depths of the glacier.' So Albert Smith afterwards described it in his book *The Story of Mont Blanc;* a book which was to bring him into some ridicule with the staider Alpinists of his time but which was to give the ordinary man a closer approach to the excitement of mountain climbing than any less imaginative writer had ever managed to give.

The summit was reached, the enormous view exclaimed at, the long descent achieved without mishap. Chamonix welcomed the returning adventurers with a triumphal entry and salutes of cannon. It was the thirty-seventh ascent of Mont Blanc, and no future member of the Alpine Club had as yet climbed it. The celebratory party given by that 'nine-bottle man' Sir Robert Peel was doubtless appropriate to the occasion, but its effect was to confirm the lofty-minded in their opinion that Mr. Albert Smith was a mere vulgar showman. 'The aimless scramble of four pedestrians to the top of Mont Blanc, with the accompaniment of Sir Robert Peel's orgies at the bottom, will not go far to redeem the somewhat equivocal reputation of the herd of English tourists in Switzerland, for a mindless and rather vulgar redundance of spirits.' Thus the *Daily News* a week after the ascent. Mr. Smith did not care. He had made his childhood dream come true, and now that it was done he saw no reason why he should not describe its wonders to the public—and, incidentally, make money out of it.

On 15th March 1852 the Egyptian Hall in Piccadilly opened with the first performance of Mr. Albert Smith's entertaining diorama 'The Ascent of Mont Blanc'. In the darkened hall a packed audience sat spellbound while a vast illuminated canvas of views drawn by William Beverley, showing every stage of the journey from London to the top of Mont Blanc, was slowly unrolled. From the stage Albert Smith himself delivered the commentary. There was something for everyone —excitement, topography, anecdotes, history, comic incident and sensational description. 'A tissue of indifferent puns and stale fast witticisms, with an incessant straining after smartness,' declared the *Daily News;* but it made no difference to the enormous popularity of the show. The diorama ran for six years and made £30,000 for its creator. Prince Albert saw it. Queen Victoria presented Smith with a diamond scarf pin after a Royal Command performance at Osborne. Mont Blanc became a London fashion gimmick, with 'Mont Blanc Polkas' and 'Chamoni Quadrilles' in the ballrooms and a form of snakes-and-ladders called 'The Mont Blanc Game' in nearly every home.

It might be thought that Mr. Smith the showman, making capital out of mountain climbing and boasting of having 'Mont Blanc in a box', would be anathema to the clerics and professors who had recently discovered the spiritual stimulus of the great peaks. Some of them, however, must have perceived beneath the surface vulgarity Smith's genuine love of mountain adventure, for he became an original member of the Alpine Club when it was formed in 1854. It can be seen as a just requital of his services to mountaineering. In the passing-on of his dream he exaggerated the terrors of the ascent but not its challenge and reward. And in unnumbered youths among his audiences he awakened the realization that there was awaiting them a field for high adventure whose existence they had never before suspected.

PRISONER'S DREAM

There is a large and popular literature of escaping. In a sense all of us are prisoners, and the tales of daring escapes from prison camps attract not only by their excitement but also by a scarcely realized symbolism. To pass by one's own endeavour from confinement to freedom is one of the more pleasant dreams, and most mountaineers think of their holiday approach to the hills as an escape. It is not often that both feats—the somewhat sordid escape from prison and the more poetic escape to the hills—are united in one action; and one of these rare double escapes was that of Felice Benuzzi, in 1943 confined in an Italian prisoner-of-war camp at Nanyuki in Kenya. At the end of his book *No Picnic on Mount Kenya* Benuzzi speaks of his mountaineering escapade as a dream, and tells how the wind brought through the window of his cell a message from the mountain: 'Only in dreams can humans approach me; only in dreams are they allowed a fleeting glimpse of my dearest secrets.' It is perhaps how many of us feel after the descent from some perfect summit. But Benuzzi's dream had been a good one while it lasted.

From PoW Camp 354 it was possible on clear days to see Mount Kenya far away, a huge black tooth of rock enamelled with blue glaciers. It was the one lovely thing in the ugly prison life that was to endure for five years, and Benuzzi, a mountaineer who had climbed in his native mountains, fell in love with it. A mountaineer thus possessed must climb the peak of his desire or suffer torture. Benuzzi resolved to get out somehow and to climb Mount Kenya before he was recaptured.

There was a book in the prison library dealing with the customs of a Kenya tribe and in it was a photograph of Mount Kenya. Benuzzi copied the photograph and gathered what information he could from the book, for he knew little or nothing about the mountain. There was not much to be learned by intending climbers from a book about tribal customs. Mount Kenya, he read, had two peaks, Batian (17,040 feet) and Lenana (16,300 feet)—the book ignored Nelion, the twin summit of Batian and the same height; there were fifteen glaciers feeding many rivers, but whether the Nanyuki river that ran near the camp was one of these rivers was not stated; the peak was roughly twenty miles from Nanyuki, and the intervening terrain was largely a tangle of rock and forest. Apart from the photograph, his own observation had shown him that the mountain was exceedingly steep and likely to be difficult, which meant that he had to have some sort of equipment and at least one climbing companion, preferably two. With great care and after several failures he found two men who would make the attempt with him: Giuan, a doctor, and Enzo. The first had considerable climbing experience, the second had none at all and was suffering from lung trouble, but there was no one else he could trust. Now for the equipment, which—besides things like ice axes and rope—would have to include food for at least a fortnight.

How this unique mountaineering expedition equipped itself, as it were out of thin air, is not the least intriguing part of Benuzzi's story. It took the better part of six months. The prisoners' one-mile exercise walk ended at a signpost marking the Equator, and here there was a large rubbish tip. Little by little, with ingenious tricks of abstraction and concealment, scraps of iron and aluminium were acquired. Two hammers and a chisel were stolen from the Indian artisans whose job it was to maintain the camp buildings. Using steel cut from the mudguards of a wrecked car on the tip, the PoW blacksmith, who had been enlisted to help, surreptitiously constructed two pairs of crampons and converted the two hammers into instruments faintly resembling ice axes. Week after week the cigarette rations were traded for bread and other scraps of food, or for pieces of cloth out of which a tent could be constructed. The climbing rope was made from the sisal used for fastening the bedding-nets to the bunks. There was even an Italian flag, which they hoped to plant on the summit—a heroic gesture in the face of the conquering British who were overlords of Kenya. Meanwhile, through the long days of waiting, the three read everything they could lay hands on concerning Mount Kenya, learning from many books and newspapers a little about the treacherous weather they might expect on the mountain and a great deal about the wild beasts they were almost certain to encounter on the approach march.

Giuan had the job of tending the prison vegetable garden, and in a three-foot hole in the floor of his tool shed the accumulated equipment was hidden. Benuzzi at last succeeded in getting an impression (in tar) of the key to the compound gate, and all was ready. The three men contrived to hide in the tool shed at nightfall and let themselves out with the key they had made, counting on the darkness to allow them to get clear before their absence was discovered. Enzo, with a temperature of 101°, refused to be left behind. It was 24th January.

By 2nd February Benuzzi, Giuan and Enzo had reached the lower limit of snow and ice below the tremendous north face of Batian. For nine days they had struggled slowly upward, through semi-cultivated farm land at first, then through tangled forest where progress was slow and infinitely laborious. None of them was fit—Enzo least of all—and the food they had been able to collect with such patience had to be severely rationed. They had beaten off a leopard's attack, encountered a bull elephant, seen wonders of beauty in plant and rock and river which (they told each other) were more than compensation for the inevitable punishment that awaited them when they returned, even if they failed to climb their peak. Uphill, always uphill, over twenty miles of trackless equatorial wilderness with no map to help them, they had come out of the weird upper world of bamboo and giant groundsel into the land of the high peaks. Already they had had some hard rock climbing in a gully. Now the real mountaineering confronted them.

Enzo, cheerful but far from well, was left at the tiny camp on the vegetation line and at 2 a.m. Benuzzi and Giuan began the climb. Their plan was to cross the face of the minor peak above them, called Dutton Peak, and gain the ridge beyond it, by which—if Benuzzi's guess was correct—the summit of Batian could be reached. It was a fine starry night and the going, over steep scree to begin with, was not difficult in the darkness. At dawn the sky was still clear, and two hours later they had put on the home-made rope and were climbing out across the sheer face of Dutton Peak with the crevasses of the César Glacier far below their clumsily nailed boots. On the ice of the couloirs the camp-made axes rang triumphantly. In struggling up a hard oblique crack below the ridge Benuzzi slipped and came on the rope, but the sisal held and they climbed on. A gully with ice pitches in it brought them to the ridge, where they looked down on the fearsome ice cliffs of the Northey Glacier on the other side. Very hard climbing up snow-covered slabs followed. They reached 16,000 feet and the cold struck deep into their bodies, thinly protected as they were. By noon they were engaged with ice-covered rocks where Giuan, in the lead, advanced only a few inches at a time; and half an hour later mist gathered with frightening suddenness and a storm of hail and snow burst upon them.

PRISONER'S DREAM

Giuan, far above Benuzzi's head, ceased to advance at all, and when his companion called up to him announced that he could move neither up nor down. Retreat down the mountain at once was essential if they were to remain alive. And it began to look as though retreat was impossible.

Giuan began to inch back down the difficult pitch. It took him forty minutes to do it, but at last he was beside his half-frozen companion, his 'anorak' (made from blankets) white with snow and as stiff as a suit of armour. The wind tore at them, the blizzard blinded them, the hairy sisal rope froze into a cranky bar inflexible as iron. And they crawled on through the storm, always downward now. When they reached the scree and safety they had been climbing on difficult rock for twelve hours. The terrible weakness of untrained, underfed men subjected to gruelling toil at high altitudes had them in its grip, but they had still to reach the little tent. Stumbling through thick and freezing mist, they groped their way down the boulders and ravines that had seemed easy enough in the morning but were now obstacles that demanded all their failing strength and confused them, in the dense and darkening fog, by their multiplicity. It was inky dark and frightfully cold. The exhausted pair began to suffer from hallucinations. Benuzzi heard bells chiming, met and talked with characters from the books he had been reading. They were at the very limit of endurance when, more by luck than reasoned route-finding, they stumbled on the tent and roused Enzo to make them a can of tea. It was ten minutes to nine; they had been on their feet for more than eighteen hours.

Just thirty hours later, at one o'clock in the morning of 6th February, Enzo was washing the insides of the little bags which had contained the hoarded Ovaltine, sugar and cocoa. The water he washed them in was the morning drink for Benuzzi and Giuan, who were about to set forth for the ascent of Lenana—16,300 feet high and a worthy 'consolation prize' for their failure on Batian. A small biscuit thinly smeared with meat extract completed their breakfast.

One day's rest had not compensated for their ordeal in the storm, but they knew that the Lenana route was less exacting and hoped it was within their powers. And so it proved. Moraine and scree, then ice-covered rocks, took them slowly upward and in seven hours of climbing they had gained the ridge of their peak, with a tremendous view on either hand. There was an easy shoulder to follow, and then the summit, just after ten. The Italian flag was hoisted on the improvised pole they had carried up with them, and left flying there on the lower peak of Mount Kenya.

Three days later the expedition, nearly starving but still jubilant, let itself into the prison compound at night and next morning reported to the Prison Commandant. They were sentenced to twenty-eight days' cells and their hard-won possessions were taken from them; but they did not complain. No one could take away their dream.

THE GULLY THAT WAS

If there are 'ghosts that darkling roam' the shores of wild Llyn Cae under Cader Idris they will be jovial ghosts and kindly; clad in tweeds and cloth caps instead of shrouds; shod with massive clinker-nailed boots and burdened with a plate camera and a coil of thick hemp rope. There will be Owen Glynne Jones with his thin eager face and strong-lensed spectacles, and burly Ashley Abraham, and George Abraham the elder and slimmer of the famous Keswick Brothers. They will certainly be gazing up at the precipitous north face of Mynydd Pencoed, Craig y Cae, where the Great Gully once gave them precisely the sort of climb that was considered, by the climbers of 1897, completely satisfying.

It was the Gully Epoch. Cragsmen looked for clefts and grooves and chimneys, the 'line of weakness', to take them up their chosen rockface, and strenuous writhings and clutchings were the order of the day rather than the balanced movement of a later era. Jones and the Abrahams, that Easter morning in 1897, surveyed the splendid crag and the gully that split it from base to crest and gloated over the prospect of good sport. The gully was steep throughout its length, very narrow in its upper half; two of the lower pitches had considerable waterfalls pouring down them. It looked strenuous and uncomfortable and was clearly a Victorian rock climber's paradise.

They had crossed Cader Idris from their inn at Dolgelley, a three-hour walk, but Jones's impatience allowed them no rest beside the icy waters of the llyn. Jones was host to these cragsmen from Cumberland, discoverer of the Great Gully and chief extoller of its merits; he could not wait to demonstrate the excellence of his taste. They toiled up the scree to the bottom of the gully and uncoiled the rope, John Buckingham's famous Alpine Club rope with the red thread down the middle of its three hawser-laid strands. Eighty feet was held to be the right length for three climbers. Jones tied on at one end with a bowline knot and George Abraham, laden with his camera, at the other, while Ashley secured himself in the middle with a double fisherman's bend. Clinker nails rang on the first foothold and set a brief echo flying between the vertical walls of the gully. The climb had begun.

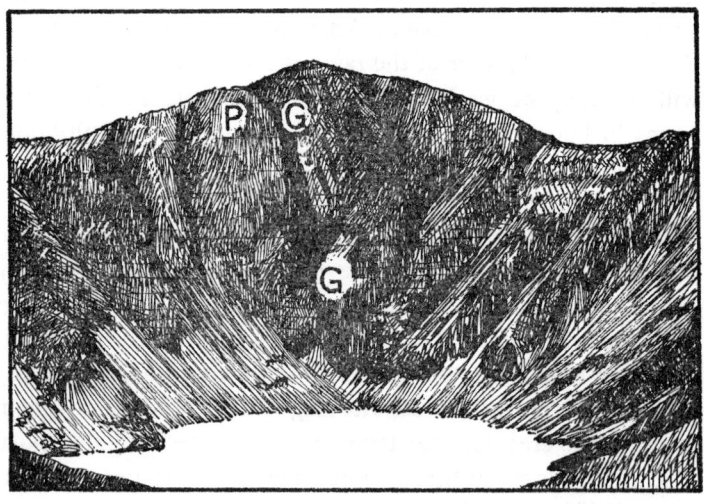

CRAIG Y CAE, CADER IDRIS,
from Llyn y Cae

P = The Pencoed Pillar   G, G = Great Gully—'The Gully that Was'

THE GULLY THAT WAS

The first pitch was forty feet high, but could be taken in two sections. The upper section, roofed in by a big jammed stone, gave the first real difficulty, and Jones took off from a foothold on Ashley's knee to climb the crack between the chockstone and the wall. There was no fussing with belaying points, no scientific mumbo-jumbo with the rope, in those carefree days; you got up the pitch somehow, you 'planted yourself as firmly as possible', you held the rope in your hands while the next man came up. Ashley followed up the crack, and his brother, carrying the bulky plate camera and its folding tripod, joined the others in a lofty cavern. The capstone overhead was passed by some grass ledges on the left wall which took them back again into the steep bed of the gully above the obstacle, thus missing the lesser of the two waterfalls. The second waterfall now confronted them. It spouted over the edge of another capstone thirty feet above their heads in the direct line of ascent; but some unstable-looking ledges on the right seemed to offer a drier alternative. Jones wiped the spray from his glasses and buttoned his Norfolk jacket tightly.

'Good gracious, Jones, you're not going to climb up the waterfall?'

'Indeed I am.'

'But ——'

But Jones was already worming his way up the fall 'like some huge amphibian', ignoring the laughter and protests of the others. He was getting on swimmingly, Ashley jested. George, searching vainly for somewhere to set up his camera, retorted that they were all in for a soaking unless their leader got washed down again like the sparrow in the spout. Now Jones was nearly at the top, directly under the solid jet of water which struck him full on the top of his head and rebounded in a gleaming fan against the gully walls on either side. Completely blinded, he clung there for several minutes groping for a handhold before retreating, defeated and half drowned, to the sound of lusty cheering from his friends below.

Amid a good deal of chaffing Jones was stripped mother-naked (it was Easter, remember, and cold at 2,000 feet) and his drenched clothing wrung out. When he was clothed again in his clammy garments he led up the crumbling ledges and the party gathered on a shelf above the waterfall. Four small and comparatively easy obstacles higher up were passed and they were at the foot of the great pitch which was Jones's pride and joy.

It was a grim and singularly forbidding place. The dark and dripping walls of the gully towered straight up like the sides of a lift shaft, fifteen feet wide at the foot but narrowing forty feet above to a mere three feet. Jammed in this inverted funnel was a pile of huge rock splinters, the largest of them jutting out in an overhang so pronounced that a stone dropped from its tip would fall outside the stony shelf where they stood. To get under the overhang it was first necessary to gain a chimney formed by a big vertical flake resting against the left wall; but the bottom of the chimney overhung and appeared impossible to enter.

'Isn't it beautiful?' said Jones ecstatically, and incontinently scrambled up into a recess in the wall to the left of the chimney.

George said cautiously that it was worth a photograph, at any rate, and untied himself from the rope while his brother followed the leader up to the recess.

Taking climbing photographs was no light matter seventy years ago. The big box camera, with its glass plates in their metal holders, might weigh anything up to six pounds and the telescopic tripod another three. The tripod was essential for steadiness, because the slow emulsions of those days needed long exposures, especially in dark places like gullies. George clambered on to some reedy ledges and called to Ashley to wait half-way up the pitch while he divested himself of the

THE GULLY THAT WAS

apparatus slung round him and set up the tripod. There was one occasion, on Lliwedd, when his photographic stance had peeled off as he was about to take a picture; fortunately he was tied on to the rope, and he had dangled in mid air—camera and tripod and all—over a 500-foot drop. This time he had a better stance, though Baedeker would have classed it as 'suitable only for those with steady heads'. He got his picture, and it can be seen (by those fortunate enough to possess a copy) opposite page 368 in *Rock Climbing in North Wales*. By the time he had descended and tied on again Jones was shivering in his wet clothes and impatient to be on the move.

The move was a delicate step out of the recess and across the wall into the undercut bottom of the chimney. There was very little foothold but a good handhold to swing on, and Jones was quickly across and wrestling invisibly with the problems of the chimney, his progress marked by heavy breathing and much scraping of clinker nails. He found good standing-place above it from which to belay the other two as they made the step across, which Ashley thought 'a sensational one'. They were now perched beneath the overhanging splinters. Peering vertically upwards, Ashley discerned a gleam of daylight at the back of the overhangs. This tiny hole, announced Jones, was the 'through route'.

'Come off it, Jones,' protested Ashley. 'You can't get through there!'

'*I* can,' returned Jones calmly, wiping steam from his spectacles. 'I don't know about you—but you'll have to follow the rope. Give me a shoulder, there's a good chap.'

Obediently Ashley leant his bulk against the narrow wall so that the leader could swarm up his body and use his shoulder as a foothold. A kick, a few seconds of violent effort and spasmodic wriggling, and Jones's legs passed from view as they were drawn up through the hole. A moment's pause, and then a breathless voice from overhead.

'It's easy enough—just deflate your lungs while you shove through.'

It was Ashley's turn. He hesitated, tugging at his moustache.

'This,' he remarked to his grinning brother, 'is the time I'd like to feel small.'

George guffawed and slapped him on the back. 'Don't worry,' he said. 'The hole will put that right by the time you're through it.'

Ashley took off his Norfolk jacket and handed it to George in silence. With some help from the rope he hoisted his fourteen stone until he could insert head and shoulders into the hole and writhe upwards using its constricting sides to obtain friction hold. Half-way through he stuck. A convulsive effort shifted him forward another six inches, but try as he might he could get no farther. There was an interval of desperate panting punctuated by brief and futile struggles.

'Deflate, man, deflate!' shouted Jones impatiently from some niche overhead.

Ashley had no breath to answer with, or he would have retorted that the part of him that was jammed was incapable of deflation. He decided that he had better wriggle backwards and start again. It took him thirty seconds to discover that he could not wriggle backwards at all.

'I'm stuck!'

They climbed for fun in those days and this was just the sort of fun they liked. Hearty jokes and loud laughter resounded in the gully. Jones was (he said) for descending to Tal-y-llyn and bringing up a can of lubricating oil. George suggested pouring water over his brother to shrink him. Methods of supplying the unfortunate man with food during the next few days or weeks were freely discussed. It was when George was recalling an apocryphal Austrian, similarly trapped on the Ortler, who had been freed at last by the use of dynamite that Ashley found strength for a last great effort. There was 'a

THE GULLY THAT WAS

grievous rending of nether garments'—the mention of breeches in print was *tabu* in the eighteen-nineties—and he emerged like a cork from a bottle.

What with Ashley's proportions and George's photography, the pitch had taken them two hours to get up. But it was the crux of the climb and they were nearing the top. Two or three easier pitches; a fork in the gully, where they chose the deep chimney of the left-hand branch and 'backed up' in orthodox fashion; then a penultimate pitch where they looked out between the narrow walls, past riven curtains of black perpendicular rock, to see the snow-powdered shoulders of Cader Idris opposite them and Llyn Cae's dark still waters very far below. The final pitch was hard, a perpendicular chimney with few holds in its lower half. Jones prepared for it in his characteristic manner, kicking his boots about on the rock and grunting noisily; he called it 'getting up steam'. He was extremely shortsighted and needed this odd summoning of the blood to give him confidence in the holds he could only see as vague blurs overhead. Then he climbed the chimney with the superb dash and energy for which he was famous, and the ascent of the Great Gully was over.

Two years later Jones was to meet his death on the Dent Blanche, dragged down by the fall of the leading guide. He was 32 years old.

The great climbers pass; and so, sometimes, do their great climbs. For the hills, proverbially eternal, are in fact nothing of the kind. Owen Glynne Jones's beloved gully, whose outward prospect George Abraham thought 'unsurpassed in Great Britain', is a climb no longer. Years ago the crux pitch vanished in a mighty fall of rock which filled the cleft with loose debris and sodden turf. And later explorers, finding there nothing worth climbing, are apt to wonder whether the ascent of the Great Gully of Craig y Cae was after all no more than a dream.

DREAM OF A VIRGIN

When we first saw her Jack and I knew that she was a mountaineer's dream come true. Like a lesser Matterhorn she rose in lovely lines of rock and snow from the glacier, a steep east ridge and a less forbidding west ridge meeting in a perfect and pointed summit against the ice-blue sky of Arctic Norway. The glacier had never been trodden by men until our little expedition reached it, so that we were the first to set eyes on our mountain, which was unmapped, unnamed—a virgin peak. True, that alluring summit could be little more than 4,000 feet above the sea, for this was about the average height of the wild North Lyngen peaks we had come to explore and survey; but mere height has very little to do with the beauty of a mountain, which is a matter of form and proportion.

'She's a real lovely,' said Jack, unexpectedly supporting my conviction of her sex.

For me the Spissthorn (the name is Norwegian for 'pointed peak' and we had already christened her) was feminine from the first, though British climbers are by custom denied the personification of their mountains. Once again they manage these things better in France, where they speak of a mountain as '*elle*'. It is a defect in our language. Whymper writing of the Matterhorn, Mallory describing Everest, were both obliged to love their loves with an 'it'—yet any seaman may without reproach cherish a graceless collier as 'she'. Our Spissthorn had a twofold appeal which was wholly feminine: she was a

DREAM OF A VIRGIN

virgin, aloof and snowy-robed; and she very manifestly invited conquest.

She was smiling, if not actually beckoning, when Jack and I crossed her white threshold on 14th July 1952. The sun was warm in a clear sky, and the traverse of the glacier inches deep in slush had not cooled our ardour. There was a white skirt of steep and folded snow striped with the blue lines of crevasses; colours nicely suited to a maiden whose bower is 220 miles north of the Arctic Circle. We kicked and cut our way upwards on it—it was not hard-frozen and the strokes of the axe were no more than love-taps. High and shadowed on our left soared the western ridge, looking from below so level and devoid of difficulty that I was secretly disappointed; no man likes his conquest to be too easy. Was our virginal Spissthorn a wanton after all?

I need not have worried. Foreshortening had played its usual trick. When at last we gained the saddle at the lowest point of the ridge, stepping from the upsurge of snow to a flat kerb of rock overlooking 3,000 feet of space on the other side, we saw that she was not going to yield without a struggle. The *arête* swept up magnificently to the final peak in scallops of yellow granite braided with dark red gabbro, and in two places there were thin towers leaning over towards us. There was distinct likelihood of rebuff; she didn't lack spirit, it appeared.

We rested and ate. The blue air of the Northland swam about us, the Arctic Ocean spread blue-green floors beyond purple islands into the northward haze. South and east and west rose the graceful Lyngen peaks, some few still virgin, some few taller than our mistress; but on her alone our hearts were set, and the wooing could wait no longer. Leaving rucksacks and axes on the saddle, for no snow or ice lay on that narrow crest of rock, we tied on the 120-foot rope. The sun was hot on our backs and the rough rock warm under our grasping fingers as we began the climb, leading in turn. Jealously I watched Jack's progress, joyously I passed him and made my own assaults. Exhilaration grew with each success. A saucy parade of delightful tricks—airy knife-edge, coy traverse, archness of bridged flakes—served only to bring us nearer to our desire. To Jack it fell to deal with the first anticipated rebuff, a grey tower like a reproving finger, inflexible and unassailable. He thrust boldly past it on the left and found the ridge yielding in a short but exposed traverse and a little chimney that brought us back to the crest above the grey tower. We were half-way to triumph now. But I remembered the second tower and wondered whether the Spissthorn was playing with us; cat and mouse was a game beloved of females.

The ridge climbed on and we mounted with it, rope's length after rope's length with little difficulty but some exposure. When we bestrode the sharp crest, as we did now and then, our right boots dangled over shattered precipices that dropped into a purple brume of shadow in the moatlike glen between us and the snowy mountain on its further side; already we could look across the shining dome of that summit to the far peaks of South Lyngen, floating like clouds on a level sea of haze. On the left we looked down past our footholds to the glacier more than a thousand feet below, narrow gullies with ribbons of ice in them plunging sheer to the shrunken blue-pencil marks of open crevasses. It was only on this side that we could hope to turn any unclimbable obstacle.

The ridge reared above us still, hiding with its successive pinnacles what lay beyond, and still there was no sign of the second tower. Perhaps we had passed it unknowingly; perhaps it had been a mere perfunctory gesture intended to provoke, not to daunt, ardent lovers. Then, when we were hardly more than 200 feet below the summit, we came suddenly round an exposed corner and saw it opposing us with unmistakable sincerity of purpose.

DREAM OF A VIRGIN

It was more of a wall than a tower, a great slab of red gabbro like the palm of an out-thrust hand, barring us from what lay beyond with the classic gesture of 'Thus far, but no farther'. It was my lead and I surveyed the problem with care and some anxiety. The red wall was not high—twenty feet at most—but it was genuinely perpendicular; more accurately, its mean angle was 90° to the horizontal, for it was convex like a shield or a saucepan-lid, lying back a little at the top and undercut at the bottom. The ridge, very narrow, ran perfectly level and flat to its base, eight feet or so from where we were perched by the little rock bollard over which Jack had placed his anchor belay, and the base was undercut on both sides as well as in front so that it overhung slightly the glacier on the left and the vertical perspective of rotten wall on the right. Diffidence or shyness, tentative pawings round the flanks, could not help us here. A bold frontal attack was the only course, and the front of the wall offered no convenient foothold in its lower section and nothing but rudimentary fingerholds higher up. But—it was gabbro, the roughest and friendliest of all the climber's working surfaces.

Jack could have given me a shoulder in the manner of the early mountaineers, but that would mean both of us performing acrobatics eight feet away from the belay. I scanned the sunlit red rock for the likeliest rugosities, cautioned Jack to give me plenty of slack, and took a running jump at the wall. There was a second or two of frantic out-of-balance scrabbling before fingers got enough hold above the vertical part to resist the friction pressure of vibram soles on the grainy gabbro. After that it was astonishingly easy, as though the Spissthorn had suddenly decided to abandon all further resistance. I could have sworn I heard a sigh.

There was a handy knob above the wall for the abseil that would be needed on the descent, and only a hundred feet of easy knife-edge, like the Crib Goch ridge, left to climb. We tightroped along the crest until it vanished and left blue space under our noses. The Spissthorn was ours.

We crowned her with a cairn. We luxuriated in the hot sunshine and our triumph, we flaunted aneroid and prismatic compass and thermometer and numbered her very feet of height. Feeling ourselves Pygmalions to this newly awakened Galatea, we took full possession. The minutes flew unnoticed, for when a dream becomes reality—as it does perhaps once in a man's life—time ceases to exist.

Four hours later, when I looked up at her from the glacier below, I knew that we could never really possess the Spissthorn. Our tiny cairn had dwindled into invisibility on her proud head; she was aloof and virginal as ever. And yet— might there not be some scrap of mastership, some particle of possession, in having been the first? Then I would find consolation in that particle, and say, with Touchstone, 'A poor virgin, sir . . . but mine own.'

THE CONQUEST OF MAC

It was in the highest degree unlikely that any party of climbers would be climbing the Muldrow Glacier, at 11,000 feet on Mount McKinley, on 15th March 1910. For one thing, the Muldrow Glacier was still unexplored and had not yet been named; for another, it was only thirteen years since a surveying party had established that the great mountain, 150 miles north of Fairbanks in the Arctic wilderness of central Alaska, was the highest peak in North America. But if there had been such an intrepid party—intrepid, because explorers had declared the mountain impossible except to Alpinists of the highest skill possessing superhuman endurance—the climbers would have come upon a line of birch poles planted up the snowy walls, leading to a choked crevasse in which a tent of balloon silk had been pitched and roofed over with snow. In the tent they would have found four bearded men: Tom Lloyd, Pete Anderson, Billy Taylor and Charlie McGonagall. Observing the complete absence of mountaineering equipment, the hypothetical visitors would have concluded that these hard-bitten specimens clad in animal skins and fur caps, with caribou hides for sleeping-covers, were not climbers. In one sense they would have been right, for Tom Lloyd and his companions had never been on a mountain before, had no experience of climbing, and had probably never heard of the Alphine Club. Yet the men in the balloon-silk bivouac were proposing to make the first ascent of a peak 20,270 feet high.

In faraway Europe all the great Alpine peaks had been

scaled and the technique of climbing mountains established as a difficult craft essential to success and safety. Freshfield had climbed in the Caucasus and the Duke of the Abruzzi and Sir Martin Conway in the Himalaya; Mummery had perfected the art of rock climbing on the Chamonix Aiguilles. Seven decades of mountaineering sport and a thousand skilled Alpinists had produced inflexible rules and conventions outside which no man could hope to get any distance up a difficult mountain. Not in their wildest dreams had the mountain experts envisioned a great ascent made by ignoramuses without guides, ropes or ice axes—let alone an attack on a peak of Himalayan dimensions, defended by a maze of glaciers and a final icy keep which is the coldest place on the surface of the earth. On Mount McKinley a temperature of 100° below zero has been noted, the lowest natural temperature ever recorded. Small wonder that the Sourdough Ascent of McKinley, its origins hearsay and its facts still debatable, has a dreamlike character, a quality of insubstantiality that has prevented it from becoming as famous as many less notable ascents.

Tom Lloyd was a 'sourdough', one of the tough pioneers who wrested a living from the Alaskan wilderness by being in in turn hunter, prospector, and trapper. He and his climbing companions were not educated men like the European mountaineers of their day, nor were they interested in recording in print their McKinley adventure. All the same, Lloyd kept a diary of the climb and allowed the little local paper, the *Fairbanks Daily Times*, to print extracts from it; and two months later the London *Daily Telegraph* reprinted the extracts. From this, and from verbal comments picked up in Fairbanks, later historians tried to reconstruct the full story.

It seems certain that the idea of climbing McKinley originated in a bet. On a night of the Alaskan winter, with the cold outside so intense that when a man spat the saliva crackled into ice in mid air, the fur-clad men who were drinking in

THE CONQUEST OF MAC

Billy McPhee's saloon were arguing about the highest mountain in North America. Someone opined that it would never be climbed. Tom Lloyd (doubtless well filled with liquor) said he reckoned he could climb it himself. His mining partner Billy Taylor braved the resultant jeers by supporting his pal, and the opposition challenged them to back their claim with a wager. Evidently Lloyd and Taylor were known to be genuine hardshells and men of their word, for the saloon keeper and another man named Dave Petree put up a forfeit of $5,000 that Lloyd or one of his party would reach the top of McKinley before Independence Day, 4th July 1910. McPhee grubstaked the party to the extent of 500 dollars' worth of food and whisky, Lloyd enlisted two other tough prospectors named Anderson and McGonagall, and on 20th December 1909—in the depth of an Arctic winter—the expedition set forth from in front of the wooden Pioneer Hotel amid derisive cheers. Alaska was buried deep in its December snows. The venturers had two dog teams, and the sleds were loaded high with crates of food and casks of whisky and an enormous quantity of rope. Tom Lloyd knew nothing about the use of the climbing rope, but he had worked out a climbing technique of his own: he knew there would be very steep snow and ice to climb, and on these parts of the mountain he intended to fix ropes by which they could pull themselves up and descend again. It is interesting to note that Ardito Desio and his party largely relied on this method for their ascent of K 2, the second highest mountain in the world, 44 years later.

In one branch of the mountaineer's craft Lloyd and his friends were past masters, though they had never used it on a mountain: all their lives they had been pathfinders, and now that it came to finding a route up a mountain they made no mistake. Lloyd headed for the foot of the great Muldrow Glacier, nearly a dozen miles in total length, which sweeps up between tremendous precipices of rock and ice to the saddle between McKinley's twin summits. It took the four sourdoughs and their dog teams eleven weeks to cross the snowy Yukon wastes and gain a footing on the glacier. In that time they camped night after night in the snow, shooting for the pot (for of course they took their rifles) and finding themselves completely at home. While the snow lay—and it would last far beyond April—they had a limitless highway they could use as a city-bred man uses a pavement, and there was no hurry. At the treeline they established a sort of base camp and began cutting saplings, trimming hundreds of them into poles for staking the route. Tom Lloyd's diary vividly reports the start of the climb:

> March 13.—Took stove, tent, and bedding up Wall Street Glacier. We called it that because you look straight up as at a wall. I would not like to estimate the height of the walls, but in places it honestly looked to me to reach 10,000 feet straight up .... It is the grandest thing I ever saw in my life, that long stretch of glacier ... the next eight miles are terrible for crevasses. You can look down in them for a distance stretching from 100 ft. to Hades or China.

When there was no snowbridge across those crevasses they carried up treetrunks and built bridges, packing snow on the transverse branches so that the dogs could haul the sleds across. They used the dogs for hauling their materials and equipment higher than 15,000 feet, higher than the summit of the Matterhorn. Above that the route was too steep for teams and sleds and it was time to use the ropes and stakes.

It had taken them a fortnight to establish and stock Pothole Camp, as they called their refuge in the crevasse. Avalanches had thundered down, blizzards had driven them back more than once, but they had reached the beginning of the real climbing. Lloyd's one dread was lest a warm spell should set in and soften the snow; and at Pothole Camp his fear was realized, for the temperature rose to zero. For four days heavy snowfalls held them in their snow hole while gigantic avalanches hurtled down the mountain walls above them with a noise that shook even Lloyd's iron nerve:

> It was like the sound of a great gun . . . the ice comes tearing down the sides of the perpendicular walls with a most awful noise, tearing and grinding its way.

But they were lucky. Their balloon fabric tent was buried deep in drifts but not by avalanches. Soon they were able to climb on hardening snow, planting stakes, fixing ropes to them, slowly creeping up towards the top of 'Mac', as they irreverently called their mountain. On 17th March they reached a saddle of hard snow where the 'tent' could not be placed but where such men as these had no difficulty in contriving a house for themselves. They drove a tunnel into the face of the snowslope 30 feet below the crest:

> If we had driven the tunnel a little further in, so as to have a back door to our house, and had we opened that back door, we would have found ourselves looking down a precipice . . . If our foot had slipped at such a back door there wouldn't have been a grease-spot left of one of us by the time we reached the bottom of that precipice.

Again snowstorms held them fast at Tunnel Camp, and for a time they were in danger of starvation. Billy Taylor, who was doing the ferrying of supplies as far as the dogs could go, was unable to get up to them. But at last the vital contact was made and with sufficient rations and a 14-foot pole to which the American flag had been securely fixed they began the last lap of their long climb.

As they had done all the way, they planted stakes to mark their route. Those stakes had been their salvation during the eighteen days they had spent on the mountain, enabling them to move up and down the glacier with certainty through mists and blizzards. Now, as the four sourdoughs kicked and clung their way up to the ice basin now known as Harper's Glacier, only 1,000 feet below the top, there were no less than 750 stakes stretching away in innumerable zigzags behind and below them. Using hatchets to cut steps in the ice, planting stakes and fixing ropes where they could, they prepared the way foot by foot and day by day, retreating at night to Tunnel Camp. From the saddle they could see Mount McKinley had two summits, about three miles apart and separated by a long dipping snowridge; and as far as Lloyd could tell these tops were of equal height. He chose to go for the north summit.

Altitude was having its effect now. McGonagall collapsed 500 feet below the highest point and stayed where he was, to recover and go down under his own steam afterwards. The others reached the top, which was of crumbling rocks blown clear of snow, and planted the Stars and Stripes:

> We dug down 15 in. into the rocks until we had found a solid spot, where there will be no question but that the flagpole will stand, and into it we stuck that flagpole, a straight, seasoned spruce sapling full 4 in. at the butt, and tapering to full $2\frac{1}{2}$ in. at the top, and is full 14 ft. long. The flag attached to it is 6 ft. by 12 ft. in size, is an American flag erected by four Americans of Welsh, Scotch, Canadian and Swedish descent, and on the flag, written thereon in ink, is the name M. W. Griffin. The flag was raised at 3.25 p.m. on 3rd April 1910.

It was 10 p.m. before they got down again to Tunnel Camp. Next day they descended the whole of the staked route that had taken so long to climb, right back to their starting-point on the treeline. 'We travelled some' is Lloyd's comment on this feat. They had accomplished an epic, a first ascent without parallel in the annals of mountain climbing. But—they had not reached the highest point of McKinley.

Though Tom Lloyd did not know it at the time, he had chosen the lower of the twin peaks. The south summit is the higher by 300 feet, not very much in a total height of 20,270

THE CONQUEST OF MAC

feet but enough to rob the sourdoughs of the somewhat academic distinction of being first *on the top* of Mount McKinley, which was accorded to Hudson Stuck, Archdeacon of the Yukon, when he reached the south summit three years later. Stuck saw the flagpole still planted on the other summit. But a false statement made by Lloyd when he returned to Fairbanks cast such doubt on the rest of his story that many people refused to believe him. By travelling at top speed with a dog team he arrived in Fairbanks, alone, eight days after the climb; and he claimed to have climbed *both* summits of Mount McKinley.

Why Lloyd made this claim is matter for conjecture. There is no real doubt that he was one of those who reached the north summit, or that he did not know that it was lower than the other. At a distance of three miles it is impossible to judge, by eye alone, a difference in height of 300 feet. It may well be that he remembered the $5,000 that his friend Billy McPhee, who had grubstaked him, would have to pay out if someone proved that other distant summit to be the real top, and that he decided to claim both of them in case this happened; that, probably, would not have seemed unethical to Tom Lloyd. But he had not primed his companions with the story, and when some enterprising reporters made the trek to Lloyd's mining camp, where he had left them working, Taylor and Anderson and McGonagall all said they had only climbed one summit.

And that is why a man whose achievement merited honorary membership of the Alpine Club is not even credited, today, with the first ascent of the north peak of his 'Mac'. Anthony Huxley's *Standard Encyclopaedia of the World's Mountains*, published in 1962, states that only 'Pete Anderson, Billy Taylor and Charley McGonogol' took part in the Sourdough Ascent of Mount McKinley. The name of Thomas Lloyd has vanished like a dream from the pages of mountaineering history. It seems not unlikely that Thomas Lloyd himself wouldn't give a damn.

THE DREAM OF ETERNITY

It is an odd thing, and non-climbers must find it an odder thing still, that so many mountaineers should find themselves moved by what are sometimes termed 'religious' feelings when they are high on a mountain. It has long ceased to be the fashion to describe these feelings in print, and no modern climber writing of the pleasures of an ascent in a book or a club journal would dare to mention the name of God except as part of an oath; but now and then, from timid hint or careless implication, you perceive that someone else has experienced that fleeting revelation which is beyond reason and better than faith.

The church-going Christian (and there are still some of them among climbers) can fit his mountain-top emotions to the set terms of his creed without much difficulty. This does not necessarily mean that his is the right interpretation, any more than Edmund Hillary's desire to climb Everest meant that he accepted the Buddhist belief that Chomolungma was a sacred mountain. Men of other beliefs or none at all have felt these movings of the spirit, varying in form and degree as their motives for climbing vary. Sir Leslie Stephen, great climber and Victorian agnostic, was debarred by his belief—or disbelief—from using words like 'heaven' and 'eternity' in his classic writings about mountains, but he admits in many passages of *The Playground of Europe* to feelings bordering on the religious; speaking, for example, of

'those gigantic masses to which, in spite of all reason, it is

THE DREAM OF ETERNITY

impossible not to attribute some shadowy personality. Their voice is mystic and has found discordant interpreters; but to me at least it speaks in tones at once more tender and more awe-inspiring than that of any mortal teacher. The loftiest and sweetest strains of Milton or Wordsworth may be more articulate, but do not lay so forcible a grasp upon my imagination.'

Hilaire Belloc, a Catholic and a mountain-lover though no climber, saw in a vision of the distant Alps what many have felt on their ridges and summits, and described it in a famous passage of *The Path to Rome*. 'These, the great Alps, seen thus', he ends that description, 'link one in some way to one's immortality. . . . Since I could now see such a wonder and it could work such things in my mind, therefore some day I should be part of it. That is what I felt.' No one could call his conclusion rational. But the words interpret, as well as mere words can do, a feeling which may be irrational but is none the less a real and not uncommon experience among mountaineers. Belloc knew that there could be no satisfactory verbal explanation of his feelings. 'It is better to address prayers to such things than to attempt to interpret them for others', is his comment on his own attempt. Some men, indeed, have made a sort of religion out of their love of mountains, turning a blind eye to their quite frequent ugliness and assuming that the universal beauty of high hills—which they alone, it is implied, can perceive—produces this exalted sensation. To others such an assumption is like declaring that light has no part in the beauty of a stained-glass window; they will agree with the poet Michael Roberts: 'Mountains may be symbols or images of some other reality, but the worship of symbols as if they were something other than images is a form of superstition.'

Some other reality. That is a phrase that comes very near the mark. There are times on a mountain when perception seems suddenly to become sharpened, piercing the walls of sense and reason that ordinarily enclose us all as conclusively as the horizon, so that we *know*—though for the briefest of moments—that these surrounding peaks, real as they undoubtedly are, represent 'some other reality' beyond them. That this heightened perception may be due to heightened emotion is immaterial; there is nothing abnormal in emotional response to the stimulus of special environment. When Leslie Stephen found it 'impossible not to attribute some shadowy personality' to mountains he was aware, in some degree, of the second reality behind the first and obvious one. It is in this awareness that the blinding flash of insight comes as it did to the poet and we know that we are a part of all that we behold. And the knowledge revives those intimations of immortality which even the atheist has to keep sternly battened down. Nothing is more transient, more quickly forgotten, than this glimpse of certainty on the heights; but the impact on the spirit remains though we deny it afterwards in the valleys. The 'other reality' beyond the mountains is in us also, and our personalities, shadowy as the mountains' own, are mere projections of it in time and space—that is the thing that makes us part of them. To this feeling is joined the definite impression that the other reality is the ultimate truth. The mountains will crumble into dust at last just as men must do, but something of both, the same something, is indestructible—immortal.

Attempting to analyse such things is like trying to dissect the glow of sunrise on untrodden snow. It will convince no one who has not experienced it; and it is both safer and easier to state boldly that the mountain revelation does occur, and has recurred since mountain-climbing began. Great mountaineers like Frank Smythe (who trod, perhaps, too deeply into mysticism) and modern hard-climbing experts like W. H. Murray have received it and tried to convey its message. Some have derided them—'sees an angel on every pitch, does Bill'—

THE DREAM OF ETERNITY

but the thing happens still, as it did to Mr. Justice Wills on the Wetterhorn in 1854.

Mr. Wills, later the Rt. Hon. Sir Alfred Wills and a Judge of Queen's Bench, arrived at Grindelwald with two Chamonix guides, intent on making what he believed to be the first ascent of the Wetterhorn. It was in fact only the fourth ascent; but from it is dated the beginning of mountaineering as a pastime. Wills, you remember, had four guides, having enlisted the Oberlanders Lauener and Bohren in addition to Balmat and Simond, and Lauener carried the *'Flagge'*—a 12-foot iron pole with an iron banner at the top. They spent the night in a cave above the Upper Grindelwald Glacier and began the climb before dawn next morning; the glacier, a rock ridge, and then the dazzle of the rising sun on the snow. Behind them on the rock ridge they suddenly discerned, to the dismay of the guides, two men following them up the mountain, one of them carrying on his back 'a young fir-tree, branches, leaves, and all'. The tree-carrier was Christian Almer, who was to become perhaps the greatest of all Alpine guides. After a brief dispute it was agreed that the two newcomers had a right to be on the mountain, and soon the two parties joined up and climbed Lauener's zigzag ladder of ice steps together. The last, very steep, snowslope ended above in an overhanging cornice fringed with giant icicles. Lauener climbed up the hard snow beneath the cornice and began to cut a way through, expecting to haul himself out on to a snowy dome beyond.

'Suddenly a startling cry of surprise and triumph rang through the air. A great block of ice bounded from the top of the parapet, and before it had well lighted on the glacier, Lauener exclaimed, "Ich schaue den blauen Himmel!" "I see blue sky!") . . . and then at length we crept slowly on. As I took the last step, Balmat disappeared from my sight; my left shoulder grazed against the icy embrasure, while, on the right, the glacier fell abruptly away beneath me towards an unknown and awful abyss; a hand from an invisible person grasped mine; I stepped across, and had passed the ridge of the Wetterhorn!'

The ridge was indeed the actual summit. It was a knife-edge of frozen snow so narrow that Wills found he could not place his two feet side by side on it, and later on there was some difficulty in planting Lauener's famous *Flagge* and Almer's fir-tree securely on the crest. It was a perfect day, a perfect summit, and (so far as they knew) a first ascent. But Wills's first reaction was not one of triumph, or of relief, or even of pleasure. The vast prospect of peaks and glaciers in the upper world of mountains, so remote from Man's everyday life, so complete a contrast to the green pastures of Grindelwald 9,000 feet below him, worked its brief miracle of revelation. In attempting to describe it afterwards he naturally used the medium of his own religion; nor is his sincerity the less apparent for that.

'I am not ashamed to own that I experienced, as this sublime and wonderful prospect burst upon my view, a profound and almost irrepressible emotion—an emotion which, if I may judge by the low ejaculations of surprise, followed by a long pause of breathless silence, as each in turn stepped into the opening, was felt by the others as well as myself. . . . We felt as if in the more immediate presence of Him who had reared this tremendous pinnacle, and beneath the "majestical roof" of whose deep blue heaven we stood, poised, as it seemed, between earth and sky.'

So Mr. Justice Wills, by tradition the First Mountaineer, perceived on the Wetterhorn his unprecedented nearness to the First Cause; to the inexplicable. It is significant that the passage forms part of the Prologue to the first collection of mountain writings ever published, *Peaks, Passes and Glaciers*. Other men on other mountain-tops have felt as he felt, and found, or not cared to find, their own interpretation. But the true interpretation will only be found when it is time to write the Epilogue.

THE SUPERNATURAL

. . . it appears that the climber's view of things is in some way clarified rather than distorted; and that there are times when he is more open to extra-sensory perceptions than is the normal person.

W. KENNETH RICHMOND

THE GREY MAN

North-west of Braemar beyond ten miles of wild and lonely hills rises the second highest mountain in the British Isles, Ben Macdhui. 'The hill of the black pig', 4,296 feet high, is one of the Cairngorms, mountains distinguished for their mass and extent rather than for shapeliness, though there are several fine climbing crags on and around Macdhui. It has other distinctions: Queen Victoria climbed it (on a pony) in 1859; Mr. Gladstone climbed it (on foot) in 1884; and—though neither of these notables saw him—Ferlas Mor, the giant Grey Man, roams the mountain in the darkening mists of twilight.

Those who testify to seeing apparitions, especially in country districts, are more often than not folk of poor education with a traditional background of ancient lore and superstition. The Scottish Highlands in particular, where legend has persisted longer than anywhere else in Britain, are likely to retain as fact stories of supernatural appearances which had their real origin in the tales of long-ago bards. But the Grey Man of Ben Macdhui is a much more substantial spectre. Apart from the fact that he has often been seen or heard by climbers in quite recent years, his existence is supported by the testimony of a man of science who was Professor of Organic Chemistry at University College, London.

John Norman Collie has undisputed claims to distinction as a pioneer of mountaineering. It was Collie who revealed the glories of the Coolin and scaled the last unclimbed peak in Britain, Sgurr Coire an Lochain. He made the first ascent of Tower Ridge on Ben Nevis, was with Mummery and Slingsby on the first ascent of the Dent du Requin in the Chamonix Aiguilles, and in 1895 went to the Himalaya as one of Mummery's party who were the first men to attack Nanga Parbat. He had a keen analytical mind whose natural scepticism was apt to be expressed in sarcastic comment. A lifelong bachelor, he devoted all his vacations to rock climbing and mountaineering, and Geoffrey Winthrop Young wrote of him: 'Of all the wholehearted mountaineers I have known, Collie alone remained to the end wholly and passionately absorbed in the mountain world.' His inquiring mind and his 'whinstone common sense' are exemplified by two incidents famous in climbing history. In 1906, when climbing in the Coolin had been going on for forty years, he discovered the Cioch, one of the two most notable pinnacles in Britain; noticing a big shadow cast by the evening sun on the face of Sron na Ciche, he photographed it, closely examined the photo, and later climbed up to confirm his deduction that it was the shadow of a most remarkable rock tower which has ever since been a Mecca for British climbers. The incident of the Collie Step, which for long remained a subject of heated dispute in climbing circles, occurred when Collie was leading the first ascent of Moss Ghyll, then a 'last great problem' in the Lake District. High up on the climb Collie found his exit from a cave barred by a smooth slab which had to be traversed but gave no foothold. The success of the climb depended on that missing foothold, so without hesitation he used his ice axe to make one. Though he was a dedicated mountaineer, he was also a scientific genius, devising the neon tube and sponsoring the first medical use of X-rays. He was the last man, one would have thought, to see an apparition—unless the apparition was indisputably vouched for by his own senses.

It was natural enough that such a man could not bring himself to relate a very unscientific happening until many

THE GREY MAN

years after the event. Collie was speaking at a dinner of the Cairngorm Club in 1925 when he revealed his strange experience. He had been climbing Ben Macdhui alone, not for the first time. There was snow on the ground and mist around him as he neared the summit on a grey day with no trace of sunlight to cast shadows. A little way below the top he heard heavy footsteps behind him in the snow and halted to find out who was following him so noisily. The footsteps had stopped; no one was there. When he started up again the footsteps recommenced, stamping and creaking in the snow, a far heavier tread than the heaviest man would make. Each time he stopped the invisible follower stopped too—until the summit cairn loomed out of the mist. Then the footsteps began to come nearer and nearer. A tall shadow, darker than the grey mist, loomed more immense than any human shape. Collie turned and fled. 'I was seized', he told his listeners seriously, 'with an intolerable fright and I ran my hardest down the mountainside. No power on earth will ever take me up Ben Macdhui again.' There was some laughter but the Professor was not smiling. And afterwards two other climbers buttonholed him and confessed that they had a very similar experience on the Ben. Collie, lean and erect with lank grey hair above somewhat sombre features, accepted their stories gravely as evidence supporting his own tale. For the many who scoffed he cared nothing.

The Grey Man seems always to choose a solitary climber, and though he has—very rarely—been seen as a vague shadow human in form but three or four times human height his normal manifestation is by the sound of footsteps. In his book *Always a Little Further* Alistair Borthwick tells how he talked with two men who on separate occasions in the forties heard the Grey Man on Ben Macdhui. The first man was crossing the mountain on a calm night when the snow was hard-crusted and a hidden moon gave faint luminosity to the mist that lay across the upper slopes. He passed the summit and was descending towards the Lairing Ghru when the crunch of footsteps sounded on the snow close above him. He stopped; the other noise stopped, to start again when he went on. He noticed that the rhythm of the other steps was one step to his three, so it could not be some freakish echo. Men who cross big mountains by night are not nervous types, but this man was 'scared stiff', as he admitted—too scared to look behind him when the mist thinned. He made himself walk steadily instead of yielding to the strong impulse to race down the treacherous slope in the dark. And the footsteps stopped, a thousand feet above the glen he was making for. The experience of the second man was rather similar, except that he was crossing Ben Macdhui in summer daylight. Mist was down, and very dense, so he was using his compass as he toiled up the screes alone; alone, save for another solitary hill-walker who was evidently following him up the scree, invisible in the mist. The loud crunching of the rock fragments sounded clearly in the stillness. A big man, or one with an abnormally long stride, thought the climber, because the invisible one took only one step for two-and-a-half steps of the man in front. Then, a little below the summit, a sudden breeze blew the mist clear and the whole mountainside was plain to see. There was no one else on the scree.

The second man was long-legged and six feet tall; the first was five feet seven. If Ferlas Mor has a somewhat dubious consistency, he is at least consistent in his relation to human height.

In a later year there was a search party on Ben Macdhui in which stalkers and gamekeepers of the area took part. One of the climbers asked the local men what they thought of Ferlas Mor. Was there such a thing? Or was it just a silly story? They looked at him queerly for a moment. Then one of them said quietly, 'We do not talk about that.'

THE GREY MAN

There is never any positive proof that such things as Ferlas Mor exist. Perhaps the strongest argument for the existence of the Grey Man of Ben Macdhui lies in the behaviour of Professor Collie. After that frightening encounter Collie walked very often on the Cairngorms, the nearest hills to his home in Aberdeen. But he never once, in all the rest of his life, set foot again on Ben Macdhui.

'GEISTER' ON THE MATTERHORN

'See, Herr Mommerie—a *geist*!' Alexander Burgener, squat and bulky as a bear in the darkness, gripped his employer's arm and pointed downwards. 'On the glacier—there, moving about!'

'A lantern,' Mummery said reassuringly.

Burgener spat out an oath. 'A lantern! What could anyone want there, on the Gorner Glacier? It leads nowhere—and at this hour? It's three in the morning, *mein Herr*!'

Three in the morning of 3rd September 1879. A. F. Mummery and his guides Burgener and Venetz were on their way up to the Schwarzsee below the Matterhorn, intending to attempt the first ascent of the Furggen Ridge. It was their second start, for Burgener had been unwell the first time and they had been forced to return to Zermatt, where Mummery had the uncomfortable experience of lunching in a quiet corner of the Monte Rosa hotel while tourists were searching the Matterhorn skyline for him with the hotel telescope. This time he was determined not to turn back, ghosts or no ghosts. The queer behaviour of the light far down on the Gorner Glacier was indeed a puzzle, but there must be no delay if they were to get up the great unclimbed ridge and down again before nightfall by Whymper's route. Insisting firmly that the light on the glacier (it was wobbling in slow circles now) could be nothing but a lantern, he got the uneasy Saas men moving again. All went well until they reached the boggy ground near the Schwarzsee. Here, to Mummery's dismay, they were soon surrounded by the weird unearthly flicker of innumerable will-o'-the-wisps. The two guides were very frightened. Burgener clutched Mummery's arm again and whispered that these were the spirits of the dead, the ghosts who were seen by men about to die.

'We were marked out for the vengeance of the immortal gods. The fiends who haunt the crags of the Matterhorn were already gloating over their prey! Such was the purport of the agonised whispers of the men. I am fain to confess that the crawling bluish flames, the utter silence, and the contagion of my companions' superstitious fear, thrilled me with instinctive horror. I perceived, however, that if we were not to return to Zermatt baffled and beaten a second time, the delights of a spiritualistic *séance* must be abandoned in favour of a matter-of-fact explanation.'

His explanation, Mummery adds in *My Climbs in the Alps and Caucasus,* was so forcible that the guides must have thought that every square yard of Britain was brilliantly illuminated at night by these marsh-gas lights. Its effect was temporarily ruined by the appearance of two more lights far down the black mountainside, which were at once pronounced by Burgener to be more 'Geister'. Mummery retorted that two parties were starting up the ordinary route and these were their lanterns. Burgener refused to believe it until, urged by his *Herr*, he achieved a tremulous yodel and heard the distant voice of Peter Taugwalder reply with a cheerful yell. The situation was saved, and an obstacle that might easily have prevented Mummery from getting to the Furggen Ridge was almost removed. Almost, but not quite, for Burgener and Venetz still believed that they had seen at least one *geist*. It was a well-ascertained fact (attested by all the ecclesiastical authorities in the Saas, Zermatt, and Anzasca valleys) that anyone seeing a *geist* would be dead within twenty-four hours. Mummery pointed out that if this was so they might as well

THE SUPERNATURAL

go on with the climb, since it would be more shameful to be plucked by the Devil from the streets of Zermatt than from the Furggen Ridge. This logic got the men moving again, though somewhat gloomily; and when they had offered up prayers in the little chapel by the Schwarzsee, and dawn had come, they started more resolutely for the Furggen Glacier and the foot of their ridge.

Dread of the supernatural was as strong in the two guides as the courage and skill that had taken them with Mummery up the virgin peak of the Charmoz. Burgener, a devout Catholic, might invent useful dispensations for his faith; Sunday climbing, he considered, was permissible on easy mountains because there even the Devil couldn't drag you from the large firm holds. But with Geister it was another matter altogether. Geister had no mercy. And the mountain was the haunted Matterhorn.

Two decades earlier Edward Whymper had come up against the Matterhorn's garrison of Geister:

'There seemed to be a *cordon* drawn around it, up to which one might go, but no farther. Within that invisible line gins and effreets were supposed to exist—the Wandering Jew and the spirits of the damned. The superstitious natives in the surrounding valleys (many of whom firmly believed it to be not only the highest mountain in the Alps, but in the world) spoke of a ruined city on the summit wherein the spirits dwelt; and if you laughed, they gravely shook their heads; told you to look yourself to see the castles and walls, and warned one against a rash approach, lest the infuriate demons from their impregnable heights might hurl down vengeance for one's derision.'

From this passage of *Scrambles Amongst the Alps* with its unusually shaky prose it might almost be thought that Edward Whymper himself was infected by the beliefs of the 'superstitious natives'. Certainly on that tragic 14th of July 1865,

'GEISTER' ON THE MATTERHORN

when he was descending the Hörnli ridge with the two Taugwalders after their four companions had fallen to their deaths, the weird sorcery of the Matterhorn awed him unforgettably. They were clambering, slowly and uncertainly, down the easier part of the ridge—

> 'when, lo! a mighty arch appeared, rising above the Lyskamm, high into the sky. Pale, colourless, and noiseless, but perfectly sharp and defined, except where it was lost in the clouds, this unearthly apparition seemed like a vision from another world; and, almost appalled, we watched with amazement the gradual development of two vast crosses, one to either side. If the Taugwalders had not been the first to perceive it, I should have doubted my senses. They thought it had some connection with the accident, and I, after a while, that it might bear some relation to ourselves. But our movements had no effect upon it. The spectral forms remained motionless. It was a fearful and wonderful sight; unique in my experience and impressive beyond description, coming at such a moment.'

In 1879 the Matterhorn still retained its uncanny reputation, and it may have been this that distracted Alexander Burgener from his route-finding and led Mummery's party into extreme difficulties on their Furggen Ridge attempt. When they reached the crest below the final 500 feet of vertical rock (which was not to be climbed direct until 1941) it was late in the day and a gale was raging. The only escape from an impossible situation was by traversing right across the East Face, on sloping slabs which were swept by falls of rocks and ice, to the Shoulder on the easier Hörnli Ridge. They accomplished it safely. The 'infuriate demons' hurled down their missiles but did not hit them.

Burgener and Venetz were much puzzled. They had certainly seen a *geist* on the Gorner Glacier, and yet they were alive. Back at Zermatt, they learned the true explanation of the wandering light—an explanation that enabled them to keep their superstition intact.

A party of girls with their schoolmistresses, staying in Zermatt, had spent the afternoon in cautious examination of the flat and comparatively safe Gorner Glacier. On their return it was discovered that one of the girls was missing, lost on the glacier, whereupon the whole school had set forth again at evening and scattered in all directions across the ice to search for the lost one. The result was that by midnight half-a-dozen girls were hopelessly entangled in the maze of icy hollows. The wandering light was the lantern of a guide despatched by the hotel keeper to rescue the disconsolate maidens one by one.

'I HAVE TO GO ON'

Because he is a very well known climber, I shall call him Charles, which is not his real name. He told me this story just as it happened to him a dozen years ago.

Charles was nineteen and in love with mountains. Especially he liked to wander alone on the rocky ridges of Snowdonia, where you can find hand-and-foot work on *arêtes* and pinnacles steep enough to be interesting but not hard enough to warrant the use of a climbing rope. Finding himself at Ogwen, where the A 5 cuts through the mountains north of Snowdon, he planned a day's walk that is frequently done—up Tryfan, on by the Bristly Ridge to the top of Glyder Fach, over Glyder Fawr and down into Cwm Idwal by the Devil's Kitchen path. The Idwal Youth Hostel was to be his lodging that night.

Cwm Idwal, with its pale still lake lying under the mountain walls that rise from the water's edge on either hand, has a gloomy grandeur unparalleled in Wales. The Glyder Fawr precipices on the east and the crags of Y Garn on the west provide much of the grandeur; the vertical rock wall of the Devil's Kitchen cliffs closing in the southern end of the cwm is chiefly responsible for the gloom. In the centre of these cliffs the black gash of Twll Du, the Devil's Kitchen, is the only break. It is a climber's way, once a 'last great problem' and even now not often climbed, though more than one route has been made up its dark and slimy walls. The mountain walker must seek an easier way down when he descends the screes of Glyder Fawr and finds himself on the crest of the rock wall. The way, a steep and crumbling path, starts down a grassy gully near the eastern end of the cliff top; but if you miss the little cairns that mark its beginning—as it is quite easy to do in mist, or if your mind is not on your route-finding—you come in a minute or two to another grassy gully as inviting as the first. And this gully, after leading you gently downwards with treacherous innocence, thrusts you suddenly on to the verge of space, with a vertical drop of some 400 feet under your boots. There have been a number of fatal accidents here.

Charles tramped up the track to the northern end of Llyn Idwal and then headed east over rising moorland, leaving the hollow of Cwm Idwal and making for the craggy west face of Tryfan. You can find very good scrambling on Tryfan's west face if you go straight up when you strike Llyn Bochlwyd. He climbed the muddy path beside the waterfall and saw the lake, with Tryfan soaring above on his left front and the notchy Bristly Ridge mounting rightwards above the purple buttresses of Glyder Fach. It was a quiet day on the hills and so far he had seen no one. Now he saw a small orange tent under a little crag not far from the lake shore, and a man tidying up after his camp breakfast. Charles's route lay past the tent, so he halted and exchanged greetings with the camper; a youngish man, quiet, nothing remarkable or even memorable about him. The camper seemed to like Charles's plan for the day, and Charles invited him to come along.

Charles says they talked very little together. Men meeting by chance on a mountain and joining for the day's scrambling are apt to discover nothing at all about each other except that they both like mountains. Charles felt that the stranger felt about mountains as he did; they were in accord, and speech was unnecessary. Together they clambered up the good grey rock of the west face and rested, mostly in silence, beside the two summit monoliths called Adam and Eve.

'I HAVE TO GO ON'

'Down to Bwlch Tryfan and up Bristly?'

'Suits me.'

They went on down the south ridge. Up the screes to the start of the Bristly Ridge, where you have not enough breath for conversation anyway. Up and down, and up higher next time, on the towers of the ridge to the chaos of gigantic boulders strewn on the summit of Glyder Fach. Easier going over the col between the two Glyders, past the queer isolated clumps of spikes one of which is Glyder Fawr's highest point, down the long jolting descent north-westwards. Straight below them as they descended the flanks of scree the moorland saddle lay, rising beyond into the bare steeps of Y Garn. On the right they looked down a thousand feet to the lake of Idwal, sunk deep below the long edge of the saddle which was the crest of the Devil's Kitchen cliffs. When they were down at last on the saddle there was no hint of the precipices so close on their right hand; boggy hollows and little hummocks of rock hid the approaches to the edge. But Charles knew the route, and he spotted one of the little cairns that mark the start of the one safe way down. He turned right, into a shallow gully of grass and rock.

When he had gone a few steps he became aware that his companion was not following. He turned, and saw the other standing apparently irresolute.

'This is the way down. Come on.'

'I can't go down there.'

There was something a bit queer in the stranger's tone, though Charles couldn't have described the queerness. He was puzzled. The chap had clambered over the Bristly Ridge towers confidently enough.

'It's perfectly safe and easy, man,' he said.

'I can't go down there. I have to go on.'

'Oh. Well, it's getting a bit late—and anyway I want to be back at the hostel for supper. If you're not coming ——'

'*I have to go on.*'

The way those words were spoken made them linger in Charles's mind after he had said 'Cheeroh, then' and started his solitary descent. He remembered them next morning.

'You went up by Bochlwyd yesterday, didn't you?' said the hostel warden. 'See anything of a tent?'

'A small orange tent?'

'That's the one.' The Warden sighed. 'I've got to go up and collect it—dead man's effects. It belonged to a chap who broke his neck a couple of days ago—missed the path and tried to get down the Devil's Kitchen cliffs.'

YETI

In an age when our scientists claim to have solved all the problems of the natural world it is pleasant to hand them one question which they still haven't answered: what is a Yeti?

Himalayan travellers who have made some inquiry into the gods and devils of Buddhism in those parts can define a Yeti as an earth-spirit, entirely mythological, sent forth when the gods intend harm to someone. The Sherpas from Sola Khumbu, when they find otherwise inexplicable prints in the snow, declare them to be made by a Yeti. This is how the creature called 'the Abominable Snowman', presumably a thing of flesh and blood since it leaves real footprints, has come to be identified with a quite different thing, a supernatural being called a Yeti. Perhaps this differentiation is mere purism after all, though; for in spite of expeditions dedicated to the finding of an Abominable Snowman there is still no real proof of its existence. Indeed, it could well be from the same stable as the Grey Man of Ben Macdhui, who—since he is heard crunching the scree and stamping the snow—must surely leave footprints.

Colonel Howard-Bury, leader of the first Mount Everest Expedition in 1921, came upon some curious tracks on the Lhakpa La at 21,000 feet and was told by his porters that they were made by 'the Wild Men of the Snows'. Mr. Henry Newman of Darjeeling, talking to these porters on their return from the expedition, obtained a fuller description: the 'Wild Men' had very long hair; their feet were turned back-

THE SUPERNATURAL

wards; the proper name for a Wild Man was *Metch Kangmi*, *kangmi* meaning 'man of the snow' and *metch* meaning 'filthy and disgusting'. Mr. Newman contracted 'filthy and disgusting man of the snow' into the happier 'Abominable Snowman', and so the creature received its popular name. He also suggested an explanation for both footprints and description: Tibetans did not execute their worst criminals but simply turned them out of their villages or monasteries; thus, having to live in caves and steal food in order to live, they might be the stealthy and invisible makers of prints in wild places. The objection to this (as H. W. Tilman points out in his Appendix to *Mount Everest 1938*) is that no half-naked criminal, however hardy, would or could walk about on a snow col at 21,000 feet on Everest, never before approached by men and accessible to expert climbers only after days of gruelling toil.

The fact that the Far East does produce ascetics of incredible hardiness, however, led others to maintain that the footprints could have a human source. Captain Henniker, R.E., reported that in July 1930 he and his party were crossing a 17,000-foot pass in Ladakh when they met a man completely naked except for a loincloth. It was snowing and bitterly cold. The man, an Indian, greeted him in perfect English: 'Good morning, sir, and a happy Christmas to you.' He was an M.A. of an English University, on pilgrimage. But this was on a pass comparatively low and often used. The unexplained footprints continued to be found in places much higher and more remote, such as the Zemu Gap, a 19,000-foot pass where it was inconceivable that any man could have been before the first explorers struggled up to discover it. No European ever saw the creature that made the prints, though in many widely separated villages of the Himalaya the story that he had been seen (usually by a villager recently deceased) was to be found.

The camera now took part in the investigation. Frank Smythe took photographs of some 'yeti' prints he found at

16,500 feet in the Central Himalaya and submitted them to a caucus of zoologists. Dr. Julian Huxley pronounced them to be the prints of a bear, *Ursus arctus pruinosus*. The footprints were imperfect, as spoor in snow must be even when freshly made; and since bears are vegetarians and the Himalayan treeline is at about 12,000 feet, the improbability of any bear climbing snow and ice thousands of feet above its feeding grounds led some people to distrust Professor Huxley's theory. Tilman, a more experienced Himalayan traveller than Smythe, found and measured some 'yeti' tracks on the upper Biafu Glacier. They were roughly circular, a foot in diameter, and lay in a straight line 18 inches apart. A few days later he and his Sherpas found genuine bear tracks in the valley of a lower glacier, and 'they were no more like the others than those of a two-toed ant-eater'.

I have seen the track of an Abominable Snowman myself, though without recognizing it as such. In 1954 our small expedition was trying to penetrate a maze of unexplored ridges towards the unclimbed peak of Baudha, 22,000 feet. We and our Sherpas, in two or three small parties, were ferrying loads up to a camp at 14,000 feet in the bad weather that characterized that year. I was with two others, struggling up a steep snow gully which we were using as the ferry-route to our camp site, when I noticed a line of tracks crossing a shoulder of snow high above on the right wall of the gully, and remarked that the Sherpas must have worked out a better route. Two Sherpas were at the site when we arrived and I suggested they should follow the tracks when they went down for the next load, to see if they gave a better alternative. When they came up again, in a thick snowstorm, they were both very frightened. None of the four Sherpas, they declared, had gone that way; and the tracks were 'yeti' tracks. The snowstorm had blotted out the prints by now, but I got one of the Sherpas —an intelligent man who had served in a Gurkha regiment—

to make a drawing to scale. His sketch showed an almost circular footprint 12 inches in diameter, with three toes in front and one much larger toe behind. A year later John Jackson of the 1955 Kangchenjunga Expedition photographed a very clear and recent print; it corresponded with the Sherpa's sketch—except that the impression of the large hind toe appeared as two toes.

Monasteries in various parts of Nepal are reputed to treasure portions of genuine Yeti, skins or embalmed heads. These relics, not shown even to Buddhists, were sought by the *Daily Mail* expedition led by Ralph Izzard, which was arriving in Kathmandu when my party returned there after failing to climb Baudha. Also in Kathmandu was Dr. David Snellgrove, Tibetan scholar and authority on the Buddhist Himalaya. Dr. Snellgrove confided to us, in unscholarly but emphatic phrase, that the *Daily Mail* party had not 'a cat in hell's chance' of tracking down the Abominable. News of its purpose had already spread like wildfire throughout Nepal, and every scrap of Yeti evidence down to the last hair had been carefully hidden away; for the devils of a Buddhist's theology are as sacred as his gods, and the lamas had decreed that the prying unbelievers must be sent empty away.

So even the *Daily Mail* did not succeed in giving the public the truth on this occasion. There is one more recent item of evidence. In 1958 a Russian scientist, Professor Pronin, claimed to have seen a number of simian-looking creatures running away as he climbed a snowy shoulder in the high Pamirs. They vanished before he could give chase or approach near enough to observe details; the confused footprints they left were like the Yeti prints reported in the Himalaya. No less than three Soviet expeditions subsequently visited the area to search for Yetis, but found nothing at all.

There the matter rests at present. Is there such a creature as a Yeti? Is it natural or supernatural? It seems to be anybody's guess.

THE HORNS OF ELFLAND

Precisely at midnight the sun pierced the lowering clouds. The mountain walls of the Stortindal glowed with ruby light, and the milky blue of a glacial lake in the valley bottom changed to blood-red. Five thousand feet overhead the snowcrests looked like pink neon lights. At 1 a.m. we halted and lit a fire of juniper to warm our wet socks, soaked half-a-dozen times that night in the fording of glacier torrents, and the orange flames seemed reflected in the changing hues of the high snows.

With a day to spare at the end of our little expedition to Arctic Norway, John and Dewi and I had camped beside the Jegervand, the most beautiful lake in North Lyngen, with the idea of finding a new route up Stortind. The lake is only a few feet above sea level, and the superb mountains that surround it show all their 5,000 feet of height from the birch scrub at their toes to their white heads nodding above walls of rock and hanging glaciers. Stortind is the highest of them. It had been climbed already from the west, but we thought a way might be found from the east if we could locate the glacier that fell from the mountain into the wild Stortindal; since there was no map—for the area was uninhabited and only partly explored—this might not be easy. So we had started for the climb at eight-thirty in the evening, with plenty of light for climbing although the Midnight Sun was at first lost behind clouds. Ploughing through dense birch scrub, bashing endlessly over the massed boulders of the valley floor, we took five hours to find our way up the Stortindal. It was a grim place, beautiful only when the red sunrays brightened it. The icefall of the glacier was grimmer still, an enormous wall of ice capping a strictly vertical precipice that rose above our heads for more than a thousand feet. A waterfall spouted from the junction of ice with rock, dropping through empty air to vanish in fine spray before it reached the bottom.

We toiled up moraine heaps and scree, found a zigzag route up loose ledges, and traversed gingerly on to the glacier above the precipice. It was 3.30 a.m. now and the walls and pinnacles of ice were translucent against the bright sun, blues and greens and golds like pieces of an immense stained-glass window shattered on the snows of Stortind. We tied on the rope and began to edge a tortuous way through the icefall, nicking steps up *arêtes* of glass or balancing along snow-covered ledges above crevasses whose blue-green depths were too suggestive to impress us as beautiful. It took us two hours to work our way out of the icefall on to the steep snow of the upper glacier, where we were in warm sunshine. Close on every hand the rock buttresses rose, one of them no doubt giving access to the ridges of Stortind; but one after another of them was dismissed as 'too dicey'—the lower part was always overhanging and there was a continuous bergschrund under the overhangs with not a single convenient snowbridge. It was perhaps a hasty reconnaissance, but it was obvious, in the brilliant Arctic sunlight that showed up every detail, that we would make no new route up Stortind from this side. At half-past seven we began the retreat, by the way we had come.

Four hours later I was boulder-hopping half-way down the Stortindal. The traveller in Arctic Norway does a lot of this because the lower flanks of the mountains, and often the glens below them, are jam-packed with jumbled rocks. You get along quickly by springing in continuous motion from one boulder to the next—if you are unwearied and sure of foot. I was neither. Fourteen hours of climbing had reduced me to a state wherein it was far safer to boulder-crawl than to boulder-hop; I needed a rest. By dint of neat route-finding down the moraines I had outdistanced John and Dewi, who were a good twenty minutes' going behind me. I found a boulder as big as a house with a flat ledge in the sunshine beyond it, and sat down with my back against the rock.

The valley was utterly still, and yet the stillness was loud with voices. There was the voice of the river's restless rush among its rocks a hundred feet below; the more distant voices of the waterfalls pouring from the snows; the voice of the little wind that crept intermittently along the mountainsides. I don't think I slept, but perhaps I dozed, lulled by the hushed sounds. When the music began I started awake, holding my breath.

The voices of wind and water had strangely altered. They were in harmony—not the harmony of choral music but of instruments. An orchestra was playing. I could distinguish its elements, strings and woodwind and brass, or something that produced the same effect, and in that wild and lonely place the impression was almost stunning.

Of course, I must be dreaming. I scrambled to my feet, struck my knuckles hard against the rough rock of the boulder. The music went on, a huge orchestra playing far away, its chords filling the upper valley with a glory of sound—comprehensible harmonies too, none of your modern discord. I heard, on a sudden waft of the breeze, a noble melody given out by the horns.

It was at this point that the utter impossibility of the thing struck me; before, I had accepted it because I knew it was real. I went a step or two until I could look round the side of the boulder, and saw two tiny figures scrambling down towards me a few hundred yards away. They were real enough, and so was I. There had been no alteration in myself, no shifting in time or space. I turned, listening again for the music. But it had stopped. I never heard it again.

THE SUPERNATURAL

By the time John and Dewi came down to the big boulder I had reached the stage of trying to find a rational explanation of what I had heard. John possessed a mouth-organ and had regaled us, from time to time during the expedition, with a rendering of *South of the Border*—the only tune he could play. Some freak of the wind, aided by my own imagination ——

'Been helping yourselves along with some harmonica music?' I asked casually.

John looked surprised. 'Why, no. I left the old blow-suck in the tent.'

I said nothing to them about the orchestra that couldn't have been there. We had still to get back to civilization and climbers aren't really comfortable with a companion who hears non-existent music. When we reached the tents the melody the horns had played was still sounding in my mind and I noted it down in my log.

This is a strictly true story with nothing omitted, and I shall not omit a circumstance which might suggest that I did, after all, imagine that music. Here is the melody, or theme, I heard in the Stortindal:

Some years afterwards, when I first related my experience, one of my listeners declared that Wagner had used that theme—had, moreover, allotted it to the horns. This, as I confirmed, is so. It does not shake my faith in my own senses. I *know* I heard music in that far wild valley of Arctic Norway. And isn't it just possible that Wagner, too, had heard 'the horns of Elfland faintly blowing'?

SOARING SPIRITS

A cheerful life is what the Muses love,
A soaring spirit is their prime delight.
WORDSWORTH

FIFTY NAMES FAMOUS IN MOUNTAINEERING HISTORY

Abruzzi, Duke of the

Luigi Amedeo Giuseppe, grandson of King Victor Emmanuel II of Italy, was born in 1873 and early in life devoted himself to a career of exploration and adventure. In 1897 at the age of 24 he made the first ascent of Mount St. Elias (18,008 feet) in Alaska and was thereafter known chiefly as an enterprising mountaineer, though he also led an attempt to reach the North Pole in 1899-1900 when members of his party attained a record latitude of 86° 34′ N.

The Mountains of the Moon—the Ruwenzori—next attracted him, and in 1906 he and his expedition to East Africa climbed no less than nineteen peaks of this vast massif. He had with him four skilled Alpine guides and also the great photographer Vittorio Sella, who brought back some of the finest mountain pictures ever taken. Scientists and surveyors formed a large part of the expedition, whose aim was to map every part of the massif and climb every main summit. In this it was entirely successful. The first ascent of Margherita (16,795 feet), the highest summit of the range, was made during this venture.

The Duke's next objective was nothing less than the second highest mountain in the world, K2, from which a strong party had already been forced to retreat in 1902. Seven years afterwards the Abruzzi expedition had also to turn back, but only after two determined attempts had taken them to 21,800 feet on the Abruzzi Ridge by which the successful assault—again by an Italian party—was made in 1954. Vittorio Sella was with the Duke once more, and his photograph of K 2 taken on the 1909 expedition is still the best picture of the great mountain ever obtained.

World War I intervened, and the Duke of the Abruzzi commanded the Italian Navy during the 1914–1918 conflict. In later life he made pioneer explorations in Somaliland and Abyssinia. He died in 1933.

ALMER, CHRISTIAN

Born in Grindelwald in 1826, 'the unsurpassable' Almer first appears in Alpine history as one of the two piratical peasants who tacked-on to Mr. Justice Wills's party on the Wetterhorn in 1854. He was at first a shepherd on the Zasenburg alp, but after his adventure with Wills he was sought out by Alpine travellers and became an officially qualified guide in 1856. From then onwards he took part in ascent after classic ascent of the Alpine peaks, most of which were still unclimbed, and his list of first ascents has never been equalled. The Mönch and the Eiger are among his earliest 'firsts'. The Aiguille Verte and the Grandes Jorasses (with Whymper) followed in 1865, and it was only because Almer had been previously engaged by two Alpine Club members on 7th July that he was not with the party that made the first ascent of the Matterhorn on 14th July of that year. He had already made a new route up Mont Blanc with A. W. Moore, doing the route-finding himself and with no other companion. In addition to his skill and strength, he was better than any other guide of the Golden Age at discerning at first inspection a route that would 'go'. Coolidge, whom Almer guided on the second ascent of the Meije, wrote: 'Almer never once retraced his steps during the whole of this difficult ascent . . . though this was of course the first time he had been on the south face of this mountain.'

Christian Almer climbed the Wetterhorn—the peak that first brought him fame—at least fifty times. In 1896, when he was 70, he climbed it with his wife Margheritha, who was 71 and had never been on a snow mountain before, to celebrate their Golden Wedding. He died in 1898.

ANDEREGG, MELCHIOR

One guide only has ever equalled Christian Almer's record of first ascents. 'Le grand Melchior', as he was often called, was a peasant of the Oberland like Almer, yet his character and intrepidity made him the friend and companion of the wealthy and educated men who employed him. Whymper called him 'a very prince among guides', and the editor of the *Alpine Journal* asserted that Almer and Anderegg dominated the Alpine world from 1860 to 1880.

Born in 1828, Melchior went at the age of 20 to assist in managing the little inn on the Grimsel Pass, and after acting as guide to mountaineering travellers for several years he undertook some glacier expeditions with Thomas Hinchliff of the Alpine Club and soon became famous as one of the great guides. He was a big man, a local wrestling champion as well as a gifted carver in wood. Among his most famous climbs is the first ascent of Mont Blanc from the Brenva side—by the Brenva ice ridge—which he made with A. W. Moore in 1865. It was Melchior who made the comment on a proposed route up the Zmutt Ridge of the Matterhorn which was dangerous by reason of falling stones, a comment still frequently quoted. 'But it goes, Melchior, it goes,' urged his eager employer impatiently. 'Yes, it goes,' said Melchior quietly, *'aber ich gehe nicht*—but I don't go.' His friends of the Alpine Club brought him on two visits to England, on the second of which he made the only error of judgement on a mountain ever recorded of him. William Mathews took him up Snowdon over the Crib

Goch ridge in snow, and when Melchior saw Y Wyddfa rising magnificently beyond the long jagged curve of the ridge he said they must turn back—'we cannot climb the final peak in less than five or six hours'. Mathews insisted on going on, and demonstrated that Snowdon summit could be reached in little more than an hour.

In 1888 Melchior was a guest of honour at the annual dinner of the Alpine Club. He died eighteen years later, aged 78.

BALL, JOHN

Lawyer, politician, and amateur scientist, John Ball became the first President of the Alpine Club when it was formed in 1858. He made few important ascents, but was at that time the most experienced of Alpine travellers, for he had for twenty years spent his vacations wandering in the range and taking notes of its topography, botany, and glaciology. In all, he crossed thirty-two passes over the main Alpine chain and a hundred lateral passes, often entirely alone and carrying his enormous knapsack full of notebooks and scientific instruments. In 1862 the Alpine Club gave him a commission to produce a printed guidebook to the Alps (nothing of the sort existed at that time) and as a result he wrote his famous *Guides* to the Western, Central, and Eastern Alps, which for nearly half a century formed the 'bible' of the Alpine climbers. It was pioneering interest rather than science that led him on most of his expeditions and to the ascent of Monte Pelmo, the first great Dolomite peak to be climbed. John Ball was born in 1818 and died in 1889.

BALMAT, JACQUES

The name of Balmat is forever associated with the name of Mont Blanc. Born in the shadow of the great mountain in 1762, Jacques Balmat was a chamois hunter and seeker of valuable crystals among the rocks of Mont Blanc's lower slopes. He seems to have been the most avaricious type of Savoyard; 'always greedy of gain', it was said of him, and 'his great fear was of having to share with others, not glory, but money'. Undoubtedly he had great courage. When Dr. Paccard, the young physician of Chamonix, discovered in Balmat the only man willing to come with him in an attempt to climb Mont Blanc for the first time, Balmat was 24. They succeeded; but Balmat took all the credit (and the monetary prize De Saussure had offered, which Paccard had agreed to give him) and boasted that he had literally to drag and carry Paccard to the top. This story he told to the novelist Alexandre Dumas, who —without troubling to confirm the details—retold it in his so-called history of Mont Blanc. For nearly a century Balmat's version was believed. Only after the deaths of both Paccard and Balmat was it discovered that a certain Baron von Gernsdorff had watched the whole of the ascent through a telescope and noted every incident, including the times of arrival at different stages of the ascent. This record, besides coinciding with Paccard's own notes, declared definitely that the doctor had been the leader throughout and had been the first of the pair to reach the summit.

In 1834 Jacques Balmat was found dead among the rocks of the Mont Blanc slopes, where he had taken to searching for non-existent gold.

BENNEN, JOHANN JOSEPH

'A perfect Nature's gentleman' was how Vaughan Hawkins, with whom Bennen made the first reconnaissance of the Matterhorn, described his guide. Undoubtedly Bennen was a cut above the normal peasant type, an individual and unusual sort of Alpine guide. He was a man of moods, sometimes rash, sometimes over-cautious; shrinking inexplicably from apparently straightforward ascents, he was yet one of the very few men who considered the Matterhorn a practicable climb.

Bennen was born in 1824, in the Oberland village of Laax, and became a carpenter. He delighted in hunting chamois in his spare time and was taken as guide by Professor Tyndall on some early expeditions. With Tyndall he reached 13,000 feet on the Italian ridge of the Matterhorn, and among his later triumphs were the first ascents of the Aletschhorn and the Weisshorn. The dramatic circumstances of his death in 1864, as related by his employer P. C. Gosset, are familiar in Alpine record. MM. Gosset and Boissonet, with three guides of whom Bennen was chief, were ascending a steep field of soft snow on the Haut de Cry, a minor peak—a route, in the prevailing conditions, which no Alpine guide should have taken. They heard 'a deep, cutting sound' of the snow splitting above them, and there was a brief pause. Then Bennen said solemnly: '*Wir sind alle verloren*—we are all lost.' A few seconds later an avalanche swept the whole party down. Bennen and Boissonet were buried and killed, but the other three survived unhurt.

BREVOORT, MARGUERITE

Miss Brevoort, almost invariably called 'Meta' by her friends and relatives, left the United States to settle in Europe in 1865, when she was 40. She took with her a nephew, William Coolidge, who was then 14 and a weakly, rather precocious boy. Meta Brevoort fell in love with the Alpine world, and her adventurous walks designed to improve William's health soon developed into an overpowering desire to climb mountains. She was a large woman, masculine in manner and outlook, very strong and determined. A Swiss writer of the time describes her as a '*grosse hollandische-amerikanische Miss*'. Young Coolidge became almost abnormally devoted to his aunt and caught the mountaineering passion from her; he was to become one of the great mountaineers, editor of the *Alpine*

FIFTY NAMES FAMOUS IN MOUNTAINEERING

Journal, honorary member of the Alpine Club, all due to Meta Brevoort's influence.

Together they climbed the Cima de Jazzi and crossed the Col du Géant. Two years later came the first employment of Christian Almer as their guide, and with him Miss Brevoort and her nephew made the first ascent of the central peak of the Meije, the first ascent of the Ailefroide, and the third ascent of the Écrins. Meta became the first lady to traverse the Matterhorn, up by the Hörnli and down by the Italian ridge to Breuil. She also took part in the first winter ascents of the Wetterhorn and the Jungfrau. Her death in 1876 left Coolidge almost inconsolable, and it was to fulfil a wish she had once expressed that he took Holy Orders.

BRUCE, CHARLES GRANVILLE

Born in 1866, Charlie Bruce—as his acquaintances called him—was an officer of the Indian Army when he first took to mountaineering. With his Gurkha regiment, he was employed in penetrating the difficult Himalayan frontier country on survey missions or punitive expeditions, and soon became passionately fond of mountains and mountain climbing. When he was 26 he took part in Sir Martin Conway's expedition to the Karakoram in 1892, and made the suggestion that Everest should be attempted. Not for thirty years was this proposal to bear fruit.

Bruce was a big man in every way. He knew the Gurkha peoples better than any man alive, spoke their language (and a dozen other dialects) and could hold his own with them at any of their native sports. When debarred from mountaineering he was accustomed to keep fit by running uphill every morning—with a Gurkha under each arm.

In 1920 he was invalided out of the army with the rank of Brigadier-General; the medical board recommended a quiet and sedentary life. Subsequently he led the 1922 and 1924

Everest Expeditions, though he did not himself go higher than 16,500 feet. He died in 1939.

BUHL, HERMANN

In the 33 years of his life—he was born in 1924 and died in 1957—Hermann Buhl became an almost legendary figure to his generation of climbers. As a boy in Innsbruck he begged a pair of worn-out climbing boots and made solitary ascents in the difficult rock peaks of the neighbourhood. He was a withdrawn young man, seeking solitude among the peaks rather than companionship, and preferred to climb alone, seeking always the narrow margin between life and death. Typical of his feats was his ascent of the Salzburg Route on the Watzmann, 6,000 feet of sheer and extremely difficult rock; Buhl climbed it alone, in winter, and at night. With one companion, he set out to climb the North Face of the Eiger. Fearful storms forced him to join forces with French and Italian parties, and when the exhausted men at last reached the summit after three terrible days Buhl set off down the easy route without a word to the others.

This *penchant* for solitary achievements persisted even on Nanga Parbat, the very difficult Himalayan peak which was finally climbed by Dr. Herligkoffer's German-Austrian party in 1953. Buhl and Kempter, the summit pair, were in the highest camp at 22,640 feet and had agreed to start for the summit at 3 a.m. Buhl announced at midnight that he was ready to start, and as his companion declined to change the plan he started alone. It took him nearly 19 hours to gain the summit and he had to spend the night at 26,000 feet, but descended safely though severely frostbitten.

Four years later Hermann Buhl fell to his death when he was descending—unroped, by his own wish, from his companion—the ridge of Chogolisa, a 25,000 foot Himalayan peak.

FIFTY NAMES FAMOUS IN MOUNTAINEERING

Burgener, Alexander

From the pages of Mummery's *My Climbs in the Alps and Caucasus* Alexander Burgener emerges as one of the most lovable and amusing characters in the whole history of mountaineering. He was born in 1846 in the Saastal, where chamois-hunting, the normal sport for young men of the valley, developed his climbing skill on the steep rocks round Saas. With Clinton Dent he undertook his first employment as guide and made the first ascent of the Lenzspitze and the first traverse of the Portjengrat. Their association is famous for the dogged assault on the unclimbed Aiguille du Grand Dru. Dent made eighteen unsuccessful attempts on this peak, and the nineteenth and successful one was made with Burgener in the lead.

Squat and immensely strong, with bear-like arms and an ugly good-humoured face, Burgener loved all the good things of life—including risk—with unquenchable exuberance. His first climb with A. F. Mummery was a first ascent—the Zmutt Ridge of the Matterhorn. And after that the two engaged in many epic struggles with steep ice and difficult rock, the difficulty and danger lightened by Burgener's simple zest and not always seemly comment. Burgener died in 1910, the victim of an unexpected avalanche on the way up to an Alpine hut.

Carrel, Jean-Antoine

Carrel, whose name is almost as closely associated with that of the Matterhorn as Edward Whymper's is, was born in 1829 at Valtournanche, at the foot of the Matterhorn in Italy. He was often called 'the Bersagliere' because of his service in the Italian Army, and he was intensely nationalist. When he returned to Valtournanche from the army in 1857 he made a lighthearted attempt to get up the Matterhorn with two companions from his village, and though they got no higher than the Tête du Lion the great peak took hold upon Jean-Antoine and became an obsession. It had to be climbed, and from the side of Italy.

Edward Whymper engaged Carrel for an attempt on the Italian ridge in 1861, and found him 'a well-made resolute looking fellow with a certain defiant air which was rather taking'. Carrel wanted an Italian to be first on top and gave Whymper little help. Four years later he slipped out of an engagement with Whymper, who was to attempt the Matterhorn again, and joined the Italian party that was to try from Valtournanche on the same day. On that day, it appears, Carrel saw the ill-fated Zermatt party on the summit above him and refused to go farther. He reached the top by the Italian ridge three days later and planted the Italian flag there.

In 1879 Carrel and Whymper joined forces again, for Whymper's long expedition to the Andes on which they climbed Chimborazo, Cotopaxi, and many lesser peaks. Carrel died in 1890, of exposure during a violent storm on the Matterhorn's Italian ridge.

COLLIE, JOHN NORMAN

The Coolin of Skye were nearly all virgin peaks in 1859, when Collie was born. Even when, on a fishing holiday in 1886, he had his first sight of rock climbers high on Sgurr nan Gillean, many of the Skye summits were still virgin. He was then 27, science tutor at Cheltenham Ladies' College, and a year afterwards he had begun to climb. With a Skye man, John MacKenzie, he reached the top of every Coolin peak—including the Bhasteir Tooth—except Sgurr Coire an Lochain, and from Mackenzie he must have learned the craft of rock climbing. Later, joining his friends Slingsby and Mummery in the Alps, he was with them on the first ascent of the Requin; but he returned always to his first love, the Coolin. As a Professor at University College, London, he continued to regard mountaineering as his second and more important life. Lofoten and the Canadian Rockies saw first ascents by Collie, usually with one or more of his special climbing companions—Geoffrey Hastings, Collier, Solly, or Slingsby. His gaunt figure and cadaverous countenance led the way on the first ascents of the Buchaille Etive precipice and of Moss Ghyll (whereon he chipped the famous 'Collie Step' with his ice axe and shocked the purists) and he returned again to Skye to climb the last virgin peak there, Sgurr Coire an Lochain. He was the first to cross the well-known Thearlaich-Dubh Gap on the Coolin Main Ridge and first up the Tower Ridge of Ben Nevis, which he compared favourably with the Italian ridge of the Matterhorn. It was his feats and explorations that launched the pastime of climbing in Scotland.

In 1895 he went with Hastings and Mummery to the Himalaya to attempt Nanga Parbat; the expedition whereon Mummery disappeared for ever. Collie died at Sligachan, in Skye, at the age of 88 and was buried there in Struan churchyard.

CONWAY, WILLIAM MARTIN

Martin Conway, later Lord Conway of Allington, was born in 1856, and by the time he was old enough to climb mountains all the big Alpine peaks had been ascended. He had, from the beginning, wealth and position; on his first climb, a boyhood ascent of Snowdon, he was too small to place a stone on the cairn—but his cousin's butler did it for him. After 1876, when he first began to climb in the Alps, he planned his life as a series of great adventures, to be achieved while he was still young enough to enjoy them. 'For all of us', he wrote, 'there are many kinds of joy as yet unexperienced, many activities untried, many fields of knowledge unexplored. We must not spend too large a fraction of life over one or the next will escape us. It is life, after all, that is the greatest field of exploration.' Tall, hardy, and with the eye of an artist for beauty,

Conway was an Elizabethan adventurer born too late. Luckily his wealth enabled him to live according to his tastes.

His many seasons in the Alps made him restless, and his dream of greater mountains took him to the Himalaya in 1891 as leader of one of the earliest exploring and climbing expeditions. He surveyed the Hispar and Baltoro glaciers and climbed Pioneer Peak, 22,600 feet, at that time the highest summit ever reached by man. After his return to England he was soon abroad again making another dream come true—the traverse of the Alps from end to end. Within the next three years he made two visits to Spitzbergen, achieving the pioneer crossing of the island and several first ascents among its peaks. The following year found him in South America travelling through the Andes, where he climbed the virgin Illimani. And then, in 1901 when he was 45, he took his young daughter on a farewell ascent of the Breithorn, the first Alpine peak he had climbed as a youth, thus formally ending his career of adventure. Though he lived until 1937, Conway set forth on no further climbs or journeys. His books *The Alps from End to End* and *The Autobiography of a Mountaineer* remain to show how truly he loved the high places and the wilderness.

COOLIDGE, WILLIAM AUGUSTUS BREVOORT

Brought to Europe by his aunt, 'Meta' Brevoort, at the age of 14, William Coolidge was a weakly child, with a precocity that was later to develop into eccentricity. Doctors had recommended mountain air for the boy, and the walks he and his aunt took from Zermatt fired them both with enthusiasm for mountaineering. During the next 30 years Coolidge made no less than 1,700 Alpine expeditions, including 600 major ascents or difficult passes.

He was born in New York in 1850 but never returned to the United States. He was short, frail, with bad eyesight and weak lungs; but the enthusiasm for mountains, which had perhaps been pumped into him by Miss Brevoort in the first place, never left him. His gift for study and scholarship found outlet in a monumental history of the Alps and in numerous guide-books. As editor of the *Alpine Jonrnal* he conducted a series of fiery disputes on all manner of details with other members of the Alpine Club; 'in his one-sidedness, savagery, and bitterness he was medieval', wrote one of them. His fierce feud with Edward Whymper over a dramatic drawing called 'Almer's Jump' in one of Whymper's books nearly led to a libel action. After Miss Brevoort's death in 1876 he took Holy Orders, in accordance with a wish his adored aunt had once expressed; and in 1926 the Rev. W. A. B. Coolidge, greatest of Alpine historians, died at Grindelwald, where for thirty years he had made his home.

Croz, Michel

Croz was born in 1830, and died in 1865 after achieving a meteoric fame as an Alpine guide. He was a native of Tour in the Chamonix valley, but had no good word for the professional guides of Chamonix and their methods, which according to him were slipshod and unskilled. But this was after Croz had reached the age of 30, for his life up to 1859 was that of an obscure porter and odd-job man. In that year William Mathews engaged him as guide for the ascent of Mont Blanc and was struck by his natural ability as a climber. After that he served as guide for men like Whymper, Tuckett, and Moore, always with notable efficiency. His first ascents in this brief period included the Écrins and Monte Viso, Mont Dolent, Aiguille d'Argentière and Aiguille de la Trélatête. To steep snow and ice he brought a kind of instinctive skill, and this allied to a natural courage and daring made him much sought after by the more adventurous Victorian climbers. He considered himself, and with reason, the supreme master of step-cutting and ice work generally, and disliked criticism.

Except at places of extreme difficulty or danger, he smoked a large pipe continuously.

Croz had climbed with Whymper several times before the successful attempt on the Matterhorn, and though he had been engaged by the Rev. Charles Hudson for the ascent it was to Whymper that Croz looked as leader of that ill-fated climb. Croz and Whymper together threw off the rope on the last snowslope and raced for the summit; and it was Croz to whom Whymper called excitedly to come up and see the defeated Italian party far below. It may be that Croz trusted Whymper, who was to descend last, to see that the ropes were properly attached for the descent. A weak rope was used. When Hadow slipped and fell, it broke. Michel Croz fell to his death with Hadow, Hudson, and Lord Francis Douglas.

DENT, THOMAS CLINTON

Clinton Dent was born in 1850. In later years he was to become senior surgeon at St. George's Hospital Medical School, but until he was 26, having independent means, he spent his youth playing games and climbing mountains. In the 1870's all the great Alpine peaks had been climbed; yet the sages of the Alpine Club frowned severely on the 'rock gymnasts' and 'reckless youngsters' who attempted the first ascents of difficult pinnacles where there was hardly any of the traditional and essential snow. Dent, writing in the *Alpine Journal*, told them plainly that they had left nothing for the succeeding generation except these same 'unjustifiable' rock towers; and promptly devoted his energies to the ascent of one of the most impressive pinnacles anywhere in the world—the Aiguille du Dru.

Clinton Dent's long siege of the Dru is an epic of persistence as well as of daring. He made his first attempt, with Alexander Burgener as leading guide, in 1873. After eighteen unsuccessful attempts he was suddenly seized with consciousness of his idle life and became, at 26, a medical student. Mountaineering still called him, and in 1878 he returned to make his nineteenth attempt—again with Burgener in the lead—and this time reached the top.

Dent afterwards made four climbing trips to the Caucasus and did many more Alpine climbs. Later he studied the causes of the increasing number of mountain accidents and was the initiator of the Alpine Distress Signal. He died in 1912.

FORBES, JAMES DAVID

An F.R.S. at the age of 23, at 24 Professor of Natural Philosophy at Edinburgh University, J. D. Forbes was attracted to mountains by the opportunity they offered for scientific study. His tours, he declared, were made 'not as an amusement but as a serious occupation'. Yet this tall, quiet scientist, intent on elucidating the geology of Alpine regions and the movement of glaciers, found his studies developing into adventures not only of the body but also of the spirit. A deeply religious man, he was stirred by the wonder and beauty of the mountain world and could not refrain from interpolating descriptions of his emotions in his records.

Forbes was born in 1809, made his first Alpine journey of note in 1839, and in his mid-thirties was seized with the crippling illness that led to his death in 1868. He would never admit that mountains ought to be climbed for any unscientific reason; but among the ascents made in the course of his investigations was the first British ascent of the Jungfrau. His Alpine journeys made him the man most travelled above the snowline in his day, and this, with his exploration of many glaciers to observe their behaviour, resulted in his being made the first honorary member of the Alpine Club.

FRESHFIELD, DOUGLAS

Freshfield's name is closely associated with the exploration of the Caucasus. He was born in 1845 and died in 1934, so that his climbing career was outside the Golden Age of Alpine climbing, and though he climbed extensively in the Alps (and occasionally in Scotland) he sought mountain adventure farther afield when he could.

'The true mountaineer', Mummery wrote, 'is a wanderer and explorer.' Freshfield was certainly a 'true mountaineer' by that definition. Geographer and historian by inclination, he liked best the sort of mountaineering that could add to the sum of human knowledge. As early as 1899 he led a party on a complete circuit round Kangchenjunga in the then unexplored Singalila region of the Nepal Himalaya. He made three visits to the Caucasus, climbing Kazbek, the second highest peak, and the lower summit of Elbruz, both first ascents. His last visit in 1889 was made with Clinton Dent, to solve the mystery of the disappearance of two British climbers —Donkin and Fox—who were thought to have been murdered by bandits. They found the last camp of the missing men high on a mountain ridge, but the bodies were never recovered.

Freshfield was a talented poet, and four lines of his—part of his Epitaph for W. F. Donkin—appear under the section-heading THE CLIMBER'S BEDSIDE in this book.

GEORGE, HEREFORD BROOKE

The Rev. Hereford George was—perhaps more than any other man of his era—the prototype Victorian mountaineer. Massively built and tall, with a fine red beard, he radiated the upper-class Victorian conviction that an Englishman should be humble before God and before nobody else. Leslie Stephen took him on a small glacier tour when he was 22 years old, about to take Holy Orders, and George was deeply impressed. 'We perceive that above and beyond all law rises the supreme will of the Almighty lawgiver,' he wrote afterwards; and 'Familiarity with the wonders of the

Alps is among the best means of originating and deepening such impressions; for their gigantic size and awful phenomena tend to produce an effect not merely on our intellectual perceptions, but also upon the moral feelings.' It was a typical reaction. Nor was it just humbug. The hearty, muscular climbers of George's time really did feel as he felt; for all but very few of them it was a large part of the reason why they climbed.

Hereford George made Alpine history by taking a large party, including three ladies and six men, on a tour of the Oberland mountains, obtaining some of the earliest photographs ever taken on glaciers and snowslopes—with the ladies in vast skirts reaching to below the ankle and wearing bustles. The men of the party occasionally escaped to make first ascents, climbing the Gross Nesthorn and the Jungfrau from the Wengern Alp. He was largely responsible for the laying-down of standards for climbing equipment, today considered an essential of safe climbing.

GREEN, WILLIAM SPOTSWOOD

The Rev. W. S. Green, born in 1847, was a Dublin clergyman of much the same type as Hereford George—a jovial muscular Christian, delighting in using mountains for his physical and spiritual recreation. Little is known of his Alpine record, and the Alpine Club of which he was a member printed no obituary of him when he died in 1919. He had climbed a number of first-class Alpine peaks with two of the best-known Oberland guides, Ulrich Kauffmann and Emil Boss, but he was too late for the Golden Age and longed for virgin peaks to climb. In 1881 he sailed for New Zealand with his two Swiss guides, intent on finding a way to the summit of that country's highest mountain, Mount Cook. The trek through unknown country, the discovery of a route up the tilted maze of rock and ice, the fourteen-hour struggle in a storm that drove them back within 100 feet of the actual top—these make one of the great epics of mountaineering. Thirteen years later three New Zealanders became the first men to stand on the summit at 12,350 feet; but Green was the real conqueror of Mount Cook.

HADOW, DOUGLAS

In 1865 Douglas Hadow, then only 19 years old, was taken by the Rev. Charles Hudson on his first Alpine tour. They had made two fairly easy ascents and had been up Mont Blanc by the ordinary route in fast time. That was all. The inclusion of a climber so young and lacking in experience as Hadow in the 1865 Matterhorn party was a major error of judgement. The Matterhorn, so many times attempted in vain by the finest climbers in the world of that day, still deemed inaccessible by many other climbers, was no peak for an untried youngster still in his novitiate.

Edward Whymper, it appears, questioned Hadow's inclusion in the party; Hudson pressed for it, because he had already told Hadow they would try the Matterhorn together. On the ascent Hadow continually required help, as Whymper records. On the descent he had no notion at all of using rock holds. 'Croz', says Whymper, 'was absolutely taking hold of his legs and putting his feet, one by one, into their proper positions.' This was just before Hadow slipped, fell against Croz, and knocked him over the edge of the precipice. Next moment Hudson and Lord Francis Douglas had been dragged down; the rope broke; and only Whymper and the two Taugwalders were left alive.

The boots Hadow was wearing were later recovered, and are in a museum. The heels are fitted with smooth metal plates, today considered a dangerous fitting on climbing footwear.

FIFTY NAMES FAMOUS IN MOUNTAINEERING

HUDSON, CHARLES

The Rev. Charles Hudson, who died in the Matterhorn disaster of 1865, was born in 1828. He began mountain climbing by reconnoitring a new route up Mont Blanc when he was 24, but then went to the Crimea as a Chaplain with the armed forces during the war with Russia. After this he made an adventurous trip across Armenia in an attempt to reach Mount Ararat. He signalized his return to the Alps in 1855 by making —with Birkbeck and the Smyth brothers—the first ascent of the highest summit of Monte Rosa. The climb could almost be called 'guideless', for their guides could not climb the final part and the amateurs, with Hudson at their head, took over the leading. In the same year Hudson made the first guideless ascent of Mont Blanc with Kennedy; a feat which was condemned by the Alpine Club but acclaimed by the less well-off mountaineers who could not afford guides. Subsequently he climbed in the Alps every year (visiting Zermatt, indeed, during his honeymoon in 1862) and his perfect competence in every branch of mountaincraft soon led him to be acclaimed as the greatest mountaineer of his generation—'almost as great as a guide'. It was Hudson, rather than Whymper, who perceived that the way to climb the Matterhorn was by the Hörnli Ridge; but he must bear a large part of the responsibility for the tragedy in which he lost his life.

IRVINE, ANDREW COMYN

Andrew Irvine was 22 years old when he was chosen as a member of the 1924 Mount Everest Expedition. He had twice rowed in the Oxford boat and had a magnificent physique, had showed excellent qualities on the Oxford Spitzbergen Expedition in 1923, and was strongly recommended by Dr. T. G. Longstaff and N. E. Odell, men whose word carried great weight with the Everest Committee. All the same, he was admittedly an 'experiment'. He had only a small experience of mountain climbing, and he was considered by many people too young to have developed the endurance and self-knowledge essential on Everest. He was still an undergraduate.

On the expedition Irvine 'pulled his weight' in a manner beyond praise. In particular, he made himself fully familiar with the oxygen apparatus they were using, which was then very imperfect, and improved it in many ways. When the time came for the final assault, Andrew Irvine and C. E. Odell were the only two remaining fit enough to accompany Mallory. Odell was the likelier choice and the better mountaineer, but Mallory chose Irvine, probably because they had the same university background and got on well together. On 8th June 1924 Mallory and Irvine started for the summit from Camp VI at 26,800 feet and were never seen again.

JONES, OWEN GLYNNE

O. G. Jones was one of the 'fathers' of British rock climbing. His own father was a Welshman who had settled in London, where Owen Glynne was born in 1867, and the young man's first rock climb was a solo ascent of the Cyfrwy Arête on Cader Idris—its first ascent—when the family were on holiday at Barmouth. Two years later a photograph of Napes Needle displayed in a shop window in the Strand attracted him to the Lake District, where his enthusiasm and skill quickly made him supreme among the habitués of Wasdale Head. For a decade he held this supremacy unchallenged. During that period he made many new climbs with the Abraham brothers and with their photographic co-operation produced his massive guidebook, *Rock Climbing in the English Lake District*, the first book to grade climbs; the classifications Jones used were Easy, Moderate, Difficult, and Exceptionally Severe.

Owen Glynne Jones was very strong in the arms but handicapped by shortsightedness, which tended to make his technique one of muscular rush rather than balanced deliberation. He was not sociable and preferred to climb alone when possible, but his long association with the Abrahams led to marked improvements in the use of the rope for belaying. Among his first ascents in North Wales were three of the classic routes on Tryfan: Milestone Buttress, North Buttress, and the Terrace Wall Variant—the last a notable feat of open climbing for its date, Easter 1899. Jones was a science lecturer at the City of London School when he began going to the Alps, where he climbed many big routes and took part in the first winter ascent of the Schreckhorn. In the summer of 1899 he went to Arolla. With F. W. Hill and three guides he started up the Ferpécle Arête of the Dent Blanche, and was killed when the leading guide fell from a rock wall and dragged all the others down with him except Hill, who survived.

Kennedy, Edward Shirley

Born in 1817, E. S. Kennedy was a man of independent means and inquiring mind. In his youth he made a study of the down-and-outs, journeying as a tramp from London to Brighton; wrote a reflective book, *Thoughts On Being*; and was captain of the London Amateur Sculling Club. He made Alpine climbing his chief pastime and by 1855, when he and Charles Hudson made the first guideless ascent of Mont Blanc, he was a master of mountaincraft. After that time he made many guideless climbs, with Hudson and others.

In 1857 Kennedy was with William Mathews, Hardy, and Ellis on the first British ascent of the Finsteraarhorn when Mathews suggested the formation of an Alpine Club, and in the autumn of that year acted as secretary at the meeting when the circulars convening prospective members were sent out. Like Hardy and Hudson, both clergymen, with whom he often climbed, Kennedy was a deeply religious man; he contemplated talking Holy Orders himself, but did not do so. He died in 1898.

LE BLOND, MRS. AUBREY

One of the founders of the Ladies' Alpine Club, the first women's climbing club in Britain, Mrs. Le Blond (or Elizabeth Main—she was three times married) was a pioneer in that she took it for granted that women had as much right to climb mountains as men and an equal capacity for doing it. This was not the view of most male climbers, who held that although the Matterhorn (for example) might be climbed by a woman it would never be climbed by a lady. Mrs. Le Blond was convinced, and rightly, that a skirt was not only an awkward but also a very dangerous garment on a mountain; but a woman in breeches was the antithesis of a lady and no hotel in Switzerland would admit such a creature, so she had a 'mountain skirt' made which could be discarded when the hard climbing began and put on for the return to the valley. On one occasion she had traversed the Zinal Rothhorn and was well on her way down to Zinal when she discovered that she had left her skirt on the other side of the mountain. Knowing that no door in Zinal would open to a skirtless female, she repeated the traverse in the opposite direction so as to descend, skirted and free from shame, upon Zermatt.

Joseph Imboden was Mrs. Le Blond's favourite guide and was with her on most of her Alpine ascents. When Joseph's son Roman was killed she decided to give up Alpine climbing; but climb she must, so she turned her attention in 1898 and 1899 to the unclimbed peaks of northern Norway, taking Joseph Imboden and another son, Emil, as guides. In this region she found her greatest pleasure. Many first ascents, particularly in the unmapped and unexplored Lyngen Peninsula 220 miles north of the Arctic Circle, give her a position second only to that of W. C. Slingsby as a pioneer of climbing

FIFTY NAMES FAMOUS IN MOUNTAINEERING

in Norway. Imbodentind, a fine peak above the Lakselv Glacier, perpetuates the memory of her guides. She died in 1934.

LONGSTAFF, TOM GEORGE

Tom Longstaff was told by his science tutor at Oxford that he had 'neither the brains nor the physique' for the career of physiologist he intended to pursue. He became a physiologist. He was a very small man, by no means strong. He became a great traveller and mountaineer.

Mountains called to Dr. Longstaff from his early youth, but he counted travel among them, rather than climbing them, the greatest happiness in the world. 'Attainment of a set objective is but a secondary matter,' he says in his Foreword to *This My Voyage*, the book that records his life of adventure. He began by climbing in the Alps, but mountains that were hidden or unclimbed appealed more strongly than difficult peaks that had been climbed before. After some fine new routes in the Caucasus he sought greater things in the Himalaya, and his first ascent of Trisul (23,406 feet) constitutes a feat unique in the annals of Himalayan climbing. With only the somewhat primitive Alpine equipment of 1907, he reached the top of a peak 8,000 feet higher than the highest of the Alps, climbing the last 6,000 feet in a single day and descending the same day to his base camp on the moraine of the glacier. It was then the highest summit ever reached by man.

Longstaff went out with the Mount Everest Expedition of 1922, but he was now 47, and illness prevented him from getting as far as the North Col. Before this he had travelled and climbed in the Karakoram and the Hindu Kush, twice visited the Rockies and made new ascents there, and made a long journey through Tibet. The year before he went to Everest he had been with the Oxford University Expedition to Spitzbergen and made the first ascent of Mount Terrier. At the age of 59, when he took part (for the second time) in an expedition to Greenland, he was with Pat Baird on the first ascent of the Devil's Thumb, a spectacular rock monolith. Throughout his long life Dr. Tom Longstaff was always (as the present writer can confirm from personal experience) ready to devote time and trouble to helping aspiring venturers in the many lands he had visited. He died in 1964.

Mallory, George Leigh

Mallory of Everest was born in 1886. As an undergraduate he met Geoffrey Winthrop Young while climbing on Lliwedd, in North Wales, and their friendship resulted in the development of his undoubted gifts as a mountaineer, both on difficult rock and on the snow and ice of the hardest Alpine routes of the early 1900's. From the first he was at home on near-vertical faces and had a tendency to regard elaborate safeguarding tactics with the rope as rather unnecessary. Mallory's Slab on Lliwedd commemorates an occasion when, having climbed down from the Bowling Green ledge with a roped party, he found he had left his pipe on the ledge and climbed up by the much steeper slab, unroped, to get it.

By 1921, when an expedition was preparing to reconnoitre the approaches to Everest, Mallory was one of the best climbers of the day and an obvious choice. He had secret hopes of actually climbing the mountain, for half a century ago little was known about the problems of high altitude climbing. The North Col was reached by the reconnaissance party and the way (as they thought) found; and the challenge of the great mountain had gripped George Mallory. He went out again with the 1922 expedition, and the trials and calamities of that attempt, of which he bore the brunt, might have deterred any other climber from trying a third time. Mallory was different. To a great many people the problem of Everest meant the contest between Everest and Mallory. In 1924 he was married, with two children, happy in his work at Oxford. 'How can I be out of the fight?' he wrote to a friend when, invited to join the third expedition, he decided to accept.

After a gruelling seven weeks Mallory, with Andrew Irvine, reached 26,800 feet and spent the night of 7th June there in the single small tent which they called 'Camp VI'. Next day they made an attempt to reach the summit, during which both men disappeared. The 1938 Everest Expedition discovered an ice axe lying on the treacherous slabs at about 28,000 feet. It was either Mallory's or Irvine's axe, and it was thought to indicate the place from which they fell.

MATHEWS, CHARLES EDWARD

One of a great mountaineering family, Charles Mathews was born in 1834 and died in 1905, filling his 70 years with a remarkable diversity of activities. He was a town councillor of Birmingham, friend of Joseph Chamberlain, founder of the National Education League; Justice of the Peace, governor of several schools, politician, historian of Waterloo and of Mont Blanc, water engineer—and mountaineer. Like very many Victorians, he had high ideals of duty towards his fellow men, and perhaps one of his greatest lifeworks was the establishing of the Alpine guides as a corporate body of skilled and self-respecting craftsmen, the equals of those who employed them on mountains. Of Melchior Anderegg, his guide and friend, he wrote: 'To say that I owe him a debt impossible to pay is not to say much.'

Charles and his elder brother William began Alpine climbing in 1856. From then until 1900 Charles climbed regularly in the Alps, reluctantly giving up the higher peaks when he was 65. He acquired a holiday cottage at Machynlleth in North Wales which he occupied at summer week-ends and often in winter, making more than 100 ascents of Cader Idris. Snowdon, which also he climbed more than 100 times, was his favourite in winter. On these occasions he stayed at the Pen-y-gwryd inn, whose fame and custom he was chiefly responsible for enlarging. Here he formed the 'Society of Welsh Rabbits', whose object was to explore Snowdonia in winter. It was the forerunner of the Climbers Club, which Mathews helped to found in 1898, becoming its first president.

MATHEWS, WILLIAM

'I want you to consider whether it would not be possible to establish an Alpine Club, the members of which might dine together once a year, say in London, and give each other what information they could.' So William Mathews wrote to his friend the Rev. F. J. A. Hort, a fellow mountaineer, in 1857. Hort replied cautiously that he feared the dining might take precedence over the information; the dinner bill, he added, might be too high for some climbers. William Mathews was not discouraged. He had climbed in the Alps for several seasons, and that year he made the first British ascent of the Finsteraarhorn with Hardy, Kennedy, and others. While they were on the mountain he put forward his idea of an Alpine Club again, and it was received enthusiastically. In the autumn of the same year half-a-dozen Alpinists met at William Mathews's house, The Leasowes, on the outskirts of Birmingham, and the preliminaries of forming an Alpine Club were dealt with. In 1858 the Club was fully established, with John Ball as its first president.

Mathews was a quieter figure than his more ebullient younger brother Charles, but he acquired a long list of fine Alpine ascents in twenty years of climbing. Born in 1828, he died in 1901.

MOORE, ADOLPHUS WARBURTON

A. W. Moore, born in 1841, was one of the most daring and enterprising Alpine climbers of the later nineteenth century.

His book *The Alps in 1864* is a very readable classic. In that year—1864—he made a famous climbing tour through the Dauphiné with Horace Walker and Edward Whymper, in the course of which the first ascent of the Écrins was made. His most famous climb was the first ascent of the Brenva Face of Mont Blanc in 1865. The route crossed the knife-edge of ice known as the Brenva Ridge, afterwards to become familiar to a non-climbing public through A. E. W. Mason's novel *Running Water*. Horace Walker was in the party, and so was Horace's 57-year-old father.

Moore went to the Caucasus with Freshfield and Tucker in 1868, and took part in the first ascents of Kazbek and the east summit of Elbruz. He died in 1887.

MUMMERY, ALBERT FREDERICK

Tall, studious-looking, with thin pinched features and thick spectacles, A. F. Mummery looked incapable of undertaking any sort of arduous adventure. Yet in the 16 years of his climbing life he planned and carried out climbing ventures whose daring rocked—and indeed shocked—the hard climbers of the 'Silver Age'. He was born in 1855, son of a middle-class industrialist who later became Mayor of Dover. His chief passions were political economy and climbing.

Eight holiday seasons in the Alps taught him mountaincraft, and in 1879 he made the first of his remarkable climbs—the first ascent of the Zmutt Ridge of the Matterhorn. This was with Alexander Burgener, the famous guide who was to be his companion on so many hazardous adventures. William Penhall, a young man of wealth and position who had been made a member of the Alpine Club at the age of 18, was attempting to capture the Zmutt on the same day. His chosen route was not a good one and Mummery, who had picked a safer and better way, was first. A few days later Mummery and Penhall were climbing in the Mischabel group together and remained close friends; but the race for the Zmutt was afterwards declared by Mummery's enemies to have been 'unsporting'—or at any rate to show that Mummery was a competitive, exhibitionist sort of climber who ought not to be a member of the Alpine Club. Edward Whymper disliked him, no doubt because of his success on the Zmutt Ridge and near-success on the Furggen Ridge of 'Whymper's mountain'; the epic rock climbs on Grépon and Requin caused the traditionalists to think of him as a 'rock gymnast'. He was blackballed—refused membership—when he applied to join the Alpine Club, and declined Coolidge's invitation to apply again. In 1888 he went to the Caucasus, where he journeyed and explored and finally climbed Dych Tau, the second highest peak (17,054 feet) and the highest remaining unclimbed. He was now so famous as a mountaineer that the Alpine Club could hardly do without him. He was invited to apply, did so, and was this time elected.

Further Alpine climbs followed, including the first guideless ascent of the Brenva face of Mont Blanc. In 1894 Mummery was persuaded to write his famous book *My Climbs in the Alps and Caucasus,* and in the following year went to the Himalaya with Slingsby and Hastings to try to climb Nanga Parbat. With one porter, Mummery reached over 20,000 feet on the difficult Diamirai face but was forced to descend—even so a notable feat, for the face has never been attempted since then and the mountain remained unclimbed for the next 57 years. In endeavouring to cross a high and unexplored ridge to begin another attempt Mummery and two porters disappeared and never returned. His great ascents on rock, of a nature in advance of his time, have caused A. F. Mummery to be called 'the father of modern rock climbing'.

NOYCE, WILFRED

Noyce was one of the Cambridge group of rock climbers who in the 1930's pushed the standard of British rock climbing yet a little higher. He climbed mainly in North Wales, making such new routes as Scars Climb on Tryfan and the Girdle of Terrace Wall. With J. M. Edwards, his climbing partner on many first ascents, he compiled a definitive guide to the Tryfan climbs. He was born in 1919. At the outbreak of the Second World War he had a list of fine Alpine ascents to his credit, and was for some time engaged in training army and R.A.F. personnel in mountaincraft in the mountains of Kashmir. He climbed Pauhunri, a 23,400-foot peak in Sikkim, and led an expedition to the Karakoram.

Wilfred Noyce was a bold climber, with a touch of Mallory's indifference to exposure and impatience with 'superfluous' safety margins. On Everest, with Sir John Hunt's victorious expedition of 1953, he showed superb qualities of resolution and endurance, being chiefly responsible for the successful establishment of Camp VIII on the South Col. A schoolmaster by profession, he was a poet and writer by predilection, and his book *South Col*, a personal record of the Everest expedition, makes a fine companion volume to Hunt's *The Ascent of Mount Everest*.

In 1962 Noyce was with the British-Soviet Expedition in the Pamirs, of which Sir John Hunt was joint leader. He and Robin Smith were descending steep ice on Garmo Peak, roped but moving together, when they slipped and fell 4,000 feet to their deaths.

PACCARD, MICHEL GABRIEL

Dr. Paccard was born in 1759 in the valley of Chamonix and became the physician of Chamonix village. He had a great and reverent love for mountains and spent his spare time wandering, exploring, and spending nights out in bivouac among them. He longed to climb the great peak that dominates all the Chamonix region, but Mont Blanc was then unexplored and unattempted. He was 24 when he discovered one other man ambitious to make the first ascent—Marc Theodore Bourrit, a journalist who planned to make himself world-famous by this one feat. They tried together, but Bourrit's cowardice was greater than his ambition and he refused to venture on the ice. Paccard went on alone for some distance to reconnoitre the route, and found what he considered a practicable way before returning.

Three years later Paccard joined forces with Jacques Balmat, a local crystal-hunter who agreed to make the attempt on condition that he received the whole of the large reward that had been offered by De Saussure for the first man to reach the summit. They spent a night on the rocks of the Grands Mulets and next day were seen on top, at 6.30 in the evening of 8th August 1786. Forty-eight hours later they were being given a heroes' welcome in Chamonix.

Balmat, a great boaster, took all the credit as well as the reward. In a short while he was declaring that he alone had reached the top—Paccard had refused to climb to it. His story, given to the novelist Alexander Dumas, was published and generally believed, especially when articles and pamphlets published by the envious Bourrit supported it. It was nearly a century later, years after Dr. Paccard's death, that evidence came to light to prove that Paccard had not only found the route but had also led the ascent and reached the summit.

Saussure, Horace Benedict de

De Saussure was a scientist with a European reputation, a man of wealth and social position. Born in Geneva in 1740, he early devoted himself to investigating the nature of glaciers and in 1760 visited Chamonix and saw Mont Blanc. His project of climbing the mountain for the purpose of scientific research on the summit was defeated when everyone assured him that no man could ever make the ascent. De Saussure, a lover of mountains, knew he had not the skill to make the attempt himself; he therefore offered a large reward to anyone who would discover a way of climbing Mont Blanc and by it reach the top.

Two years after the successful ascent by Dr. Paccard and Jacques Balmat the Genevese scientist himself climbed to the top. The party included eighteen bold Chamonix peasants, as 'guides', and De Saussure's valet. They spent four hours on the summit at 15,782 feet above the sea making scientific observations. In the same year De Saussure took a large party to the Col du Géant, on the Franco-Italian border above the Mer de Glace, and camped there for nearly a fortnight to investigate the various phenomena of high mountains and glaciers. It was these ascents more than any others that persuaded the world that climbing mountains and traversing glaciers were not merely the feats of suicidal madmen.

Though he was purely scientific in his purposes, De Saussure felt the appeal of high mountains as a mountaineer feels it. Of Mont Blanc he wrote: 'I could not even look upon the mountain, which is visible from so many points round about, without being seized with an aching of desire.' He died in 1799.

SLINGSBY, WILLIAM CECIL

The huge bearded figure of the Yorkshireman W. C. Slingsby bestrides many a page in the Alpine records of the 1870's and 1880's. He was born in 1849 and began to climb in his early twenties. Unlike most of his contemporaries, he did not see the Alps as the 'Playground of Europe' and was not much interested in gaining a reputation by repeating other men's difficult ascents. Before visiting the Alps at all he went in five successive years to Norway, with whose mountains his name is chiefly associated.

Slingsby, though a Victorian in his beliefs and way of life, had the outlook of an Elizabethan adventurer. Boisterous, hardy, revelling in conflict with storm and hazard, he left the impression of a strong and lovable personality wherever he went. Even today his name is remembered in many a remote Norwegian hamlet where tourists are unknown. His mountain adventures in Norway, where his first ascents are dotted all over the great area of mountain and glacier from Bergen as far as Lyngen, 220 miles north of the Arctic Circle, are recorded in his fine book *Norway, the Northern Playground*. In the Alps he often climbed with Collie and Hastings, preferring whenever possible to do without guides. He took part in the first ascent of the Requin and the first traverse of the Aiguille du Plan.

Turning his attention to British mountains, he found plenty to satisfy his zest for adventure. He climbed much in the Lakes and Scotland; Slingsby's Chimney on Scafell, Slingsby's Chimney on Ben Nevis, and Slingsby's Crack on Pillar Rock commemorate three of his many first ascents. With a large party of Alpine Club members he visited Skye in 1890, a campaign which resulted in the opening-up of the Coolin as a climbing ground. He was one of the founders of the Yorkshire Ramblers Club. He died in 1929.

SMYTHE, FRANCIS SYDNEY

To a great many people, the name of Frank Smythe was almost synonymous with 'mountaineering' during the years between the two World Wars. He was born in 1900, and began a career in the Royal Air Force which was terminated by ill health. Invalided out in 1920, Smythe went to Austria and Switzerland in the course of studying for an engineering diploma and was at once very strongly attracted to mountains and climbing. On foot and on ski, he made several adventurous journeys, and was soon using his gift for writing to produce extremely readable books about them. Before long he was doing very difficult climbs in the Alps. Two fine new routes on the Brenva face of Mont Blanc with T. Graham Brown, the Red Sentinel route and Route Major, established his reputation as one of the best all-round mountaineers of his day. In 1930 he gained hard Himalayan experience with the international expedition that attempted Kangchenjunga in that year, and in the following year he led the expedition that climbed Kamet (25,447 feet) at that time the highest summit ever reached. He was a natural choice as a member of Hugh Ruttledge's 1933 Everest expedition, the last of the British attempts to be made by way of Mallory's North Col route. On the final assault Smythe and Eric Shipton began the long traverse across the treacherous slabs of the North Face, whence Mallory and Irvine had fallen to death. Shipton had to turn back with acute stomach trouble; Smythe went on alone. With great labour he succeeded in reaching a point less than 900 feet below the summit—the same point reached by Norton in 1924—before being forced to stop by the instability of the snow.

In later years Frank Smythe turned his attention to mountain photography and published several volumes of fine mountain pictures, of British hills as well as of the Alps, Himalaya, and Canadian Rockies. These and his many other books made him the best-known writer on mountains since Edward Whymper. Before his death in 1949 he had developed very strongly the mystical outlook on mountains which is discernible in his writings.

STEPHEN, LESLIE

Born in 1832, Leslie Stephen was perhaps the greatest of the many men of letters who have made mountaineering their pastime. His background was indeed doubly literary, for his first wife was the daughter of W. M. Thackeray and the novelist Virginia Woolf was his daughter by his second wife. Eton and Trinity Hall brought him distinction in athletics as well as in scholarship, and by 1859 he was beginning the eight Alpine seasons which made him one of the foremost climbers of the Golden Age in the Alps.

Stephen was a critic, historian, biographer and philosopher. Unlike Whymper's *Scrambles Amongst the Alps*, his book *The Playground of Europe* is much more than a record of travel and adventure. It holds its place today among the two or three best books ever written about mountaineering, and expresses with grace and clarity the mountaineer's attitude to life. He took Holy Orders, but intellectual doubts caused him to leave the Church in 1875. Among his first ascents were those of the Schreckhorn and the Zinal Rothhorn. Like most of the Victorian climbers, he was a tremendous walker, and thought nothing of walking forty miles in a day. On one occasion he walked the fifty miles from Cambridge to London in twelve hours to attend an Alpine Club dinner. A few months before his death in 1904 he received the K.C.B.

STRATON, MISS

Miss Straton (Christian name unknown to history) was one of the earliest women climbers. She came to the Alps in about 1860 with her constant companion Emmeline Lloyd-Lewis, who appears to have been ardent in the cause of female emancipation and climbed mainly to show that women could not be kept out of a man's sport. Miss Straton, however, emancipated herself from this anti-masculine crusade by marrying her guide, Jean Charlet of Chamonix, and although he was a peasant and she had £4,000 a year of her own the pair discomfited all their critics by living happily ever after. The Charlets settled in a small house near Chamonix and had two sons, one of whom climbed Mont Blanc at the age of 11.

TSCHINGEL

A mongrel bitch 19 inches high, with a brown silky coat

and large brown eyes, Tschingel holds the all-time mountaineering record for dogs. Born in 1865, she was bought by Christian Almer and crossed the Tschingel Pass with Almer and Hereford George that same year, as a six-months-old puppy. The pass provided her name. Three years later, when Coolidge (then 18) and his aunt Miss Brevoort were turned back by bad weather on an ascent of the Eiger, Almer presented the dog to young Coolidge to lessen his disappointment. After that Tschingel took part in all except the hardest ascents made by that curious pair W. A. B. Coolidge and Meta Brevoort. She never achieved the Matterhorn, which Coolidge had planned for her, but she climbed Mont Blanc and the Jungfrau and collected a total of 66 big Alpine peaks and about 100 minor ones. Miss Brevoort was intensely fond of Tschingel but would never admit her sex, referring to the dog as 'him' even after she gave birth to a puppy. In 1879 Tschingel died, aged 14. 'She was so much more a companion than a mere dog,' wrote Coolidge to Charles Mathews, 'that I feel her loss very deeply.'

TUCKER, CHARLES COMYNS

Born in 1843, C. C. Tucker is one of the less famous names, possibly because he rarely climbed as leader of a party or wrote accounts of his adventures. Yet he was a persistent and lifelong mountaineer with literally hundreds of fine ascents to his credit. He was with A. W. Moore and Douglas Freshfield in the Caucasus when they traversed Kazbek and climbed the east peak of Elbruz, and—again with Freshfield—explored the Pyrenees and the Eastern Alps. The two made an attempt to climb Ararat in 1868, but were forced to turn back 1,000 feet from the summit. Tucker died in 1922.

TUCKETT, FRANCIS FOX

Tuckett, 'the irrepressible', was a Bristol Quaker and business man who climbed in the Alps with phenomenal energy between 1856 and 1874. As a young man he had met the great mountaineering scientist Professor J. D. Forbes, and Forbes had impressed upon him the urgent need for contributions to the body of scientific knowledge. Tuckett took the words to heart, and travelled and climbed with a vast amount of apparatus for taking observations and making notes on a variety of matters. Notebooks and pencils were carried in a dozen ingeniously contrived pockets so that a note could at once be made on botany, topography, glaciology, temperature, pressure, and many other subjects. F. J. Hort described him in 1861: 'He was a sight to see, being hung from head to foot with "notions" in the strictest sense of the word, several of them being inventions of his own. Besides such commonplace things as a great axe-head and a huge rope and thermometers, he had two barometers, a sypsieometer, and a wonderful apparatus, pot within pot, for boiling water at great heights, first for scientific and then for culinary purposes.'

Tuckett was, however, a pioneer climber as well as a scientific observer. He climbed with most of the mountaineers of his time, and there are 57 new expeditions included in his record of 165 Alpine peaks and 376 Alpine passes. He had many adventures, including being twice arrested on the Austrian frontier, first as a spy and next as a 'Panslavist agitator'. With Forbes and Tyndall, he believed that mountaineers of the Golden Age, opening up (as they were) a new world, were morally bound to equip themselves as well as they were able for the observation of its new phenomena. Before he died in 1913 F. F. Tuckett received from the King of Italy the Order of St. Maurice and St. Lazarus for his work in the Alps. He had earlier refused the presidency of the Alpine Club.

FIFTY NAMES FAMOUS IN MOUNTAINEERING

TYNDALL, JOHN

'Herein consisted the fascination of the Alps for me; they appealed at once to thought and feeling, offering their problems to one and their grandeur to the other, while conferring upon the body the soundness and the purity necessary to the healthful exercise of both.' Thus wrote John Tyndall, who was born in 1820 and did not begin to climb until he was 36. He was a scientist, deeply concerned in the current controversy over 'the theory of glaciers', but he did not see the necessity of pretending to a single purpose in the mountains. He took his work very seriously indeed, but he declared, in speech and in print, the enjoyment he got from climbing for its own sake. Unlike Forbes, how was wealthy and religious, Tyndall was poor and agnostic. He was more of a modern in his physical approach to the Alps than any of his contemporaries: he tramped 'on the cheap', as a student, from Marburg to Heidelberg and from Heidelberg into Switzerland, doing his regular fifty miles a day on foot until he saw the Jungfrau. Seven years afterwards he was in the Alps again, with Professor Huxley on a tour of glacier investigation, and the following year he climbed Mont Blanc. This was the beginning of the split in John Tyndall's personality between the sober and dedicated scientist and the lover of dangerous mountain ventures.

Tyndall's classic book is called *The Glaciers of the Alps,* and much of it is a record of scientific observation and theory. Between these solemn pronouncements are sandwiched accounts of mountaineering bold to the point of rashness. With Bennen he climbed, unroped, to the summit of the Finsteraarhorn. He climbed Mont Blanc again after an autumnal storm, in heavy snow, and spent four hours on the top when the temperature was minus 14° F. In 1858 he climbed Monte Rosa alone, with only a bottle of tea and a ham sandwich for food. By 1860 he was an aspirant for the first ascent of the Matterhorn, one of the very few men who believed it could be climbed, and reached 13,000 feet on the Italian ridge. In the next year he made the first ascent of the Weisshorn, a peak which both Leslie Stephen and C. E. Mathews had attempted unsuccessfully. He was elected an honorary member of the Alpine Club in 1887, six years before his death from chloral poisoning during an experiment.

WALKER, LUCY

Lucy Walker was the most famous woman mountaineer of the Victorian age; she would have preferred the term 'lady mountaineer'. She invariably wore proper feminine garments on a climb, a voluminous print dress reaching to within two inches of the ground. It was an age when ladies were barely tolerated on respectable snow ascents and not tolerated at all on difficult rock pitches where they were likely to 'disarrange their clothing' in their efforts. One lady, returning flushed with triumph from the ascent of a big peak, met one of the Alpine Club traditionalists. 'You said that no woman would ever manage it,' she accused him smilingly. 'No, madam,' he corrected her gravely. 'I said "no lady".'

Lucy's father and brother were famous climbers and she did not doubt that it was right for her to climb too. She was born in 1831. When she was 28, plump and spectacled and with her dark hair in ringlets, she made her first climb, an ascent of the Altels with her father and Melchior Anderegg, and after that she climbed in the Alps every season for twenty-one years. She was not interested in any other kind of open-air activity, remaining determinedly feminine and indulging only in an occasional game of croquet. On the mountains she ate nothing but spongecake and drank only champagne. Her most famous feat was the first ascent of the Matterhorn by a woman, the nineteenth ascent on record, which she made in 1871 with her father, F. Gardiner, and five guides.

FIFTY NAMES FAMOUS IN MOUNTAINEERING

WHYMPER, EDWARD

Edward Whymper was born in 1840 in London where his father owned an engraving works at Lambeth. He was apprenticed to this trade, eventually making sketches for the engravers, and in 1860 was sent to the Alps to make the originals for some illustrations to the first volume of *Peaks, Passes and Glaciers*, shortly to be published by Longmans. Whymper had an ambition to explore in the Arctic and saw the mountain journey as a form of preparation for this adventure. He was not greatly attracted to the Alps on the first visit. Of the Matterhorn that was to become the ruling passion of his life he wrote: 'Saw, of course, the Matterhorn repeatedly. What precious stuff Ruskin has written about this! . . . It may be compared to a sugar loaf set up on a table; the sugar loaf should have its head knocked on one side.' Nevertheless, he found that the Alps called him back, and he returned in 1861.

He was barely 21 years old. Already he had the characteristics that were to remain with him all his life; he was opinionated, intolerant, bold to the point of rashness, preferring his own company to anyone else's and never relinquishing any project he had decided to carry through. He resolved to be the first to climb the 'inaccessible' Matterhorn and made his first attempt that same year, getting to 12,650 feet on the Italian ridge. In the next four years he made seven other attempts. It is typical of Whymper that they were all on the Italian side, in spite of the fact that three different parties had tried the Hörnli Ridge and—though driven back by bad weather—had considered it a practicable route. The story of the ascent on 14th July 1865, which was both a triumph and a disaster, is the most familiar in mountaineering annals. Deprived of Jean-Antoine Carrel's services by what he considered treachery, Whymper hastened to Zermatt determined at any cost to get up the Matterhorn before the Italian party which Carrel was to lead on the Italian side. He joined himself to two other parties, one of which included the novice Hadow. The unwieldy rope of seven men reached the top with unexpected ease and jeered at the Italians who could be seen far below. On the descent Hadow slipped and fell, dragging the guide Michel Croz, the Rev. Charles Hudson, and Lord Francis Douglas down with him. The rope broke above the last-named and all were killed.

The controversy over the broken rope (which, it was widely rumoured, had been cut) raged for years and left Whymper an embittered man. There is still a mystery surrounding the circumstances of the accident. Lord Conway wrote later that Dr. G. F. Browne, to whom Whymper went immediately after his return to England, said many years afterwards: 'I am the only living man who knows the truth about the accident, and the knowledge will perish with me.' It seems not impossible that one of the party was in some way to blame and that Whymper decided to shield him.

However that may be, Whymper made no more great climbs in the Alps. He made a journey in Greenland, and in 1879-80 went to Ecuador, where he travelled among the Andes (with Carrel as his companion) and made many ascents including the first ascent of Chimborazo. In later life he became very sharp in money matters and resentful of criticism. He returned to Zermatt, unapproachable, drinking a good deal, taking bitter satisfaction in his reputation as 'the Lion of Zermatt'. In 1911, when he was 71, he visited Coolidge at Grindelwald, afterwards paying a last visit to Zermatt and going on to Chamonix. There he took a cheap room and was almost immediately taken ill. He refused all medical help and was dead within a few days.

WILLS, ALFRED

Wills was to become the Rt. Hon. Sir Alfred Wills, Judge

in the Queen's Bench Division, and to preside at the trial of Oscar Wilde. Born in 1828, he came to maturity in the era when it was fashionable to travel in Switzerland, and for many years he went there without attempting anything more than the customary tourist expeditions on glaciers and over easy passes. He made the acquaintance of Auguste Balmat, a guide of more than common intelligence and ability, who became his close friend. Wills's classic book *Wanderings among the High Alps* is dedicated to Balmat, 'my guide and friend, my tried and faithful companion in many difficulties and some dangers'. Balmat was his chief guide on the ascent of the Wetterhorn in 1854, an ascent from which it is usual to date the beginning of mountaineering as a sport. Though Wills did not know it, it was not the first ascent of the mountain but only the fourth. Nevertheless, Wills's description of the climb in the *Wanderings*, published in 1856, was a major milestone in the progress of climbing towards its general acceptance as a legitimate pastime. He was on his honeymoon when he made his Wetterhorn climb, and later his wife was attracted to the sport and made many minor ascents with Balmat and her husband. Wills himself made many other ascents, notably the ascent of Mont Blanc with Professor Tyndall. He built a house, called The Eagle's Nest, in the Valley of Sixt, where he and his wife were to live after his retirement; but Lady Wills died before she had ever entered it. Wills himself lived until 1912.

WORKMAN, WILLIAM HUNTER and FANNY BULLOCK

These two Americans, man and wife, whose names are inseparable, made a lifelong hobby of travel and exploration in the Himalaya. They were wealthy and took with them trained Alpine guides and many porters and local men, and carried surveying equipment. The first decade of the twentieth century was the period of their explorations in the Karakoram and Nun Kun ranges, where they carried out some remarkable journeys. Unfortunately their records were often inaccurate and their surveys valueless, though their enterprise and resolution took them to points where accurate observations would have been very valuable to the Survey of India then being made. In 1906 Mrs. Bullock Workman reached the summit of Pinnacle Peak, 22,810 feet, a record height for a woman at that time; but she persisted in her statement that it was 23,300 feet and therefore higher than Kun, the second highest of the Nun Kun range. Similarly, the Workmans frequently claimed first discoveries of features previously discovered by other travellers. Their exploration of the Siachen Glacier in 1911–12, however, was a fine achievement. With the surveyor Grant Peterkin to help them, they fixed the positions of many great peaks along the Shaksgam watershed, including Saltoro Kangri, 25,400 feet. Dr. Workman died in 1932 and his wife in 1925.

YOUNGHUSBAND, FRANCIS EDWARD

Among the thousands of young soldiers maintained in India by the British Government in the late nineteenth century was Lieutenant Francis Younghusband of the King's Dragoon Guards. Younghusband was an athlete and sportsman with a craving for adventure which his station on the Himalayan frontier could satisfy. On the small military expeditions by which the law of the British Raj was carried into the remote gorges he had ample opportunity for exploration and scrambling. In 1887, when he was 24, he made a daring crossing of the Karakoram by the 18,000-foot Muztagh Pass. In 1897, when he was in Chitral with another young army officer, Charles Bruce, the two planned to cross Tibet and climb Everest. Lack of funds and influence made this impossible at the time, but the idea persisted in Younghusband's mind.

FIFTY NAMES FAMOUS IN MOUNTAINEERING

Just after the First World War Captain J. B. L. Noel, who had in 1913 explored the Tibetan mountains just north of Everest, lectured to the Royal Geographical Society in March 1919 and suggested an expedition to Everest. The British Government was unwilling to risk upsetting relations with Russia by sending such an expedition and the plan was temporarily shelved. Younghusband, now Sir Francis and a man who had much influence in high quarters, became President of the R.G.S. next year and began to push the idea through with great energy. He was now 57 and too old for high mountaineering, but when the project was approved his old friend Charles Bruce, now General the Hon. C. G. Bruce, was asked to lead the 1921 reconnaissance expedition. Bruce was unable to do so for military reasons that year and did not become expedition leader until the next year, when he directed the first climbing attempt.

As chairman of the Mount Everest Committee, Younghusband was the driving force behind the expeditions of 1921, 1922 and 1924 which are well described in his book *The Epic of Mount Everest*. He died in 1942.

ZURBRIGGEN, MATTHIAS

'He was turned out to shift for himself as a child—I believe seven years old—his sole stock-in-trade being an imperfect knowledge of a very restricted *patois* and the capacity to herd goats.' Thus Martin Conway wrote of a man who is the most remarkable figure in the gallery of famous Alpine guides. Zurbriggen's ambition was to know as much about everything as possible. When he reached his prime he could speak English, French, German, Italian, Spanish, and a little Hindustani. He worked at different times as a labourer on the Rhone Embankment, a tassel-maker in Italy, a postillion on a *diligence*, a gentleman's gentleman in Tunis, and a stonemason in Algeria. He also accompanied travellers all over the world as a courier and went to Australia to speculate in rabbit-skins. Towards the end of his life he wrote his autobiography, from which it appeared that he had been a hill farmer and managed a sawmill at the same time. Meanwhile, he was making a reputation as an Alpine guide.

When he had learned his craft on the big Alpine peaks, the great climbers who had discovered his skill and courage engaged him for long expeditions. He was with Conway on his long journey from end to end of the Alps, climbing 21 peaks and crossing 39 passes. Conway's friend and disciple Edward Fitzgerald took Zurbriggen with him to South America in 1897. They attempted the first ascent of Aconcagua, 22,835 feet and the highest peak in the southern hemisphere, and though Fitzgerald was overcome by altitude and fatigue 1,000 feet below the summit Zurbriggen went on alone and reached the top. Five years before this one of the earliest Himalayan expeditions from England took Zurbriggen with them to the Karakoram. Conway was the leader, and he, with Bruce, Zurbriggen, and two Gurkhas, climbed Pioneer Peak, 22,600 feet, the highest summit ever reached at that time.

Utterly reliable on a mountain, Matthias Zurbriggen was unpredictable in the valleys. He was tough and lusty, a hard worker and a hard drinker, a chestnut-bearded gold-earringed giant who retained his own violent personality through all the vicissitudes of his colourful career. He remains a unique character among the sturdy men who played so important a part in the events of mountaineering history.

NIGHTMARE

*I would not spend another such a night
Though 'twere to buy a world of happy days;
So full of dismal terror was the time!*
                                        SHAKESPEARE

THE PROPHECY OF DOCTOR HAMEL

On a morning in the year 1860 two men, oddly contrasted, moved together from showcase to showcase in the British Museum. One was very tall and immaculately dressed, with sidewhiskers and a fringe of beard framing a thin intellectual face; the other's short and immensely broad figure was clad in rough brown cloth, and the keen black eyes set in a weather-beaten face followed intently his companion's pointing finger as the two paused before each exhibit. Professor John Tyndall was showing the wonders of the museum to his guide, friend, and guest Auguste Balmat. They moved across the room through the sparse throng of sight-seers, Balmat's curious glance roving everywhere. Suddenly the guide touched Tyndall's arm.

'The gentleman who has just come in,' he said quietly. 'You know him, monsieur? It is Doctor Hamel.'

Tyndall nodded. 'I remember. The avalanche on Mont Blanc—nearly thirty years ago, I believe. His guides were buried in a crevasse, were they not?'

'That is so, monsieur. Tairraz, Carrier, and Balmat—Pierre Balmat, my uncle. They were ——'

Auguste stopped. Doctor Hamel was approaching them. He was an elderly man, white-bearded but very erect. He and Tyndall bowed to each other and exchanged polite greetings, Hamel introducing himself in English with a marked foreign accent. Then the Doctor turned to Balmat.

NIGHTMARE

'You come, I think, from Chamonix, Monsieur—ah—Balmat?'

'Yes, monsieur.'

'Yes. And they have not yet discovered the bodies of my guides?'

'No, monsieur.'

Doctor Hamel showed yellow teeth in a grin. 'They will, Monsieur Balmat, they will. Within a twelvemonth—you hear?—within a twelvemonth the glacier will render up their three bodies. The Chamonix people must watch the snout of the Glacier des Bossons. Eh, M. le Professeur?'

'It is probable, Doctor,' Tyndall agreed coldly.

'Probable? It is certain! You will see.' The Doctor gave a little cackle of laughter. 'It will be a very good thing for Chamonix. They must open a museum—like this one. The—ah—relics will attract the tourists. Make them pay, Monsieur Balmat, make them pay!'

With a final bow Doctor Hamel stalked away.

It was in August 1820 that Doctor Hamel's party had set out to ascend Mont Blanc. At that date only eight parties had reached the summit since the first ascent in 1786, and there had been no fatal accident. Their route was to be the same as Dr. Paccard's—from the rocks of the Grands Mulets, where they would bivouac, up into the snow cwm of the Grand Plateau and then leftwards on an ascending traverse across the steep snowslope under the summit to gain, beyond the Rochers Rouges, the final ridge. Fourteen men in all left Chamonix on 17th August.

Doctor Hamel was a Russian, one of the Emperor Alexander's councillors. He proposed to make the usual scientific observations on the summit, and took with him besides other instruments a barometer fixed to a long board, and a carrier pigeon, caged for convenience in a cooking pot. With him

THE PROPHECY OF DOCTOR HAMEL

went a Genevan optician named Selligue and two Englishmen, adventurous students from Oxford, Joseph Durnford and Gilbert Henderson. The experienced guides Couttet and Balmat organized the party, which also included eight other young Chamonix men as porters and subordinate guides. The weather was perfect and appeared settled; but during the bivouac night at the Grands Mulets storms of rain and sleet assailed them and the leading guides counselled a retreat in the morning. Hamel berated them for cowards, and they agreed to wait another day. Two men were sent down to Chamonix for more provisions, taking with them Selligue, who had had enough. Snowstorms continued during the day, but at midnight the sky cleared suddenly and dawn showed a cloudless heaven with every promise of fine weather. As the sunrise turned the summit snows of Mont Blanc pink and then gold, the eleven men started up the glacier from the Grands Mulets.

The morning was sunny and windless. By half past ten they had begun the Ancien Passage (as it was soon to be called) across the snow face below the summit. Underfoot the new snow lay deep, falling on their left far down to end in an ice cliff where the glacier fell over vertical rock in its hidden bed; for this steeply angled snow lay on ice, the feeder ice of the long glacier that wound away thousands of feet below the toiling party. They were not roped—it was not customary to use a rope in 1820—and the men supported themselves on the slope with the long poles called *bâtons*. In case they met with hard ice, several of the guides carried hatchets thrust into their belts. Six porter-guides broke the trail, with the three 'tourists' and two guides following. The sun smote hot and brilliant down the dazzling slope that reared overhead on their right towards the summit, invisible beyond the white rim far above against the blue sky; Hamel and the Englishmen covered their faces with the long green veils they wore tied round their hats. Now and then they looked down the increasing length of the slope, where a long blue line stretched right across the tilted whiteness 400 feet below. That very long fissure had been noted by all the previous parties, and was known as the Grande Crevasse.

The white upper world smiled in the sunlight. The air was still, and there was no sound except the minor noises of their own progress—the rhythmic crunch of boots, the quick breathing of lungs striving to overcome the shortage of oxygen in the air of 14,000 feet. And then the silence ended in a brief, dull, splitting sound. The snowslope fractured along the line of their footprints and slid downwards, taking them with it. A moment later the snow higher up was pouring down in a tossing, roaring sea. All eleven men were swallowed up in the fury of the avalanche.

The waves of snow raced down upon the Grande Crevasse, poured into it, filled it, and sped on. The last white spray slid over the crest of the ice cliff and the tumult ceased almost as suddenly as it had begun, leaving absolute silence. The great white slope was spotless once more, unmarked now by the line of footprints, empty of the men who had stamped out that vanished line. It remained thus for perhaps two minutes. Then an arm, followed by a head and shoulders, broke laboriously through the snow; it was Doctor Hamel. Twenty paces away young Henderson was struggling out of the close-packed mass. The avalanche had not been entirely merciless.

One by one Durnford and three of the Chamonix men dragged themselves out. They flung the snow from their faces and bodies and looked round for the other five. They themselves had been carried down nearly 400 feet in the avalanche, but the snow had stopped sliding before they reached the Grande Crevasse. The mighty chasm was only 20 feet below them—and from its depths came faint cries. Hamel, Durnford, and two others climbed gingerly down to the edge. The green

THE PROPHECY OF DOCTOR HAMEL

walls of ice dropped to a mass of snow jammed in the throat of the crevasse, and the guide Couttet was pulling himself out of it. Near him Devouassoud, the porter who had been carrying the long barometer, was suspended between the pillars of ice; the barometer slung on his shoulders had saved him. Axes were thrown down to them and the exhausted pair were assisted to climb out. They were unhurt, but three men—Tairraz, Pierre Balmat and Carrier—were still missing. Undoubtedly they were beneath the snow that choked the Grande Crevasse. Hamel and Durnford had courage enough to climb down on to the bridge of avalanche debris, though it was likely to collapse at any moment. They probed with their *bâtons*, shouted, held the thrust *bâtons* between their teeth the better to hear any faint cries from the depths. There was no cry, no sound. An hour's vain search made it impossible that the three men could be alive.

The eight survivors descended to Chamonix the same evening.

On 12th August 1861, almost precisely forty-one years after the accident to Doctor Hamel's party, a guide arrived at the Mairie of Chamonix carrying a sack. In the sack were human remains which he had found in an ice fissure near the snout of the Glacier des Bossons. The authorities listed these relics. Besides pieces of clothing, a lantern and a pigeon's wing, there were:

Portions of three human skulls.

A human jaw with fine white teeth.

A forearm and hand, the flesh white and fresh and still flexible.

A boiled leg of mutton—the only flesh that exhaled an unpleasant smell.

Only two of the Chamonix men who had been with Doctor Hamel's party were still living, and they were now old men.

NIGHTMARE

They were called to try to identify the remains. Devouassoud, he who had been saved by the barometer, was over 80 and senile, hardly able even to recall the accident; but Couttet retained all his faculties at 72 and was strongly moved. He identified part of a skull as Balmat's, by the tuft of yellow hair still adhering to it, and another skull as that of the black-haired Carrier. The hand—a right hand—he recognized as Pierre Balmat's. Couttet grasped the smooth youthful fingers in his own withered paw, greeting with this loving handshake the dead youngster who had long ago been his friend and comrade. On the flesh of the living Couttet time had wrought its usual change; on the flesh of the dead Balmat, prisoned for forty-one years in the ice, time had failed to mark a single wrinkle.

Some months later a tourist came upon another severed hand. Later still a guide, prowling for relics among the dingy ice of the glacier snout, saw an arm, clad in a sleeve, jutting from the flank of the glacier. 'The nails of this white hand were still rosy, and the pose of the extended fingers seemed to express an eloquent welcome to the long lost light of day,' says M. d'Arve's record. This, like both the others, was a right hand. The three vanished men were now all accounted for; and the prophecy of Doctor Hamel was fulfilled.

THE SURVIVOR

The enormous rock tooth of the Aiguille du Géant, more often called the Dent du Géant, is the sort of sheer and dizzy rock tower that one would expect to attract a modern rock climber but not an Alpine guide of the nineteenth century. It sticks up most improbably from the skyline of the Mont Blanc range as you see it from Courmayeur, its 13,166 feet of height lifting it far above the Col du Géant whose guardian it is. It looks and is, as Mummery observed, 'quite inaccessible by fair means'. Yet it was an Italian guide who made the first ascent—or rather, an Italian family. Jean-Joseph Maquignaz of Courmayeur coveted the first ascent of that huge Pisa-tower of black rock and with his son and nephew spent four days fixing iron pegs and ropes up its north face. When all was ready, he climbed it, leading to the top a numerous party of male Maquignaz relations. This was in 1882. It was thirteen years later when Carson Roberts decided to climb it with the famous guide Emile Rey.

Roberts was one of the leading rock climbers of his day, and though still in his twenties was a very experienced mountaineer. He had been the first Englishman after Mummery to lead the Mummery Crack on the Grépon, and in this very year had climbed the Dru with Rey. They were a well-matched pair. Both men were exceedingly sure of foot on exposed rock and regarded the rope as a safeguard necessary only on glaciers or unstable snow; they had made the ascent of the

NIGHTMARE

Dru without roping-up except for the crossing of the glacier below it.

With Emile Rey and a Chamonix porter, Roberts made a bivouac on the grassy slopes above the Mer de Glace on the night of 23rd August. Rey had mentioned that he was feeling fatigued—an unusual circumstance with him—and that was why they had not camped higher up. Roberts had designs on the Aiguille Verte by the Moine Ridge, but the guide pointed out that it was too far and suggested the Dent du Géant instead. At five next morning they sent the porter back to Chamonix and started across the glacier; it was none too early a start for the ascent of a high peak, but after the descent they could reach the hut on the Col du Géant in less than two hours. By 1.15 they were at the foot of the huge pinnacle. According to their custom, the rope was not used. Roberts led the way up the column of rock, sheer as the side of a house, stepping unconcernedly on the very exposed sections between the pitons and fixed ropes left by Maquignaz. They were on the summit, a platform of rock uniquely isolated in space, after only three-quarters of an hour of climbing; satisfactory proof, they told each other, of the excellence of their system of unroped climbing. Now they could spend a long time admiring the stupendous view of Mont Blanc and the Aiguilles.

Far down below them was the snow-streaked rock of the Col du Géant, with the hut a tiny dot on the Italian side of the pass. Beyond it the Péteret Ridge, one of Emile Rey's 'firsts', sprang in scallops of black and white to the snow dome of Mont Blanc. Bad weather was brewing behind that ridge, but the two men lingered talking of old climbs and new routes for nearly an hour and a half before beginning the descent. As usual, they climbed down unroped, and got safely to the foot of the Dent at a little after four. They roped up now, for there was a tricky ice-slope to cross to gain a rocky promontory jutting from the plinth from which the great tower rose. Once this was passed, they had only to get down the rocky face of the promontory, very steep but only a few hundred feet in height, to reach the snowfield and walk up it to the col and the shelter of the hut. It was fortunate they had so short a distance to go, for now the storm-clouds were brimming over the Col du Géant and the wind was rising every minute.

They untied the rope, without comment. The scramble down the rocks would be easy and men like Roberts and Rey could hardly put a foot wrong on easy rock. Rey descended first. He came to a short chimney below which was a sloping slab leading to a traverse to easier ground above the precipice. Roberts, watching, heard Rey give a grunt as he let himself drop the last three feet on to the slab. The guide staggered and fell on his side, loosing his axe and making no apparent effort to recover himself. There was a projecting rock close to him but he made no attempt to catch hold of it and slithered slowly from the slab on to an incline of hard snow. It was a frozen chute above a vertical drop in the shallow gully below. Emile Rey's slide accelerated swiftly. At the verge of the drop he was flung clear, into space. Roberts saw his body 'like a cartwheel in the air' silhouetted for a moment against the crevassed snowfield far below and then he was gone.

Roberts was doubly stunned by the accident. It had happened without warning; it had been entirely unexpected. As soon as he recovered he shouted, hoping to hear a cry or a groan from below. He could see nothing of the foot of the precipice from where he stood, and the wind was now roaring among the crags and driving volleys of hail before it. Obviously he must get down to the fallen man as quickly as possible. Between the blasts of hail he took a compass bearing of the hut on the col; he would probably have to go there for help. Then he began to climb down.

On the verge of the snow chute he was brought to a halt by

an impassable wall dropping more than 200 feet from his boots. But he saw Emile Rey. The fall had ended on steep snow at the foot of the precipice and Rey had slid down this to land on a bank of snow where the slope eased. He lay still, with one leg doubled behind his back.

Roberts shouted against the wind, and shouted again. There was no response, no movement. He clambered up to the foot of the chimney and began to traverse along the crags looking for a way down. Snow was driving thickly in his face, blinding him, making the dense grey mist almost opaque. He could find no way of descent. At last a route appeared below him—a short snow gully that would land him on the snowfield. He had come so far from the scene of the accident that he was nearer to the hut than to Emile Rey; and it was more than likely that he would be unable to find where Rey was lying. It was a nightmare position, alone there in the fast growing violence of a storm at nearly 13,000 feet, with darkness falling above the whirl of the blizzard, and the decision Roberts had to make was the kind that haunts a man in nightmares. Rey had fallen a total of seven or eight hundred feet, but he had fallen on snow. He was conceivably still alive. Ought the survivor to try to reach him at once? If he found Rey—and in the storm that was no more than an even chance—might he not discover that Rey's only hope lay in the fetching of help from the hut on the Col du Géant?

Roberts made his decision. He kicked steps down the snow gully, took a hurried compass-bearing at the bottom, and set out through the storm across the crevassed snowfield towards the hut. Staggering in the furious blasts, unable to see more than a few feet ahead, reeling back on the brink of crevasses, he made terribly slow progress. Night was upon him when he crossed the rocky saddle of the col and saw below him, looming out of the ceaseless blast of snow, the dark rectangular shape of the hut. Sobbing and exhausted, he dragged himself to the door and wrenched at the handle. The door was locked.

The two young climbers from Geneva who had left Montenvers in the morning proposed to go as far as the hut on the Col du Géant and spend the night there. Both Baumann and Jacottet were apprentices in mountain craft, but they were fast goers on the mountainside; much earlier that afternoon, below the Géant *séracs*, they had overtaken and passed the slow caravan of six Dutch tourists—three men and three women—with their six guides. It was the thought of this cumbrous and inexperienced party that worried them when they reached the hut. For the storm had broken, with savage gusts of hail and snow sweeping across the pass and down the long highway of the glaciers up which the Dutch tourists were toiling. The hut, a poor structure very unlike the palatial Torino Hut of today, shook and rattled in the gale. Darkness fell. The driven masses of snow piled against the outer walls and rustled loudly on the roof. Baumann and Jacottet, a little frightened, made themselves as snug as they could, locking the rattling door and brewing tea on the stove. Their faces were anxious as they remembered the ill-equipped Dutchmen and their wives stumbling upward still through the night and the snowstorm; the elements of another Mont Blanc tragedy were there.

So loud were the voices of the storm that they did not at first hear the banging on the door. When they opened it they half expected to see one of the Dutchmen's guides come to seek a rescue party. It was Carson Roberts—'covered with snow,' Baumann writes, 'his hair disordered, his eyes haggard, his jacket torn'. Through his frozen lips Roberts managed to get out a few words, telling them of Rey's fall. They made him sit, revived him with tea. He implored them to go out with him at once and find Rey. Baumann and Jacottet looked at

NIGHTMARE

each other in silence, while the storm roared on outside. Again Roberts begged them to help him. Then Baumann explained (with difficulty, because the Englishman had little French) that he and his friend could not go out looking for a man who must surely be dead by now, when they might have to set forth to the rescue of the Dutch party lost on the glacier. 'Better to search for the living than the dead.' Nothing would move them from this stand.

The nightmare was back again. Roberts was in despair. Out there below the dark tower of rock was Emile, perhaps alive, perhaps to be saved if he could be brought into shelter. Alone he could do nothing—it would be worse than useless to make a solitary attempt at rescue—and he knew the argument of the young Genevese was reasonable. There was one spark of hope: with the Dutch party were six guides, and if they reached the hut a strong rescue party could set out to find Emile. He roused himself and told the young men that they must do all they could to find the guides. At first all Baumann and Jacottet would do was to go outside at intervals and shout, to guide the party who might be looking for the hut. Then, as a last effort, the three put on all their equipment and left the hut to grope a way towards the crest of the pass, shouting as they went.

The blackness filled with whirling white flakes closed round them and the hut was lost below. But only a little way below the col they stumbled into the missing party, the guides—themselves exhausted—dragging their charges, half dead from exposure and fatigue.

The urgency of Roberts's demands had to give way before the necessity of getting the Dutch tourists into shelter and dealing with frozen extremities and the other dangerous effects of their ordeal. Half mad with anxiety, he put his request to the leading guide as soon as the essentials of first aid were completed. The guide refused absolutely to go out again. His men could do no more, he declared. Their first duty was to their employers, and if they were to bring the caravan safely down to Courmayeur next day they must have all the rest they could get. Against this resolution Roberts argued and pleaded in vain. His last hope of saving his friend was gone.

He accepted, like a man in a dream, the suggestion of the two Genevese that they should send a rescue party up from Montenvers in the morning. He agreed to remain at the Col du Géant hut to guide the rescuers to the body—there was no doubt, now, that it would be a body. And for the rest of that night, while the violence of the storm slowly lessened, he lay wakeful on a palliasse in a corner of the hut thinking of the crumpled figure on the snow beneath the Dent du Géant, with the white mound building against it as the snowflakes drove out of the dark.

For Carson Roberts there was to be lingering sorrow, but not the haunting nightmare of failure. He could have done nothing, after all. When the searchers found the body of Emile Rey, half buried in snow where it had fallen, they saw that the neck was broken. Death had been instantaneous.

THE COLD HELL

There were four men in the crevasse. They sat huddled together on ice axes and frozen ropes laid on the floor of snow. It was pitch dark and the intense cold pressed on them, into them, like the thrust of iron. Though their bodies touched, each man was withdrawn from the rest in his own cell of suffering, suffering that was mercifully numbed by cold and exhaustion. Outside, above the twisting tunnel that led down through 30 feet of snow and ice into their burrow, the wind shrieked across the north face of Annapurna, driving before it blinding squalls of powder snow. If they had continued to struggle down through that storm, instead of sheltering in this chance-found hole, they would all have been dead by now. It was small comfort; at the back of their numbed minds was the conviction that they would never escape alive from this hell of cold.

It was the night of 4th June 1950. On the previous day Maurice Herzog and Louis Lachenal had reached the summit of Annapurna, 26,493 feet—the first mountain over 8,000 metres ever to be climbed. They had descended (Herzog bare-handed, having lost his gloves) to Camp V where Lionel Terray and Gaston Rébuffat awaited them as support party. Lachenal had fallen 300 feet and was badly shaken and concussed; Herzog's feet and hands were frozen, stiff and hard as blocks of wood. All four men had driven themselves to the limit in seventeen days of severe climbing on the mountain. And that night at Camp V the storm had risen, the icy gale and the fury of the snowfall. In the morning the wind had dropped, but the snow still fell out of a dense mist that made the enormous face of the mountain with its ice walls and *séracs* and rooftop slants of snow one featureless blur of blinding white. The climbers were unable to strike the two little tents or pack their equipment, for their hands were useless and they had barely enough strength left for the effort of descent to Camp IV. They had started down the steeps of new snow, snow that was ready to avalanche, unable to see more than a foot or two ahead and moving very slowly because of their frozen limbs. Lachenal became light-headed and attempted to rush straight down; then he wanted to lie in the snow. They persuaded him that either meant certain death and climbed on, cautiously treading the treacherous snow above the ice precipices invisible below in the mist. Once and again they had to retreat from the brink of a bottomless wall of *séracs*, painfully retracing their steps to what they thought was the right line of descent. Afternoon came, and with it a renewal of the storm. They knew they must be near Camp IV but unless they actually fell over the tents they would never find it in the whirling, blinding whiteness. They shouted above the rising whistle of the snowstorm, together: 'One, two, three—*help*! . . . One, two, three—*help*!' It was futile. They had lost all idea of time, and the coming of darkness surprised and appalled them. To dig a hole in the snow and huddle there through the night—at more than 23,000 feet above the sea—was now their only hope of survival. And even that hope was vain, they found. The last food they had eaten had been the previous night; their strength was so reduced that they could not dig a hole with the axes.

It was then that Lachenal, stumbling a few yards away to look for softer snow, fell headlong into a hidden crevasse. It had seemed the end of hope. Weak and almost helpless from frostbite, the other three could not possibly pull him out. But Lachenal's voice came faintly and cheerfully up from the

NIGHTMARE

bowels of the snow: 'I'm not hurt! This'll do for the night—come along!'

So they had come into the crevasse, dropping one by one down the 30 foot tunnel into a cavern floored with new snow and big enough—when the icicles had been broken from the roof—to hold the four of them. And the night passed very slowly, without speech. Terray massaged Lachenal's dead feet, Rébuffat stirred from time to time to rub his own feet. Herzog could do nothing. His hands as well as his feet were quite dead. Literally dead. He knew the flesh of fingers and toes was already like that of a corpse; that the deadly gangrene was slowly eating its way up his limbs, would kill him unless it could be checked. Oudot, the expedition surgeon, was at Camp II. But Camp II was far, far below them beyond 4,000 feet of the most terrible mountainside Herzog had ever seen: ice slopes, *séracs*, vertical walls of ice where they had placed fixed ropes on the ascent. How, wondered Herzog dully, was he to get down a fixed rope with hands that could not take hold and feet that could not feel any contact?

The darkness in the crevasse lightened at last to greyness. The morning had come. But what of the weather? Rébuffat managed to move his frozen lips. 'Too early yet.' A few minutes after he had spoken there sounded overhead a long hiss that became a roar. The grey light vanished as a mass of snow poured into the crevasse, burying their meagre equipment and half smothering the four men. The noise of the avalanche passed and they dragged themselves feebly out of the piled snow, aware that if they had been outside their hole when it came down they would have been swept away with it to death. Another avalanche could fall at any time; but there was no point in delay. Lachenal wormed his way out through the tunnel, and his voice came down to them in a shriek of triumph: 'It's fine—the sky's clear!'

Terray and Rébuffat climbed out, but Herzog could not.

THE COLD HELL

Somehow they pulled him up on the rope and he fell on his face in deep new snow. Pain and anxiety had gone, thrust out by the knowledge that he would never move again. He was dying.

Terray came slowly towards him across the steep slope, staggering oddly. He had just succeeded in stopping Lachenal from running madly down to destruction. Herzog spoke calmly: 'It's all over for me. You've still got a chance if you leave me. Go on—please.'

'If we get away, so will you.' Terray paused. 'Can you see anything, Maurice—anything of the route? I'm quite blind, and so is Gaston.'

There was nothing to be seen except the endless slant of whiteness above and below, under a cloudless dark-blue sky. Somewhere in the tilted chaos of ice cliff and snow hump were the tents of Camp IV, but there was no sign of them. And there was Lachenal, off again in his madness, staggering alone down the slant of snow. He stopped suddenly, and his cracked voice rang strangely. He was shouting for help, waving a feeble arm—was it possible that he could see Camp IV from where he was? The other three, too exhausted to go down to him, began to shout too. And there came a faint answering cry.

Up the slope, waist deep in the new-fallen snow, came the first of a rescue party, Marcel Schatz. In another half-hour the summit party, two of them blind and one of them helpless, had been assisted down the slope and round the corner of an ice wall into Camp IV. Their bivouac crevasse had been only 200 yards from the tents.

The rescue had not brought the four men to safety; it had merely given them a renewed chance of life. For Lachenal and Herzog—particularly for Herzog—that chance depended on the winning of a race against time.

NIGHTMARE

The 4,000 feet of very difficult descent to Camp II, where the surgeon Jacques Oudot could take charge of the patients, had to be done in one day. The snow-blindness that affected Terray and Rébuffat was not permanent; it would make their descent fearfully hard and perilous, but it would pass in a few days and leave them none the worse. But the cold had bitten deeply into Herzog and Lachenal. It had sown the seeds of death in them. Hour by hour the gangrene was eating its slow way along their extremities, and unless it was halted very soon Herzog, at least, could hope only for life as a limbless trunk; another storm on Annapurna, a prolonged delay at Camp IV, would mean death.

But the weather was at its best. The dark sky of high altitude was clear, the sun blazed down as Schatz and the four Sherpas arranged the ropes for the descent. The brief pause for warm drink and food at Camp IV had restored the power of movement to Herzog, and though he could not hold an axe he was able to lower his lifeless feet in turn into the big steps the Sherpa Angtharkay cut for them, while the rope held by another Sherpa above supported him. Very slowly the nine men crept down the vast flanks of snow, sinking up to their knees in the incoherent stuff, knowing full well that they were taking chances that were justifiable only by the vital urgency of the circumstances. The avalanche that swept down upon them was almost inevitable.

The maddened waves of snow tossed four human bodies like corks in a surf before finally submerging them in its headlong rush. Herzog, Rébuffat and two Sherpas had been borne away, the others left far above. Herzog felt the suffocating pressure of the snow fall from him and found himself hanging upside down in the jaws of an ice couloir with a drop of 1,500 feet below him. The rope had caught across a ridge of ice and saved them. With great difficulty the Sherpas pulled him up. Without pause, almost without comment, they continued the

THE COLD HELL

descent. They had fallen 500 feet. Rébuffat had blood running from his mouth but was still able to climb down, blindly, placing his feet by feel alone. Herzog was bruised and cut and his left elbow was dislocated, but he was past feeling pain. His sole conscious thought was that he must get down quickly—he must reach Camp II and medical aid.

They came to the first ice step and the fixed rope. The Sherpas could lower Herzog, but he could not grasp the rope. He wound it round his bare, dead hands and let himself slide. The skin stripped off, the flesh tore and hung in red strands, but he felt no pain. Remembering dimly that if he lost all the flesh from his finger bones it would be difficult to heal his hands, he tried to avoid tearing off the flesh altogether. He got down. Rébuffat followed more easily, sightless but able to hold on. They traversed a dangerous slope, ice covered with powder snow, and came to the second ice step. Herzog repeated his method of descent; neither he nor the Sherpas could bear to look at his hands now. On the slopes below he seemed to feel the pain of frostbite spreading to his elbows and knees, and wondered in an oddly detached way whether Oudot would amputate all his four limbs as soon as he got down to Camp II. . . . *If* he got down to Camp II.

For the dark-blue sky had vanished behind a swirl of grey mist, and out of the mist drove the snow. Annapurna, wrathful goddess robbed of her virginity, made a final bid for revenge. But the last long and dangerous traverse was somehow made, and through the mist they saw, still far below, the men from the lower camp starting up to help them. So they came down to Camp II at 19,350 feet, the conquerors of Annapurna: Herzog half dead, supported by the Sherpa Phutharkay, his dreadful hands mere tatters of red flesh; Rébuffat and Terray, stumbling and groping like the blind men they were; Lachenal carried between two Sherpas, crazed and 'pedalling' in the air with his frostbitten feet.

NIGHTMARE

Oudot was there, with his drugs and his hypodermic needle. And his surgical scissors.

Injection followed injection for Herzog and Lachenal. For Rébuffat too, for he had frostbitten feet and was unable to walk. There were now three men who would have to be carried, but Camp II had to be evacuated quickly, for the monsoon was already upon them—the storms higher up had been its vanguard—and they dared not wait to be caught and cut off at nearly 20,000 feet. So the long retreat was begun at once, down snowslope, crag, and gully; through precipitous gorges where the path was a couple of feet wide above a sheer drop into the river; across tightrope bridges, through dripping jungle, by narrow tracks between the paddy-fields of isolated villages. It took five weeks.

Five weeks to get to the nearest hospital, where Oudot hoped to bring his patients before operation, so that they would have some chance of retaining their limbs. Every day he injected, cleaned, bandaged, fighting the creeping gangrene. In the fourth week he knew it was beating him. The deadly toxin was spreading. It might turn from dry gangrene into gas gangrene; it might lead to general septicaemia or concentrate in one organ. He could not keep Herzog alive any longer without removing at least part of the source of evil—without amputation. He began to operate. At halts beside the track, in jungle clearings, whenever he found opportunity, he cut off the putrefying flesh from the tips of fingers and toes. It was not enough. Herzog got worse and Lachenal was in bad case.

The long journey was nearing its end. Roadhead—and lorries for transport to Nautanwa, where there was a railway station. There would be two days in the train, and then the last stretch of road to Katmandu; to Katmandu and the big modern hospital with anaesthetics and all the aids to safe amputation. By then it might be too late. Oudot had already

THE COLD HELL

saved Herzog's life and he was not going to let it slip away from him. And he was determined to save his arms and legs.

At Nautanwa he got Lachenal and Herzog into a railway carriage. The train started, jolting and jerking through the terrible heat. At each stop Oudot took out his surgical scissors and the bandages. There was no anaesthetic. Sweat streamed from surgeon and patients as he cut away decayed flesh and rotted bone. At Gorakhpur station two Sherpas were summoned to sweep out the carriage, and (says Herzog in his book *Annapurna*) 'an amazing number of toes of all sizes were swept on to the platform before the startled eyes of the natives'.

The venture into the cold hell of Annapurna cost Louis Lachenal all his toes. Maurice Herzog lost all his toes and all his fingers.

NO WAY BACK

I do not know that climbers are more susceptible to nightmare than other adventurers. But if they were, then there is a moment, possible on all very hard ascents, that could breed the worst of bad dreams: the moment when retreat, essential to the party's survival, is discovered to have become impossible. In a dream you would attempt the impossible descent, slip, fall and wake up sweating. In the nightmare reality of July 1936 there was no waking for three of the four men involved; and for the fourth man there was a second nightmare, excruciatingly prolonged, before he too sank into endless sleep.

It was a Saturday, 18th July, when the big telescopes down at Grindelwald and higher up at Kleine Scheidegg became the focal points for excited crowds of tourists. Four men starting up the North Face of the Eiger! It was the thrill of the season. The great Eigerwand had not yet been climbed. A lot of people thought it never would be climbed and more people still thought the attempt to climb it was worse than madness. Only last year the two young Munich climbers Sedlmayer and Mehringer had died on the Face, frozen to death in their 'Death Bivouac' at 11,000 feet after five days of climbing and clinging to icy ledges. And already this year two more Austrians, Edi Rainer and Willy Angerer, had spent a night on the Face and retreated safely when weather conditions became bad. That had alerted the Press and the sensation-seekers, and it had been no secret that Angerer and Rainer were going to try again. The new thrill was the appearance on the scene of a second pair of contestants, from Bavaria this time: Andreas Hinterstoisser and Toni Kurz. These young men were both 23 years old. Hinterstoisser was a leading expert in the technique of rope and piton which was essential on the Eigerwand's 6,000 feet of vertical rock walls and ice slopes. Kurz, curly-haired and boyishly goodlooking, was a professional guide. Among the lookers-on who impatiently waited their turn at the telescopes there were some—those who would make money out of News and a small fortune out of Death—who hoped the affair would develop into a race: Austrians *v.* Germans—Who Will Be First Up the Eigerwand? The mountaineers and the guides, however, knew that there would be no race. Those four young men up there knew what they were tackling. Even if they were fools to take such risks, at least they were fully aware of those risks; only an out-and-out madman would want to double them by starting a race.

The weather had improved since the abortive attempt of Angerer and Rainer twelve days earlier. It was by no means perfect for the Eigerwand climb, being a little too warm, with melt-water from the ice fields and the summit snows glistening on the bare slabs; but there was no definite sign of it worsening, and with a precipice whose condition could change from good to bad in a matter of hours there was little point in waiting for perfection. The four climbers had as good a chance of success as anyone could have on that enormous and repellent wall of ice and rock; one chance in a hundred, perhaps. As the hours of the first day passed, experienced mountaineers among the watchers began to think the odds were not so heavy as that.

For these men were undoubtedly superb climbers. Moreover, they were trying a different route from that taken by the ill-fated Munich men. Sedlmayer and Mehringer had tried to gain the First Icefield—the lowest considerable wall of ice on the Face—by climbing straight up to it, and they had succeeded. But that route had meant spending a whole day climbing 600 feet of terribly steep and difficult rock, a day's work that must have kept them at the limit of their strength from dawn to sunset and used up the reserves they needed for the upper part of the Face. Hinterstoisser and Kurz were leading the way, with Angerer and Rainer following on a separate rope. They were all moving with remarkable speed, considering the severity of the climbing, making upwards to the right of the First Icefield. The experts muttered uneasily. That line would bring them to the base of the great red wall, the Rote Fluh, an impassable obstacle. But beneath the Rote Fluh the leader, Hinterstoisser, began an extremely exposed traverse back to the left, a traverse that depended on fixing pitons and swinging across holdless rock with the aid of the rope. The Hinterstoisser Traverse was to be his memorial, the key passage in the ascent of the Eigerwand. It was a memorial also to his mistake, which no climber would ever make again: when they were across the traverse Hinterstoisser recovered the traversing rope. To return along that passage was now impossible. Their retreat was cut off.

The four men were not thinking of retreat. They gained the edge of the First Icefield, climbed across it with extraordinary skill and speed, and reached the steep little barrier between it and the Second Icefield. This was late in the afternoon, but they were already far above the place where Sedlmayer and Mehringer had spent their first night on the Face. At this rate, murmured the watchers, they might well need only two bivouacs before reaching the summit.

Through the telescopes the tiny figures could be seen, even identified. With the naked eye there was nothing visible on the gigantic vertical mass, capped with snow, patched with the streaks of white that were huge shields of ice hundreds of feet wide, glistening dully with the water streaming down the sheer slabs from the snowcrest far overhead. Even the windows in the Face could only be seen with the telescope: one window cut in the rock wall at the Eigerwand Station of the Jungfraujoch Railway, the other lower down and to the right, a gallery window on the railway at the point known as Kilometre 3·8. For the Eigerwand, unique among Alpine precipices in its structure, is unique also in having a railway tunnel cut into its bowels, behind its grim façade. The window at Kilometre 3·8 is some hundreds of feet below, and some hundreds of feet to the right of, the Hinterstoisser Traverse.

The telescopes were pointing high above both these tunnel windows now. Something was happening up there on the Second Icefield. The second rope had stopped though the leading rope was still moving. Then the leading rope halted too. It could be seen that one of the lower climbers—it was Angerer, someone declared—had been injured, no doubt by a falling stone. The lower part of the Second Icefield is repeatedly swept by stone fall. The upper pair were lowering a rope; and presently, to the intense relief of the watchers, the four men all began to climb upwards again, linked by one rope. They made for the rocks at the right-hand side of the Second Icefield, and there stopped. It was twilight, and they were making their first bivouac—more than half-way up the Face.

The telescopes were deserted now for the night. But the crowd of watchers was back at first light, and saw all four men leave their bivouac site at 7 a.m., climbing on two ropes once more. Evidently Angerer had recovered sufficiently to go on. It was a dull morning with the sky overcast. The gleam of wet rock was ominous on the overhangs above the icefield. They crossed it, climbing diagonally upwards, moving far more slowly than they had done previously; perhaps the injured man was holding them back, and they had resolved to stay together at all costs. It took them all that day, Sunday, 19th July, to reach the upper edge of the Third Icefield at about 10,900 feet—a little below the place where Sedlmayer and

NIGHTMARE

Mehringer had died in their bivouac. Here they prepared to spend the night. Monday morning came. The dull damp weather was unchanged. The watchers saw Hinterstoisser and Kurz start to climb the steep ice slope leading from the upper rim of the Third Icefield towards the 700-foot rock groove known as the Ramp; but the second rope did not follow them. There was a long pause. The leading rope had halted. Then the Germans began to climb down again. They reached the other two at the bivouac site, paused there a long time; then all four men started to descend together, back across the gleaming shields of ice, down the steep rock—on a doubled rope—to the First Icefield. This latter part of the descent took them a long time, and it seemed that Angerer had to be helped and carefully safeguarded all the while. The shadow of twilight crawled across the Face. Night swallowed them shortly after they had halted, well above the window of the Eigerwand Station, for their third bivouac.

With the realization that a fearfully hazardous retreat had begun, the watchers gathered almost in silence at the telescopes in the early morning of 21st July. No one knew just what had happened or how badly Angerer was injured, but it was obvious even to the non-climbing tourists that if one of the four was incapacitated in the slightest degree the chance of retreat was immeasurably reduced. The experts, those who had experience of Alpine rock faces in bad weather, were silent. For the weather had got worse in the night. The temperature had fallen, an icy wind was blowing across the Face; little puffs and threads of white—avalanches of powder snow—could be seen writhing down over the black rock. And the rock, for three days wet with melt-water, would now be covered with a thin hard glaze of ice. The condition of the men after a freezing night at nearly 10,000 feet in soaked clothing could easily be guessed.

Yet the four climbers renewed the descent at first light in

NO WAY BACK

good style. Yesterday they had come down hardly 1,000 feet and 3,000 feet still remained to be descended. The sight of the four tiny dots moving resolutely down the lower part of the white wall towards the traverse brought new hope to the watchers; perhaps they would after all get down safely before nightfall. The descent was all rock climbing now and all four men were expert rock climbers.

Grey mist wreathed itself across the Face and the dots were lost to view. When it cleared they could be seen again, three men together at the start of the Hinterstoisser Traverse and the fourth, Angerer, motionless and apart. The mist closed again, finally. The curtain had fallen before the end of the tragedy.

Albert von Allmen, a sector guard on the Jungfraujoch Railway, was on duty at Kilometre 3·8, where the gallery window opened on the rock face of the Eigerwand. He knew the four climbers were coming down the towering wall outside. At about noon on that fourth day, 21st July, he opened the heavy wooden door and stepped cautiously out on to the ledge of rock. The cold grey void was below his feet, icy mist hid all but a few yards of glistening vertical wall on either hand. Above the weird shrilling of the wind he could hear the rattle and scream of falling stones. Von Allmen knew little of mountain climbing, but he thought of the 4,000 feet of sheer precipice overhead and the men trying to get down it and he shuddered.

A faint sound came to his ears through the other noises of the Face. It might have been a man's voice. Von Allmen shouted—once, twice. And an answer came, from quite near: 'All right! . . . Climbing straight down!' The voice was only a few hundred feet away, above and to one side of the gallery window. Von Allmen let out a sigh of relief. The four men were nearly down, making for the haven of the gallery window.

NIGHTMARE

He didn't quite see how they were to reach it down the overhangs high above, but no doubt these modern climbers had their own newfangled methods. One thing was certain—they would all be exhausted and half frozen. He himself was already numb from clinging there on his safe platform of rock. He took a deep breath and shouted: 'I'll have some hot tea ready for you!' Then he went back into the shelter of the tunnel, to his electrically lit hut by the gleaming slant of rails in the heart of the Eiger.

An hour passed. Two hours. Von Allmen began to wonder if the climbers had somehow missed their escape route to the gallery window. He made his way along the side tunnel again and stepped out through the wooden doorway he had left open. The weather was getting worse, outside on the darkening Face. The shriek and roar of the wind through the crags, the hiss of sliding snow and the crash of stonefalls, made continous uproar. But out of the noisy twilight came a man's voice. It was crying for help. Von Allmen could just make out the words: 'The others . . . all dead . . . only one left. . . . Help! Help!'

Von Allmen, who was an elderly man and no climber, could do nothing himself. He hurried back to the telephone in his hut and rang through to the Eigergletscher Station at the foot of the mountain. There were three guides there. A special train would bring them up at once with their rescue equipment. Von Allmen could tell them nothing of what had happened, up there above his window; only what that desperate voice had shouted. It had been the voice of Toni Kurz.

What had happened was this.

Hinterstoisser, with Rainer and Kurz, had spent most of the day trying to find a practicable way back across the Hinterstoisser Traverse. Angerer, injured by a falling stone during the first day's climbing, was now so weak from exhaustion and exposure that he could only hang helplessly against the rock, supported by a rope passed through a snaplink clipped to a driven piton. The vertical slabs of the traverse, bulging out above the 2,000-foot drop to the screes invisible in the mist below, had been iced and absolutely impassable. Had the fixed rope been left there when they crossed four days ago they could have saved themselves; but now the only hope —an infinitesimally small one—was to climb out above the traverse and find some point of attachment whence they could lower themselves straight down the overhanging rocks. Painfully, inch by inch, they had edged across. A tiny anchorage was found, but not directly above the narrow ledge whence they could gain the gallery window. Hinterstoisser, the technical expert in these matters, had left the others secured to pitons and moved farther across above the overhangs. It was about this time that they had heard von Allmen's shouts and replied that they were on their way down. A little while— perhaps half an hour—afterwards, Hinterstoisser slipped and fell, straight down through the empty air below the overhangs. His three companions were dragged from their meagre holds. Rainer was snatched up, pulley-wise, against the snaplink and piton that supported him; in an hour he was dead, frozen. Angerer hurtled down in a loop of rope that hitched itself round his neck and strangled him. His dead body hung from the same piton that supported the living Toni Kurz, the sole survivor, who dangled in mid air 30 feet higher up. The body of Andreas Hinterstoisser, freed somehow from the rope, fell 3,000 feet to the foot of the Eigerwand.

The chief guide of Grindelwald had previously issued a warning to Eigerwand aspirants that no Oberland guide would undertake rescue operations on the Face. Adolf and Christian Rubi, with Hans Schlunegger and Arnold Glatthard, disregarded instructions. They climbed out from the gallery window of Kilometre 3·8, into the dark mist. They were

NIGHTMARE

Alpine guides, not daring young rock gymnasts with a taste for the ultimate risk; yet they edged a way diagonally upwards, by ice-glazed ledges on the vertical face, until—guided by faint shouts from Toni Kurz—they were about 300 feet below the survivor hanging invisible on his rope above. There was no possible way of getting up any higher. The gusts of powder snow whipped in their faces, the wind screamed across the slabs. They could hear Kurz's faint shouts. He was telling them that the only way to reach him was from above—by climbing to a place 500 feet above him and roping down. Even in daylight and dry conditions such a feat would have extended Hinterstoisser himself. In darkness, on ice-glazed rock, it was a physical impossibility. The guides had to tell Kurz this. They had to tell him that he must hang there until it grew light enough to make a second attempt to reach him. As they retreated, climbing with infinite care down the dark wall with that tremendous drop under their bootsoles, they heard his cries diminishing far overhead in the night.

With dawn they were climbing out on the Face again. The conditions were terrible. A hard glaze of ice covered the huge vertical slabs, the wind blew half a gale, the mist whirled in freezing blasts. The guides had brought rockets and lines, hoping by this means to send up a rope on which Kurz could lower himself. For, against expectations, Kurz had survived the night. They could just see him moving, one arm—gloveless and frozen—a useless lump, great icicles hanging from legs and feet. The rockets were useless, for the gale hurled them far out from the face. The guides resolved to make the attempt to climb up to him.

Hammering in pitons, chipping the ice from the slabs, they inched up the Face. They were only 130 feet below him when impassable overhangs barred the way finally and completely. Kurz was invisible now above the great bulge of rock over their heads, but they could communicate by shouts between the howling gusts of the wind. He must lower himself to them somehow, they told him. If he could manage to climb down to Angerer's body, hanging on the rope below him, he could perhaps cut the body free and make use of the 30 feet of rope thus provided. The three strands would have to be untwisted and joined, then lowered so that the guides could send up a spare rope.

Kurz had one arm to work with; and his teeth. It took him five hours of agonizing and dangerous work to win his last hope of life. Waiting below, trying to keep the circulation going in their freezing limbs, the guides saw a big snow avalanche go falling past them through the grey emptiness outside their perch beneath the overhangs. Then something smaller and darker hurtled past: the body of Willy Angerer. A long time afterwards the end of Kurz's improvised line came down to them and they attached their spare rope to it. Very slowly it was drawn up. The man above was nearly at the end of his strength. It was another hour before Kurz began to lower himself down the fixed rope, sitting in a sling because he could only hold on with one hand. The guides, craning their necks backwards, saw his boots appear at the edge of the overhang, then his legs. But he came no farther. The knot joining the two ropes which ran through the snaplink had jammed.

The four rescuers were powerless to help him. With an ice axe reached upwards at the full stretch of an arm they could almost touch Kurz's boots, but they could not gain another inch of height. They saw his feeble efforts to free the rope, for he was leaning forward, using his teeth to grip the strands. His left arm stuck out from his body, dead and frozen. His right hand was useless. The guides tried to encourage him. One more try—he was nearly there—six feet more and he was safe. They could not understand his replies, for his lips were black and frozen. Then, quite suddenly, he spoke in a clear firm voice.

'I'm finished.'

His body sagged forward. The rope sling dropped an inch or two below the edge of the overhang, so that they could touch the stiffened legs with the tip of an ice axe. But Toni Kurz was dead.

DAWN

Night's candles are burnt out, and jocund day
Stands tiptoe on the misty mountains' tops.
                                    SHAKESPEARE

WITH THE GOAL FORGOT

The Glacier de la Brenva, mounting north-westward from the Italian Val Veni, climbs 8,000 feet in the 5 miles of its length to the icy sources of its flow on the Brenva Face of Mont Blanc. The flanking walls of the glacier in this upper basin are gigantic, mountain ranges in themselves; the Péteret Ridge on the south-west with its Aiguille Noire and Aiguille Blanche, on the north-east the long crest of the Arête de la Brenva, a wall of snow and ice rising into needles of rock. But the Brenva Face dwarfs even its huge retaining walls. From the long snow ridge linking Mont Blanc summit with its outlier Mont Blanc de Courmayeur the stupendous precipice falls sheer to the glacier basin, a vertical maze of ice cliffs and snow couloirs and jutting buttresses that are the naked ribs of the great mountain. One of these ribs, well over to the right as you look at the Face (it is too far to the right to appear in the diagram), begins low down and ends higher up in snow slopes less formidable than those between the two summits; this is the 'old Brenva route' by which the Face was first climbed in 1865, the route of the Brenva ice-ridge described by A. W. Moore in *The Alps in 1864* and used for an exciting episode in A. E. W. Mason's novel *Running Water*. To the left of it the main Face shows three distinct though discontinuous ridges—if near-verticality can form a ridge—mounting straight from the glacier to the white snow-hammock slung between the summits 15,000 feet above the sea: a pear-shaped buttress separating two impassable icefalls near the flank of the Péteret Ridge; a central and massive buttress on its right; and to the right again beyond a long avalanche couloir a thinner rib, less well marked and broken by a snowslope at mid height. The Face is aloof despite its vast scale, a mountainside attractive only to mountaineers and rarely even seen by tourists. In 1926, when Graham Brown first saw it, Moore's route was the only way up it. Seven years later there were three more magnificent routes up the Brenva Face. Graham Brown had completed his long-planned 'triptych'.

It was twenty minutes past midnight on 5th August 1933, when three men came quietly out of the door of the Torino hut on the Col du Géant. The two guides, Alexander Graven and Alfred Aufdenblatten, were not big men, but they looked big beside the small figure of Professor T. Graham Brown, their friend and employer. The little man was the leader and planner, the spirit of the enterprise. If all went well and Mont Blanc did not produce some of its notorious bad weather, this day would see the fulfilment of a desire born long years ago and cherished passionately since. In the mountains the professor of physiology vanished and a poet took his place; a poet with the eye of an artist. Graham Brown had seen the Brenva Face of Mont Blanc as a triptych of sculptured rock framed in ice and snow. Since he was a mountaineer, it had to be a triptych of great routes. Today he hoped to climb the last and greatest of the three. And yet it was not the achievement of the summit above, not even the 'conquest' of an extremely difficult climb, that drew him on. These things had to be there; but it was the action, the engaging in the great attempt, that was for him the meat and drink of life. In his verse this creed is recurrent time and again: 'The Way is greater than the End.' In his poem *The Triptych* he wrote:

> *A quest is but a game which holds the mind*
> *Thralled by the action, with the goal forgot*
> *And everything adventured in the means.*

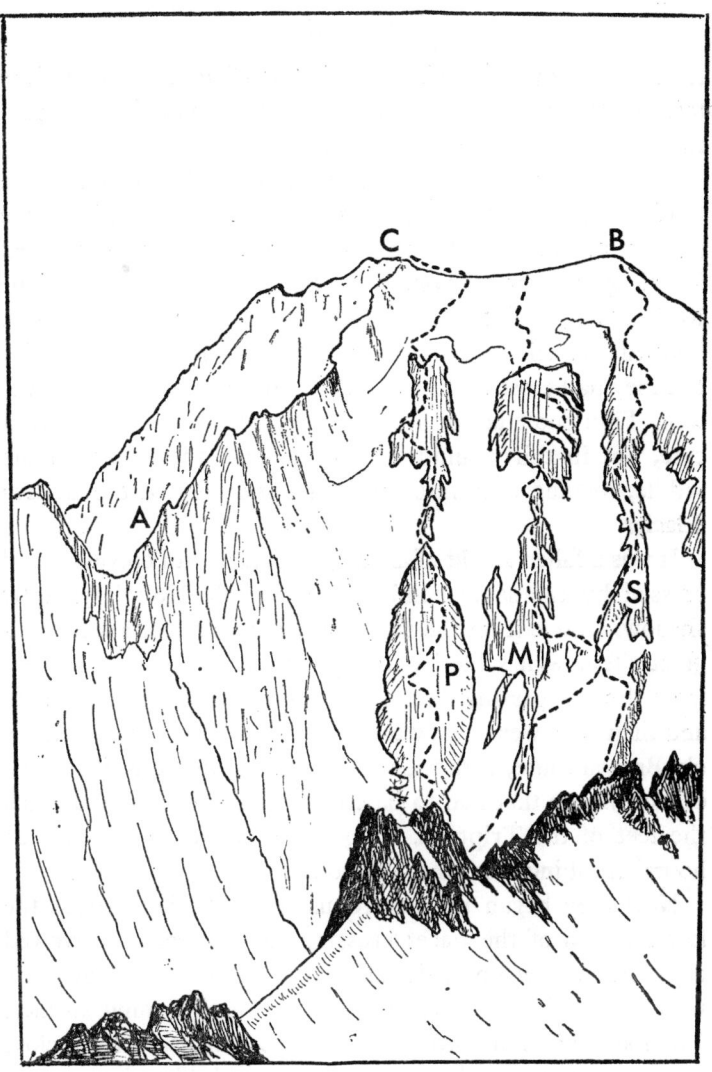

THE BRENVA FACE OF MONT BLANC
showing Graham Brown's 'Triptych'

P = Via della Pera
    (Pear Buttress)
M = Route Major
S = Route de la Sentinelle

A = Peteret Ridge
C = Mont Blanc de Courmayeur
B = Summit of Mont Blanc

DAWN

As he trudged across the moonlit snowfield with his guides towards the final triumph of his threefold quest he felt again the thrill of 'everything adventured in the means'.

It was a night of full moon and they needed no lantern. The familiar black shapes of the peaks on the frontier ridge came in sight as they rounded the base of the rock pinnacle called La Vierge and trod the pale gold snowslopes towards the Tour Ronde. The wall of snow to the east of the Tour Ronde's pointed summit looked vertical, dazzling in the moonlight, but they had crossed this col a dozen times before and knew it well. Thin snow lay on ice and the ascent to the col needed care, but in thirty minutes from its base they were on the saddle, looking over into the vast upper bay of the Brenva Glacier.

It was a fallen shield of argent, engrailed with crevasses and crossed by the sable bend of the Aiguille Noire's gigantic shadow. Above it on the right soared the Brenva Face, like a giant's tent wall sable-barred. They made the steep descent from the col, passing from shadow into full moonlight again, and then they were below the lesser ridge projecting from the old Brenva route, with the ice slope rising to the white saddle of Col Moore that had to be crossed before they could reach the feet of the Triptych. They were on the saddle after $2\frac{1}{2}$ hours' climbing from the Torino hut.

Now they began the hazardous traverse, right across the lower steeps of the Face; crossing, as it were, its furrowed chin. Far below on their left the crevasses of the glacier's western bay lay in black wrinkles on the gleaming surface. Crampons bit into hard snow steep as a mansard roof, close under sheer crags that loomed overhead like skyscrapers. Couloirs, deep chutes down which the ice walls under the summit discharged their loosened blocks, had to be crossed, Graven, in the lead, nicking steps very quickly with his axe and the others following him at top speed; the great Face was held in the grip of frost and night, but even in sleep the giant might shift a little and sweep these pigmies from his knees. Above them now, but invisible beyond the jagged shapes of nearer crags, was the rock called the Red Sentinel. Beneath that rock Graham Brown and Frank Smythe had made a cold bivouac in 1928, before their ascent of the Route de la Sentinelle, the first route of the Triptych. They were entering fully into the Brenva Face, into its deep shadow. To the left, across the far-sunken glacier, the crest of the Péteret Ridge brooded against the milky darkness of a moonlit sky. Its facets of snow glittered silvery white, but there was no moonlight on the great Face. 'We went ever deeper into shadow, until distance and size were no more,' says Graham Brown in his book *Brenva*. 'We seemed to be penetrating the very essence of a grandeur which knew no measure and had no form.' There was no sign yet of that slight lifting of darkness which precedes the dawn.

It was about 4.15 a.m. when, treading always on steep slopes falling to the glacier, they came to the great ice couloir beyond the central line of rocks. Peering high overhead, they could see on the right of the dim white trough the massive buttresses up which Route Major wound its perilous way. Graham Brown had climbed this, the second route of the Triptych, in 1928 with Frank Smythe; he remembered now that wonderful day—fourteen hours of continuously exposed and difficult climbing from their second bivouac under the Red Sentinel.

The ice couloir was split at its foot into several branches, hard and hazardous obstacles to the average mountaineer but mere incidents in a climbing approach to these three. Only the last steeply angled trough, whose father side was below the first rocks of the Pear buttress, gave them pause. It was a 60 foot ice slope, a very probable track for anything falling down the vast expanse of rock and ice above. Graven, safeguarded by the rope, ran across it on the points of his crampons and the other two followed one at a time. The thousand-foot buttress shaped like a pear, which caused Graham Brown to name this route Via della Pera, was still far above them. They began to climb up very steep ribs of rock and narrow snow *arêtes*, conscious now that the grim shadows were turning from black to grey. When they paused at some difficult passage Graham Brown looked upwards to the great dark loom of the Pear overhead, perhaps foreseeing dimly the adventures that were to come with daylight: the blinding sun on vertical rock walls, the struggle in icy chimneys, the incredibly dramatic views and the sensational positions; and the triumphant emergence above the last huge ice-cliff, with the Triptych complete. But if he allowed the hope of success to enter his mind at all, it was only for a fleeting moment. For this—the being here in the immensity of the Face, the engaging with its unexplored defences—this was the real success.

The three men were nearly up to the point where the great slabs steepened and swelled into the towering rocks of the Pear. They could see each other's features now. Very soon they would be clinging high up on that tower, with its overhangs and verticalities hiding the upper part of the Face. Graham Brown looked upwards for a last glimpse of the hoped-for final steeps. For, far overhead the white snow-rim of the summit hung in a sky of paling blue, flushed with faintest rose-petal pink. Dawn had come.

THE WEST FACE

In the neighbourhood of Chamonix there are a hundred mountains with west faces. In the summer of 1952 there was only one West Face—the overhanging, inviolate, West Face of the Aiguille du Dru, 3,600 feet of impossibly steep rock. It is not just a great rock face; it is the summit precipice of a mountain more than 12,000 feet high, with its base merely a steepening to perpendicular of the lower precipice of ice couloirs and avalanche slopes. On this lower precipice skilled Alpinists could move with some degree of safety, if it were not for the frequent falls of ice and stones from the face overhead which make this one of the places where skilled Alpinists do not go. On the West Face itself only a very few men can hope to gain a first precarious footing. These men must be expert to the last degree in the technique of 'artificial' climbing, possessing iron nerves and steel-wire muscles. They must be able to exercise their skill, calmly and with certainty, while hanging back-downwards above 3,000 feet of empty air. They must be prepared to spend three nights suspended from slings and dural pegs on the Face; for if they climb as much as 1,000 feet between dawn and sunset they will be lucky. And they must have great reserves of endurance to cold and foul weather. The Dru, standing superbly above the Chamonix valley as the terminal peak of the range that includes Les Droites and the Aiguille Verte, has a touch of the Matterhorn's defiant isolation and attraction for Alpine storms.

There had been eleven attempts to climb the West Face

before 1951. In that year a tremendous rock fall took place, shearing off some of the features which aspiring teams had climbed before retreating. The few horizontal ledges on the lower facets were piled with tottering debris. A new way had to be found; and after four determined attempts Guido Magnone and his party found it. He, with Marcel Lainé, Adrien Dagory, and Lucien Berardini, made the first ascent of the West Face on 16th-18th July 1952. All four men had come to know the Face well, almost to feel at home on it. A dozen times they had made precarious bivouac on the vertiginous granite walls, a dozen times waited impatiently for the coming of first daylight so that they could continue their infinitely slow upward progress, hammering and clinging above the abyss that grew ever deeper under their bootsoles. The descent after each failure, swinging down in the long *rappels* like spiders on their threads of nylon rope, had been as hazardous as the ascent; and when on the last day Magnone realized that the final difficulty was past, his triumph was the sweeter for the knowledge that they would this time be able to descend like reasonable climbers. He remembered with a shudder the descent from the 1950 bivouac.

The 1950 attempt had begun unpropitiously. From their preliminary bivouac at the Rognon, the pile of huge boulders perched high above the ice of the Mer de Glace, they had seen shortly before midnight a light, a pinprick of yellow, on the face of the Dru's dark spire. Another party had stolen a march on them—they were going to be robbed of their 'first'! They could do nothing about it until morning, and then they were off at first light: Guido Magnone, large and imperturbable; little Adrien Dagory, who when he was not climbing was the director of a biscuit-manufacturing firm; Marcel Lainé with his long stride, and the compactly muscular Lucien Berardini. They were heavily laden. In addition to food for three days and a stove for heating drinks, they carried 400 feet of rope, 90 alloy pitons, 30 wooden wedges, 8 *étriers*, 50 snaplinks, 2 mauls, 1 piton hammer, 1 hammer-axe, 1 collapsible ice axe and 1 pair of crampons. On top of his sack Dagory had fastened a plastic bag full of water.

They climbed up to the big cone of snow under the footrocks of the West Face. Above them rose a great precipice, a thousand feet of rock and ice swept by stonefall from the Face. This was only the approach to the start of the problem; the West Face soared up from the top of the precipice, three times its height and far too steep for ice to stay on. By couloirs where the stones flashed down like bullets, up ribs and slabs and icy ledges, they came rope's-length after rope's-length to the place where 'free climbing' had to give way to 'artificial'. It was no longer possible to stand in balance on the smooth walls. A long series of vertical chimneys brought them to a line of disconnected shelves on the smooth perpendicular face. Three hundred feet overhead the first barrier of overhangs jutted out, looking quite impassable; but three men were roping down the wall from the overhangs, where they had spent the morning placing pitons. They were Vignes, Guenot, and Dubost, from Lyons.

The rival parties greeted each other warily.

'How's it going?'

'Not bad, if we weren't so thirsty.'

'No snow in the crannies up there?'

'Not a granule. May have too much before long—the weather's looking nasty.'

Dagory secured himself to a peg and got his 'water-skin' off his shoulders. It held 9 litres, and the seven men shared it equally, thus sealing a silent compact that from now on they would share the hazards and triumphs of the climb.

But the weather was indeed worsening, so swiftly that further climbing was plainly impossible that day. Magnone's party found a narrow ledge, a few metres across the wall from the Lyonnais, where four men might conceivably manage to sit with their legs dangling over the depths. By the time they had arranged themselves, roped to a well-driven piton, it was growing dark though evening had scarcely come. A black mass that looked too solid to be merely a storm cloud was driving straight towards them across the sky. Magnone's four had only their cagoules for shelter, while the three Lyonnais had brought a large vinylite sheet. Vignes shouted above the whine of the rising wind: they could get two more on their ledge, under the waterproof sheet. Lainé and Berardini dangled across on the rope and crawled under the shelter. Hardly had they done so when the storm broke in fearful fury on the West Face, ringing the Dru with chains of lightning and deafening the seven men with continuous thunderclaps.

Magnone had already climbed out across the wall to one side of the ledge and driven in a piton to support the sack of 'ironmongery'. Even so, he and Dagory, cowering together a few feet away from all that metal, felt they could not escape the blue spears of lightning that drove at them every few seconds. When the hail came it was worse. In a few minutes they were half-buried under the pile of hailstones. Water came pouring down the wall above, drenching them completely. Each time the lightning flared they felt the prickling shock of the electrical discharge on their wrists and faces. That ordeal lasted for six hours before there came a lull—a temporary cessation of hostilities that allowed them time to make a drink. It was not a hot drink; the thunder and hail were followed by a violent wind, cold enough to turn their soaked clothing to an icy armour, and the wavering flame of the stove —a wan spark of comfort in the black night—could do no more than melt the gathered hailstones. They gulped down ice-cold Ovaltine and prepared to face the return of the storm.

It came back, slowly at first and then with an unbelievable

THE WEST FACE

fury. Wind, lightning, thunder; another savage hailstorm; and then, unexpectedly, sheets of rain. Somewhere far up on the Face, invisible in the howling darkness, the downpour was collecting in a crack or chimney whose bottom was dammed by a mass of rubble. The dam burst and a cascade of muddy water fell on Magnone and Dagory, half drowning them and nearly washing them off their narrow ledge. The rain turned to snow whirled by a bitterly cold wind, and they had to move arms and legs and bodies continuously to break the icy carapace that kept forming over them.

The thunder gradually died away but the wind and snow continued. Slowly the night hours crawled, while the huddled men began to feel the insidious numbness, a mockery of ease, which succeeds a long agony of cold. Magnone thought of the lost ropes of climbers; those whose bodies had never been found. They had started, perhaps, for some enterprise like this, saying nothing of their aims in case they failed. They had strode laughing out of the hotel at the Montenvers and no one had ever seen them again. He thought of the Montenvers with its warmth and lights and steaming food—within sight of their ledge in clearer weather, thousands of feet down through the empty, impassable air. He thought of the little train that took tourists down from the Montenvers to the cafés and comforts of Chamonix. At that moment he would have exchanged his chance of heaven to be sitting in that little train, safe, going down to the valley. . . .

The snowfall seemed to be ceasing. It was powder snow whirled by the gusts of wind that assaulted them now, and between the gusts he could discern, across a few yards of vertical rock, a ledge with a mound of snow on it. The mound was Vignes and his three companions, buried under their vinylite sheet. That he could see it at all meant that the night had ended. Dawn was here.

DAWN

Dawn. Livid, ghastly, revealing surroundings entirely unfamiliar. It was as though they had died in the night and awakened in some limbo beyond the world. There was no earth or sky or valley or mountain; only space filled with a sort of whitish foam. The snow, beginning to drive at the West Face again, was almost welcome because it proved that they were still on the earth. And still on the Face. If they did not get down quickly they would be there for ever.

One by one the men stirred, shaking off the snow, breaking the skin of ice that covered them. It was a long and very painful business, bringing the circulation back to dead limbs; to move at all was torture, to begin the fearfully hazardous descent with frozen feet and fingers seemed madness. They had 360 metres of rope between them and they would need it all. Magnone fixed the first piton and rove the sling for an abseil. Stiffly, only half alive, he and Dagory launched themselves in turn over the edge of their shelf and dangled down into the white obscurity. From Guido Magnone's book *The West Face* it seems that the terrors of that descent impressed him even more than the extreme difficulties they overcame two years later on their successful ascent—the '90-metre dièdre', the daunting overhangs, the screw pitch. They were all weakened by the ordeal of the night, and the precipice they had climbed so lightheartedly yesterday was glazed with ice and swept by volleys of powder snow. The repeated actions of drawing in the rope, coiling it, securing and throwing down the doubled line demanded all their strength. Every metre of every rappel was exquisitely painful to raw and frozen fingers. Once Dagory all but loosed his grip and would have fallen a thousand feet but for Magnone's desperate clutch at his cagoule. At the foot of the vertical chimneys they found the narrow couloir of onward descent a trough of green-grey ice; and as they hesitated an avalanche swept down it. A second such avalanche, while they were engaged in the couloir, could end it all for them, but there was no other way down. 'Nothing could impress us any more,' writes Magnone. They were beyond fear now.

There were avalanches as they roped down the couloir, but fortunately they were small ones, of loose powder snow. No one spoke. They had not spoken since starting down from the bivouac ledges. The snow had turned to rain, the grey light of dawn had given place to wan daylight when at last Magnone and Dagory saw below their dangling feet a blur of whiteness —the snow cone at the very foot of the West Face.

Ten minutes more, and all seven men were standing on the easy snowslope, peering at each other's blue unshaven faces. Out of the mists far below came a short, shrill whistle.

'Get a move on, chaps,' said Dagory. 'The puffer's waiting for us, down at the Montenvers.'

HIGH TABLE

With the possible exception of Rum Doodle (40,000½ feet) Himalayan summits do not offer good camp sites; not, that is, on their highest points. Welsh summits, however, provide unexpectedly complete amenities for the camper who is content to be solitary in a one-man tent of minimum proportions. Tryfan, for instance, boniest of peaks, has a six-by-three space of flat peat—the only such space—beside the twin summit-pillars of Adam and Eve, and a perpetual spring of water just 3½ minutes from the site. Helmet-headed Y Garn has no spring higher than the waters of Llyn y Cwn 800 feet below the top, but a little judicious levelling on the tip of the summit cairn enables you to sleep with your tent perched as a 'crest unto the crest', increasing the O.S. height of 3,104 feet to a temporary 3,107.

I would not go on record as recommending others to camp on mountain tops. Nowadays campers swarm increasingly on the mountainsides, and sanitary as well as aesthetic considerations demand restriction. With a sigh for the liberties of the past, we resign ourselves to the lesser evil of properly organized camp-sites in the Snowdonian valleys with all mod. cons. But in the thirties campers were very few—a couple of inconspicuous ridge tents pitched a bowshot from some hospitable farmhouse—and no one thought of camping on mountain tops. My own plan of camping on the summits of all the Welsh 3,000-footers was conceived as a penance and a propitiation. On a day of mental aberration I had galloped over all those fourteen peaks in record time, using them shamefully as a means of boosting my ego instead of enjoying their ridges and rock faces in the quietude which is their especial endowment. A nostalgic four lines by Lascelles Abercrombie used to haunt me at this time—

> *Would now the tall swift mists could lay*
> *Their wet grasp on my hair,*
> *And the great natures of the hills*
> *Round me friendly were!*

It seemed to me that the 'great natures' had withdrawn their friendliness because of that ill-advised rush from end to end of the Three Thousands. Some kind of atonement was required before I was accepted as of old. To 'do' the fourteen peaks as slowly as possible instead of as quickly as possible would be suitable reparation but was hardly practicable. To sleep on the tops, sharing daylight and darkness with each summit in turn, would be an adequate and adventurous act of repentance. I devised and constructed a very small tent and laid down certain rules: there should be no hasty bivouac but a proper home-making on each summit; I would accept the mountain's gifts of water and fuel, using no stinking stove; and I would cook, on a fire, a sufficient supper and breakfast, not outraging the hospitality of the peaks with emergency rations. In 1938 I made three summit camps, on Tryfan and the two Glyders. Then the Second World War intervened, and it was 1950 before the rest of the tops—all but one—had seen the glow of my camp-fire. The last top was Crib Goch, 3,020 feet. I carried my heavy rucksack to the sharp summit of Crib Goch on an afternoon of July 1951.

From north and east the steep hand-and-foot ridges, from westward the long knife-edged *arête*, stretch up to meet in a sharp little knob of bare rock. A little way along the knife-edge from this summit there is a sloping slab, its edge tilted towards the cliffs that fall to Llyn Llydaw, the only flat surface on the peak but no place for a tent. Horizontality, not flatness, is the camper's desideratum. Two feet below the highest point, where a very small cairn perches on the pinnacle, there is a shelf two feet wide and three feet long, its lower edge ending above a gravelly gully. I spent an evening hour climbing round the rim of the precipices and carrying up loose rocks to build an extension of the shelf, while the blue shadows rose higher in the trough of the Llanberis valley 2,000 feet below. In the end my tent platform was 5 feet long; I could get most of the tent floor on it and achieve a degree of comfort in a light sleeping-bag with spare clothing beneath it to mollify the hard mattress of stones.

In many a traverse of Crib Goch I had failed to notice the stunted growth of juniper that clings on the southern precipice, between the summit and the Pinnacles. Now I made precarious trips along the crags, Llyn Llydaw still and dark far below my bootsoles, and collected enough dry juniper root for two cooking fires. I had carried water up with me; not until next day did I discover that even here, on the slenderest, steepest peak of my camping programme, there was a spring not far away. If you scramble over the Pinnacles and go a hundred feet down the gully on the Cwm Glas side of Bwlch Glas, there is the clear water sparkling out among the mosses.

The evening was utterly calm. After sunset the black serrations of the Pinnacles stood against a sky of pale translucent blue-green, and away beyond the sparks of yellow light in the valley the sea rose darkling to the sharp horizon line with the Wicklow Mountains like a school of leviathans in the ultimate distance. The juniper fire burned brightly in a niche on the edge of the precipice, its red flame banishing distance and creating a circular wall of darkness round my rock needle. Crouched above the homely glow, I fried eggs in the billycan lid; carefully, for a tilt of the lid would have sent the eggs spinning down through 500 feet of empty air. Fruit cake was all the sweet I had to follow this statutory cooked meal, but coffee and cigar on my airy veranda confirmed the feeling of having dined. I turned in early, secure in the knowledge that my narrow bedroom was anchored with a turn of the climbing-rope round the summit. A gale in the night, an unconscious shift and roll, might dislodge the little tent and leave it dangling over the Llanberis Pass, but I would dangle safely inside it, for it had a sewn-in groundsheet. It was beyond all cavil a summit camp. I could reach out through the tent doorway and touch the pile of stones on the highest tip of Crib Goch.

There is no sleep so sound as mountain-top sleep when the night is calm, and this night was very calm. The murmur of a hundred streams and waterfalls, muted by depth and distance, was in my ears as I pulled the sleeping-bag round them. When I woke it was to the same faint music. There was a grey light inside the tent, and a gentle stirring outside, a going and coming of the murmur, that told of the dawn wind wandering among the peaks. I crawled out and stood up balancing on the crest of rock.

The great cone of Y Wyddfa loomed mysterious across the gulf of Cwm Dyli, unawakened in the shadowed west. But eastward the land was astir, thrilling with expectation. Moel Siabod humped its long black shape above low-lying mists, a whale stranded in a lake of milk. Beyond it the dark furrows of the moorland hills stretched to a blacker rim, sharp as cut paper on the clear pale green of the sky. I watched and shivered in the little chill wind of dawn while brightness climbed from below the edge of the world and rivulets of fire ran like lava along the black rim. Night drained from the spaces of cliff and cwm, colour flowered on green slope and red scree. Over the rim struck the blinding rays of gold, touching all the summits with radiance, gilding the cloth of the

DAWN

little tent. Ten minutes more and I was warm in the embrace of the risen sun, though it was only 5 a.m. and for hours yet the valleys would lie in cold shadow.

The smoke of the juniper fire was incense on the altar of Phoebus Apollo, and to its heavenly odour was presently added the earthlier smell of cooking porridge. I breakfasted like a prince throned above all the kingdoms of the world. But not in princely loneliness, for

The great natures of the hills
Round me friendly were.

DAWN ON EVEREST

The tent at Camp IX was a two-man Meade tent, a design preferred for this highest camp on the highest mountain in the world because of its extra roominess, in spite of the fact that Colonel John Hunt's expedition had brought three different types of lightweight mountain tent for the high camps on Everest. Edmund Hillary and Tenzing blessed the choice as they wriggled laboriously into their sleeping-bags at sunset on 28th May 1953; a little extra space eased their writhings, lessened the conscious effort of breathing. They were preparing to spend the night, perhaps even to sleep, at 27,900 feet above the sea.

Seven months of concentrated preparation, two months of hard and dangerous work, had been needed to get this one little tent to its sloping platform in space. Nearly four hundred men had shared the toil of getting the expedition to the mountain and pushing its narrowing spearhead higher and higher up the Western Cwm and the Lhotse Face to the South Col. That morning the spearhead had consisted of five men only: George Lowe, the primary school-teacher from New Zealand; Alf Gregory, director of a Blackpool travel agency; Ang Nyima, who alone of the three chosen Sherpas remained fit enough to carry up Camp IX; Edmund Hillary the New Zealand beekeeper; and Tenzing Norkhay Sherpa, the 39-year-old climber who with Raymond Lambert had reached 28,000 feet on Everest in 1952. It had taken them six hours to climb from the camp on the South Col, at an average rate of

DAWN

300 feet in an hour, breathing oxygen through the masks of their apparatus at 4 litres a minute. But others beside the men of Hunt's expedition had lifted the Meade tent to within striking distance of the summit of Everest.

From Colonel Howard-Bury's reconnaissance of 1921 to H. W. Tilman's expedition of 1938 the climbers had tried, and failed, by the route up the north ridge. Without oxygen, Colonel Norton had reached 28,000 feet; Mallory and Irvine had died on the 1924 attempt; Smythe, Shipton, Odell and a dozen other famous climbers had driven themselves to the limit and been beaten back. Though their attempts were unsuccessful and their chosen route eventually abandoned, they were the pioneers of Everest and the success that awaited Hillary and Tenzing was their success too. For they had shown that a way other than the ridge from the North Col had to be found; and—more important—they had by the hardest of hard experience learned the lessons which had resulted in the specialized equipment of 1953, the triple-skinned boots, the windproof clothing, the oxygen apparatus. When they left Camp IX for the final assault Hillary and Tenzing would be climbing on the shoulders of an army of pioneers.

In the morning of the 28th May the five men had toiled slowly up the ice, rock, and loose snow of the ridge. They had passed the tattered ruin of the tent where Tenzing and Raymond Lambert had spent the night—without sleeping-bags—before their abortive attempt in the previous year. At 27,350 feet they had paused to add to their loads the food and fuel and oxygen carried up that far by Hunt and Da Namgyal two days ago. By 2.30 p.m. they had reached the only spot that looked like providing a site for the little tent. Feeling rather lonely, Hillary and Tenzing had watched the other three descending again. Then they had set to work to prepare their night's lodging.

DAWN ON EVEREST

With their ice axes they scratched the ice from a part of the rock slope that was tilted at a mere 30°. Prising up the frozen rocks with the picks of the axes, they contrived to make two steps in the slope, each 6 by 3 feet, one above the other. Over these they pitched the tent. There were no rock hitches for the tent guys and the soft snow would not hold pegs, so they sank several of the precious oxygen bottles in the deep powder and secured the guys to these dubious anchors. The work took them more than two hours. When they turned, gasping for breath, to look outwards from their perch, they saw the immense white depths of the upper Western Cwm at their feet; the long ridge of Nuptse, its knife-edges of snow looking almost horizontal, far higher but still below them; and on the farther side of the Nuptse crest a vast boiling sea of cloud stretching to the remote horizon, with a range of great peaks—unnamed and unclimbed—floating on it like some fantastic silver galley of the gods.

The primus roared cheerfully in the tent, thawing out a frozen tin of apricots. With the apricots they ate sardines on biscuits, dates, jam and honey, and drank lemon juice in melted snow-water. Darkness flooded up, submerging the upper world. The tent was dark. Tenzing had established himself on his air mattress on the lower 'step' and was trying to sleep. Hillary reclined on the higher ledge, bracing his feet on the lower one; the wind was rising in fierce gusts, and he found that in this way he could brace himself against the flapping tent fabric and feel rather more secure. Those precarious anchorages in the snow outside would not hold the tent if a real Everest gale arose. One savage gust from the north-east, and tent and men would be flung out into the void, to fall 7,000 feet—or perhaps 8,000, it would make no difference—into the Western Cwm. The high rising whine of wind across the ridge overhead warned him of the coming of the gusts so that he could brace himself in time. Meanwhile, he thought anxiously of the shortage of oxygen, for the fact that only one Sherpa had been able to carry to Camp IX meant that the assault party had barely enough cylinders to get them to the top and back, while some of that limited supply must be used to help them obtain a minimum of sleep. If they were to have energy for the final climb they had to have sleep. He decided on using the oxygen apparatus for two night periods of two hours, at the reduced rate of 1 litre a minute. That night and all next morning (says Hillary in *The Ascent of Everest*) this oxygen 'mental arithmetic' was one of his main preoccupations.

The gusts of wind died gradually away, to the relief of the men in the tent. From 9 to 11 p.m., and from 1 to 3 a.m., they put on their oxygen masks and were able to doze a little in some degree of comfort. Without the life-giving oxygen they were miserable and cold, for the temperature inside the tent during the night was minus 27° centigrade. At four in the morning Hillary willed his cramped limbs to move and crawled gasping outside into the thin air and the darkness.

Night was draining down the flanks of their pinnacle 5 miles above sea-level. It was perfectly still, not a sound of any kind. The sleeping valleys of Nepal lay dark, far down to south-westward beyond the ragged peak of Lhotse, and a milky dawn light was already setting the ranks of icy peaks agleam. Everything was crystal clear, even in the deep troughs where the brownish-purple shadows brimmed.

'Thyangboche,' said Tenzing beside him, pointing.

And there, just visible on its spur above the valley, was the monastery of Thyangboche where they had paused two months ago on the approach march, 15 miles away and 16,000 feet below their present height.

Swiftly now the snowcrests were paling, flashing red, paling again to gold. There was much to do before the start—breakfast (sardines, biscuits, and pints of lemon-water) to be prepared and eaten, frozen boots to be thawed out over the primus, oxygen sets to be tested and strapped on. At 6.30 a.m. the two men crawled out of the tent at Camp IX for the last time. The morning was perfect, with a dark-blue sky of infinite depth overhead, and no wind. Tenzing led off, kicking steps in the soft powder up to the snowslope of the main ridge. Overhead the crest dazzled in brilliant sunshine. Now the South Summit appeared beyond the crest, the farthest point ever reached; Tom Bourdillon and Charles Evans had got that high on the first assault three days ago. Beyond it, for Hillary and Tenzing, waited the ultimate success.

THE MOUNTAINS WAIT

Steadfast and stern, as in those days of gold . . .
Steadfast and stern, the mountains wait for him.
T. H. PARRY-WILLIAMS

ONE HUNDRED NOTABLE MOUNTAINS

(The mountains are listed in alphabetical order and the heights are given in feet.)

Aconcagua (22,835) in Western Argentina is the highest mountain in the western hemisphere. The peaks of the Andes in its neighbourhood do not approach its height, so that it has a notable isolation and character. Technically it is an easy mountain to climb, for the vast slopes of stones and scree which buttress the summit are kept free from heavy deposits of snow and ice by the wind; yet this same wind, with frequent storms of hurricane violence, makes the ascent of Aconcagua as great an ordeal as the ascent of a high Himalayan peak. It was first climbed in 1897 by the Swiss guide Matthias Zurbriggen, whose employer, E. A. Fitzgerald, had to give up at 22,000 feet. A small hut has now been placed at this height, but ascents are infrequent.

Aiguille du Dru (12,320) rises above Les Praz in the valley of Chamonix and was first ascended by Clinton Dent in 1878 after eighteen unsuccessful attempts. There are in fact two Aiguilles, the Grand and the Petit Dru, often spoken of collectively as 'the Drus'. Seen from Les Praz, they are the epitome of the idealized mountain peak—one single upthrust of naked rock. On this side the Petit Dru appears as a tremendous near-vertical precipice, and its angle does in fact average 80° of inclination throughout its 3,500 feet of height. This is the West Face, one of the 'last great Alpine problems', which was climbed in 1952 by Guido Magnone, Marcel Lainé, Adrien Dagory and Lucien Berardini, using modern artificial methods.

Aletschhorn (13,774) stands above the Aletsch Glacier—the largest in the Alps—in the Bernese Oberland. It is a snow peak with three fine ridges and was first climbed by F. F. Tuckett in 1859, who thus included in his long list of first ascents that of the second highest Oberland peak.

Amne Machin (about 25,000) was for a time, in the 1950's, thought to be a great mountain perhaps higher than Everest. It is in fact a peaked ridge or spur of the Kun-Lun Range in the southeast Tsinghai province of China, with more than one summit. It is exceedingly doubtful whether any of the summits attain 26,000 feet, but since access is denied to Western climbers and surveyors it will be long before an exact height can be obtained.

Annapurna (26,492) is the highest summit of a lofty ridge 35 miles long in the Nepal Himalaya. It was the first of the *achttausenders* (peaks over 8,000 metres high) to be climbed. In 1950 a team of nine French climbers, led by Maurice Herzog, reconnoitred the mountain and found a difficult but feasible route. The ascent, completed by Herzog and Lachenal with Terray and Rébuffat in support, extended the climbers to the limit and left them with little in reserve for the ordeal of descent. Lachenal slipped and fell 300 feet but was rescued. Shortly after this a storm broke on the mountain and they were forced to spend the night in a shallow crevasse, where a mass of snow buried them. They extricated themselves, snowblind and suffering from frostbite, and were barely alive when a party from a lower camp came up to rescue them. During the journey back across India the summit climbers' frostbitten extremities had to be amputated to save their lives. Lachenal lost all his toes and Herzog all his toes and fingers.

Assiniboine, Mount (11,870), called 'the Matterhorn of the

Canadian Rockies', is an isolated rock peak of spectacular form, two days' back-packing journey from Banff. It was first climbed by Sir James Outram with the Alpine guides Bohren and Hasler in 1901. The peak dominates a very beautiful region of lake and forest and meadow, with convenient tourist cabins and many fine camp sites.

Ben Nevis (4,406) the highest mountain in Great Britain, rises immediately behind Fort William in Inverness-shire. Motor-cycles and wheelbarrows have been to the summit by the normal track, and there is an annual race to the top by the same route, but the great feature of Ben Nevis is its splendid north-east face, nearly 1,500 feet from base to crest and nearly a mile long. Here the buttresses and the gullies between them give long and superb climbs, especially at Easter when the snow is likely to be good. Modern ice-climbing in Britain developed chiefly from the harder ice-routes on Ben Nevis, and most of the British climbers whose feats on the severe Alpine faces made history in the 1960's gained their early experience here.

Bogdo Ola is a vast massif in Sinkiang, China, with the Turpanat-Tagh (17,946) as its highest summit. The range is glaciated, and on its south side the Turfan Depression lies at 1,000 feet below sea-level. This contrast of heights and temperatures results in savage winds on the mountain, which defeated Tilman and Shipton when they attempted to climb it in 1948. It is still unclimbed.

Carrantuohill (3,414) is the highest mountain in Ireland. The chief summit of Macgillicuddy's Reeks in County Kerry, it has little mountain character, being easy to walk or ride up, but of course provides a very fine view.

Changabang (22,520) is a remarkable peak in the near neighbourhood of Nanda Devi in the Kumaun Himlaya. From the Rishi Gorge it presents the appearance of a gigantic needle. W. W. Graham claimed to have ascended it in 1883 'with no great difficulty', but his description of the peak was so utterly unlike the real Changabang that his claim was not accepted. Graham was the first traveller to come out from England with the object of climbing Himalayan peaks 'more for sport and adventure than for the advancement of scientific knowledge', and the great lack of topographical information in his day is excuse enough for his mistake. In 1967 Changabang remains unclimbed.

Chimborazo (20,577) is the highest peak of the Andes of Ecuador, an extinct volcano with a great icecap on its summit from which large glaciers descend the flanks. Known in Ecuador as 'The Watchtower of the Universe', it was thought in the eighteenth century to be the highest mountain in the world. Edward Whymper made the first ascent in 1880.

Chomolungma ('Goddess-Mother of the World') was the name originally given to Mount Everest by those who considered that the highest mountain in the world should have its proper Tibetan title. Unfortunately, Chomolungma is only one of its many names, which vary according to the districts from which the mountain can be seen. One such name is Mi-Ti-Gu-Ti-Cha-Pu-Long-Nga ('You cannot see the summit from near it but you can see the summit from nine directions and a bird that flies as high as the summit goes blind.') This seems sufficient warrant for sticking to the name Mount Everest, or just plain Everest.

Cho-Oyu (26,967), the sixth highest peak in the world, is in the Nepal Himalaya within sight of Everest. From 1921, when the mountain was surveyed by the first Everest Reconnaissance Expedition, Cho-Oyu was familiar to Himalayan mountaineers, but not until 1954 was it climbed, by a small Austrian expedition led by Dr. Herbert Tichy.

Cotopaxi (19,344) is the highest active volcano in the world. Edward Whymper climbed it during his travels in the Andes of Ecuador in 1880, but it had been first climbed eight years earlier by Dr. Reiss with the native guide Escobar. In spite of its frequent eruptions Cotopaxi is snowcapped on its upper 4,000 feet. A very symmetrical mountain, its ascent is made by comparatively easy slopes of volcanic ash and boulders to the final slopes of snow lying at an angle of about 30°.

Dent Blanche (14,304), in its own way a peak hardly less notable than the Matterhorn, was climbed three years earlier, by T. S. Kennedy and W. Wigram with the guide Jean-Baptiste Croz. It stands only a few miles west of the Matterhorn and—like it—has four superb ridges, all of which are more difficult than Whymper's Hörnli route up the Matterhorn. It was on the west ridge that Owen Glynne Jones, pioneer British climber, was killed when he and one of the guides formed a 'human pyramid' to hoist Furrer, the leading guide, up an exposed rock wall. Furrer slipped and fell, dragging to death everyone except Jones's climbing friend Hill, who was saved by the breaking of the rope. Hill finished the climb alone and descended safely after spending two nights out on the mountain.

Devil's Tower (865 feet, base to summit) is an extraordinary tower of rock, a volcanic neck or plug, protruding from the horizontal plain in North Wyoming, U.S.A. It was the first of the U.S. National Monuments to be established. For many years it was thought to be completely inaccessible, its shape and appearance being that of an enormous cork, but it is now one of the most famous rock climbs in North America. It has been climbed frequently. During a national Mountaineers' Week in 1956 no less than 81 ascents were made, and more recently the sheer north and west faces have been climbed by artificial methods.

Dhaulagiri (26,795) ranks as seventh of the world's high peaks in order of height. The name indicates a section of the Himalayas in Central Nepal, and there are three other summits over 25,000 feet named Dhaulagiri II, III, and IV. Dhaulagiri

THE MOUNTAINS WAIT

I was the first mountain found to be higher than anything in the Andes, and for a time was thought to be the highest in the world. Many attempts to climb it were made before a party led by Max Eiselin succeeded in 1960. This Swiss expedition included a postal worker, a doctor, two students and an author; Eiselin himself was a sports writer.

Disteghil or *Disteghil Sar* (25,868) is a bold and striking peak, double headed, in the Karakoram range between Hunza and Nagar. The summit was first reached in 1960 by Diether Marchant and Gunther Starker of the Austrian Karakoram Expedition, without using oxygen.

Djebel Toubkal (13,578) is the highest of the Atlas Mountains of North Africa, a chain extending for more than a thousand miles and still possessing some unclimbed peaks. Toubkal has been climbed many times. It is not an easy mountain and includes some snow climbing.

Dom (14,942) in the eastern Pennine Alps, a peak of the Mischabel range which includes Täschhorn, Lenzspitze and Nadelhorn, is the highest mountain entirely in Switzerland and was among the first Alpine peaks to be climbed. The first ascent was made by the Rev. Lloyd Davies in 1858.

Dykhtau (17,049) was first climbed by A. F. Mummery in 1888, with the guide Zurfluh, after a long and difficult journey into the then almost unknown Caucasus. 'Every peak in Europe, Elbruz alone excepted, was below us,' he wrote of his arrival on the summit. The second highest Caucasian peak, Dykhtau is about 1,400 feet lower than Elbruz, the highest, and 1,600 feet higher than the more famous Ushba.

E 61 (23,890)—the only Himalayan peak apart from K 2 which is still known by the letter and number given it by the Survey of India. The first ascent was claimed in 1865 by the adventurous surveyor W. H. Johnson when he crossed the Kun-Lun range, after being ransomed from his captivity with the rebel ruler of Chinese Turkestan. The claim was disallowed—

rightly, as it appears—and E 61 still awaits (in 1967) a first ascent and a proper name.

Écrins (13,461)—Barre des Écrins, Pic or Pointe des Écrins—is the highest and most beautiful mountain of the Dauphiné Alps in south-eastern France. It is a 'hidden peak', showing its full height and character only after a tortuous approach, and its existence as a separate peak was not known until F. F. Tuckett discovered it in 1862. Two years later it was climbed for the first time by a famous quartet—Edward Whymper and A. W. Moore, with Michel Croz and Christian Almer as guides. The traverse of the Écrins, with convenient C.A.F. huts at either end, is one of the classic Alpine climbs of today.

Eiger (13,306) rises immediately above Grindelwald, the northernmost of the famous trinity of Eiger, Mönch, and Jungfrau that forms the northern retaining wall of the Bernese Oberland. It was first climbed by an Englishman, Charles Barrington, in 1858; Barrington had never been to the Alps before, but when his guides wished to abandon the ascent he refused to turn back and led them to the summit himself. The Eiger's most remarkable feature is its huge North Face (Eigerwand, Nordwand) sunless, swept by avalanches and falling stones, more than 5,000 feet of vertical precipice. The ascent of this was first attempted in 1935 by the German climbers Sedlmayer and Mehringer, who were frozen to death after spending three days on the Face. Five other climbers were killed on the Face before it was successfully climbed by Heckmair, Vorg, Kasparer and Harrer during 21st–24th July 1938. At least a dozen other aspirants have lost their lives on the Eigerwand since then, including the American climber John Harlin who fell 4,000 feet during an attempt in 1966 to make a direct route up the centre of the Wall; after his death one of his climbing companions, Dougal Haston from Britain, joined forces with four Germans and finished the climb, which has been named the John Harlin Route. The first British ascent of the Eigerwand was made by Bonington and Clough in 1961. *Elbruz* (18,481) is the highest mountain in the Caucasus. If, as is usual, the Caucasian watershed is taken as the boundary between Europe and Asia, Elbruz is the highest mountain in Europe, since it stands on the European side of the watershed. The higher of its twin peaks of volcanic rock was first climbed by Crauford Grove, Gardiner, and Walker in 1874, six years after Douglas Freshfield and his party made the first ascent of the lower peak. Today large organized parties of Russian men and girls climb Elbruz every year. In 1956 400 Soviet climbers made the ascent as one party to celebrate a national festival.

Erebus (13,202), generally linked with Terror (10,750) is the higher of the two volcanoes on Ross Island in the Antarctic, named after the two vessels of Sir James Ross's expedition of 1841. Erebus was first climbed by T. W. E. David and a party from Shackleton's expedition in 1908.

Everest (29,002) the highest mountain in the world, was first climbed in 1953 by Edmund Hillary and the Sherpa Tenzing Norkay of Colonel John Hunt's expedition. It was the ninth attempt to climb Everest, the first six attempts—all British—being made on the north side, since Nepal was closed to foreigners. In the second of these Mallory and Irvine lost their lives. The seventh and eighth attempts, made by the Swiss in 1952, were made from the south-west via the Western Cwm, a route suggested by Eric Shipton after his reconnaissance in the previous year. Raymond Lambert and Tenzing reached the South Col and climbed to about 28,000 feet, thus pioneering the way for the British victory in the succeeding year. In 1963 American climbers of an expedition led by Norman Dyhrenfurth ascended Everest by its West Ridge and descended to the South Col, thus traversing the peak. The ascent from the north claimed by a Chinese party is not generally accepted by mountaineers owing to the discrepancy between its recorded description and the known features of the route.

ONE HUNDRED NOTABLE MOUNTAINS

Finsteraarhorn (14,032) first climbed by three Swiss guides in 1812, is the chief summit of the Bernese Oberland. The peak, a striking needle-pointed pyramid, is not an easy one and the ascent was made by the difficult south-east ridge, a very remarkable achievement for its period.

Fuji (12,389) or Fuji-yama, meaning 'Fuji mountain', is the highest peak in Japan. An extinct volcano, it is a regular cone, snow-capped, with a base 65 miles in circumference. The ascent is long and laborious but made very frequently indeed because of the mountain's sacred character and the merit of a pilgrimage to its summit; between 100,000 and 200,000 people reach the summit every year. A motorable road has been built to the 7,000-foot level and there are ninety mountain huts on the six trails to the top.

Gasherbrum (26,470) in the Karakoram in northern Kashmir has three other summits besides the highest one, all over 26,000 feet. In 1958, after attempts by two other expeditions had failed, an American party led by Nicholas Clinch reached the summit of Gasherbrum I.

Gauri Sankar (23,440) is on the Nepal-Tibet border in north-eastern Nepal. For a short time it was identified with Peak XV—Everest—and during this period the name Gauri Sankar was applied to the highest mountain in the world. A large Japanese expedition attempted to climb this beautiful peak from the Nepalese side in 1959 and confirmed that it cannot be ascended from the south. In 1964 Whillans and Clough of a British expedition got to within 220 feet of the top. The peak is still (1967) unclimbed.

Glittertind (8,095) the second highest peak in Norway, is in the Jotunheim. Its summit is a snow plateau where the winter deposit varies in depth. In 1959 observations in winter revealed its height as 8,101 feet, three feet higher than the accepted height of Galdhöppigen, Norway's highest. It would thus be better described as '*usually* the second highest peak in Norway'.

Gosainthan (26,291) is one of the fifteen *achttausenders*—summits over 8,000 metres. It is in the Gandaki region of the Nepal Himalaya, on the border between Nepal and Tibet, and bears the Tibetan name Shisha Pangma. It was climbed in 1964.

Grandes Jorasses (13,799) is a peak of the Mont Blanc massif on the Franco-Italian frontier. It has a superb North Face, a great rock wall dropping to the Leschaux Glacier 4,000 feet below. The highest summit was first reached by Horace Walker in 1868, though Whymper had climbed to the lower, western summit, three years earlier. The North Face of the Jorasses later became a 'last great problem' and was eventually climbed by Meier and Peters, two Munich climbers, in 1935. The extremely difficult Walker Spur on the North Face, climbed by Cassin's Italian party in 1938, ranks nowadays as the least formidable of the Big Three—Walker Spur, Matterhorn North Face, and Eigerwand.

Grépon (11,447) is a famous granite pinnacle in the range of Mont Blanc above Chamonix, highest of the points on the pinnacled ridge originally known as the Aiguilles des Grands Charmoz. After several attempts by other parties, it was first climbed in 1881 by A. F. Mummery with his guides Burgener and Venetz, the latter first leading the difficult crack now known as 'the Mummery Crack' which is perhaps the best-known rock pitch in the Alps. Mummery himself led the Crack in 1893 with a guideless party which included Miss Lily Bristow, thus justifying the heading of the chapter on the Grépon in his classic book: '*An inaccessible peak—The most difficult climb in the Alps—An easy day for a lady.*'

Grossglockner (12,460) on the ridge of the Hohe Tauern that runs eastward from the Brenner Pass, is the highest mountain in Austria. Though not a difficult peak, its two summits are connected by a narrow snow ridge which has to be crossed to reached the higher point. The lower summit was reached in

ONE HUNDRED NOTABLE MOUNTAINS

1799 by the Bishop of Gurk, who in a later year attained the true summit also. It is now a popular tourist peak with a large hut only 1,000 feet below the top.

Huascaran (22,205), an extinct volcano in the Cordillera Blanca and the highest summit in Peru, was first climbed in 1908 by Miss Annie S. Peck, an American, with two Swiss guides. The mountain is simple of access and has been climbed many times since 1908. Two high camps are normally taken on the ascent.

Illimani (21,185) in the Andes of Bolivia, is a difficult peak with twin summits. Martin Conway climbed the lower summit in 1898 thinking it was the highest point. The other top, only 100 feet higher, was not established as the true summit until 1950. Meanwhile, in 1938 a party of young Nazis climbed the mountain and planted the Swastika flag on top; De la Motte of the British Alpine Club went up with a young Bolivian in 1940 and after two days' hard climbing removed the Nazi flag and brought it down.

Jungfrau (13,653) is the highest of the Eiger-Mönch-Jungfrau trio in the Bernese Oberland above the Grindelwald valley. It was first climbed by the brothers Meyer, from Aarau, in 1811. The Jungfraujoch railway, completed in 1912, tunnels up through the rock of the Eiger and terminates at the big hotel on the saddle between Mönch and Jungfrau at 11,412 feet, so that the last 2,200 feet of the original ascent route via the Rottal Sattel can now be climbed after a rail journey and a comfortable night in a hotel.

K 2 (28,250) is the second highest mountain in the world, in the Karakoram of northern Kashmir. Considered quite inaccessible at a time when Everest was thought to be a practicable ascent, K 2 was nevertheless attempted eight times before the final success. An elaborate expedition led by the Duke of the Abruzzi in 1909 reached 21,800 feet on what was afterwards known as the Abruzzi Ridge. During the sixth, American, attempt Arthur Gilkey was stricken with thrombophlebitis at Camp VIII at 25,500 feet, when the party there was in the gravest danger after being stormbound for six days; he perished during the descent. Compagnoni and Lacedelli of Professor Ardito Desio's Italian expedition reached the summit in 1954.

Kabru (24,002) in the Sikkim Himalaya was first ascended by C. R. Cooke in 1935. Cooke had a theory that winter was the best time for Himalayan climbing and made his ascent with G. Schoberth and six Sherpas in November, taking 21 days from base camp to summit. The weather was fine throughout and the lowest temperature recorded was minus 11° F.

Kailas (22,028), in south-west Tibet, was said by the explorer Sven Hedin to be the most famous mountain in the world, since it has been from time immemorial the most sacred peak of both Hindus and Buddhists. It is unclimbed and permission to climb it is very unlikely to be obtained. The four great rivers Ganges, Sutlej, Indus and Brahmaputra all have their sources within forty miles of Kailas. To the Hindu or the Buddhist the 25-mile circuit is a pilgrimage of the greatest merit, especially if performed—as it often is—by touching every foot of the way with one's prostrate body.

Kamet (25,447) was the first Himalayan peak over 25,000 feet to be climbed. The Sherpa Lewa became the first man to set foot on the summit when he accompanied Frank Smythe, Eric Shipton, and R. L. Holdsworth on the successful ascent in 1931. The mountain, which is in the Kaskar range and in India, was the scene of a remarkable attempt by Adolf and Robert Schlagintweit in 1855. These two pioneer surveyors reached a height of 22,250 feet on Kamet at a time when many Alpine mountains, including the Matterhorn, remained unclimbed.

Kangchenjunga (28,146) is the third highest mountain in the world. In 1955 the famous modern rock climber Joe Brown, with George Band, overcame the rock nose which guards the summit. Brown turned and shouted down: 'George, we're there!' The pair were the spearhead of a resolute and well-organized party led by Dr. Charles Evans. Kangchenjunga stands in eastern Nepal and is a complex of long ridges, all crowned with ice and extremely difficult. Its name means 'The Five Treasures of the Snow'. The first attempt to climb it, made in 1905 by a party of British, Swiss, and French climbers, reached 20,000 feet before an avalanche swept four men to death. There were three subsequent attempts before the two reconnaissances, in 1951 and 1954, which led to the success of Evans's party by the south-west face. The Sikkim people regard Kangchenjunga as a sacred mountain and wished its summit left inviolate; for this reason Charles Evans agreed that no one should set foot on the actual summit, although they proposed to climb from the Nepalese side. 'There in front of us', Band wrote afterwards, 'twenty feet away and five feet higher than the ground on which we stood, was the summit, a gently sloping cone of snow. We had come as far as we were allowed.'

Kilimanjaro (19,565) near the Kenya border of Tanganyika, is the highest mountain in Africa. An icecap 200 feet thick lies on the summit dome of Kibo, the higher of the two tops, surrounding a crater more than a mile wide. The first ascent was made by Hans Meyer in 1889. Mawenzi, the lower summit, is a rugged cone of volcanic rock 17,300 feet above the sea.

Kosciusko or Mount Kosciusko (7,305) is the highest mountain in Australia. In reality an unimpressive knob, one of several knobs over 6,000 feet rising from a high plateau, it was discovered and named by Sir Paul Strzelecki in 1840. Small snowfields lie even in summer on the eastern slopes, making it a popular ski resort as well as a centre for fishing, walking, camping and other outdoor sports.

Lhotse (27,890) rises about 3 miles south of the summit of Everest, separated from it by the South Col and a long ridge over 25,000 feet high. It is a mountain in its own right and not, as is sometimes stated, the 'south peak' of Everest. It was first climbed in 1956 by Reiss and Luchsinger, members of the Swiss party which made the successful second assault on Everest.

Makalu (27,824) the fifth highest mountain in the world, is in the Nepal Himalaya about 14 miles east of Everest. Its isolation and great steepness make it a particularly impressive giant. Sir Edmund Hillary made two unsuccessful attempts to climb it, in 1954 and 1961, after the first expedition from the Sierra Club of California, led by William Siri, had failed on the south ridge. The French party led by Jean Franco, who made the first ascent in 1955, was probably the best organized and selected party ever to climb in the Himalaya. Without any mishap or dramatic event, they gave great care to every detail, including proper acclimatization. Nine men reached the summit—three parties on three days in succession—and no one was frostbitten, injured, or even unduly distressed.

Maladetta (11,168) is the highest peak of the Pyrenees. The French name is Pic d'Anéto, and the name 'Maladetta' is often used for the massif from which it rises. It is not a difficult peak but there is a snow ridge that calls for rope and axe.

Manaslu (26,658) in the Nepal Himalaya is the ninth highest mountain in the world. Twice attacked by large Japanese expeditions in 1953 and 1954, it was climbed by a third and even larger Japanese expedition in 1956.

Matterhorn (14,701) shows its world-famous obelisk shape on the northern, Zermatt, side but has a comparatively simple route up the Hörnli Ridge by which it was first climbed in 1865 by Edward Whymper's party. Though two English parties had examined this ridge and thought it practicable, all Whymper's attempts were made up the steeper Italian ridge until the first ascent, on which Hudson, Hadow, Lord Francis Douglas and Michel Croz were killed when the rope broke after the inexperienced Hadow had slipped and fallen. The peak has four ridges and four faces, all of which have been climbed. The severe and dangerous North Face, first climbed by Franz and Toni Schmidt in 1931, is usually considered the second most difficult of the Alpine 'Big Three'—Eigerwand, Matterhorn North Face, and the Walker Spur of the Grandes Jorasses.

Mauna Kea (13,825) is a dormant volcano on Hawaii, with the distinction of being the highest island mountain in the world.

Meije (13,081) in the Alps of Dauphiné is a difficult rock peak, or more correctly ridge, which was the last big Alpine summit to be climbed. The young American climber W. A. B. Coolidge attempted it with his aunt Meta Brevoort in 1870, but it was the French climber Boileau de Castelnau who first reached the higher western summit in 1877. The traverse of the Meije is today one of the great classic routes.

Minya Konka (24,900) a fine peak in the Tahsueh Mountains on the China-Tibet border, was at one time rumoured to be higher than Everest. In 1932 a mixed team of Americans and Chinese led by Richard L. Burdsall went to investigate the rumour and ended by climbing the mountain. The ascent was made during fierce storms and terrible cold, in October, and was a fine achievement. The height of the peak was finally determined by Burdsall's party. This was the first big mountaineering venture of Americans in the Asiatic ranges, forerunner of the attempts on K 2 and other expeditions from the United States to the Himalaya.

Mont Blanc (15,781) is the highest peak in Europe excluding the Caucasus. It rises above Chamonix in the French Alps, but its southern flank is in Italy. H. B. de Saussure, who wished a way to be found to the summit so that he could make scientific observations there, offered a reward for the first man to reach the top. Dr. Paccard, physician of Chamonix, climbed to the summit with Jacques Balmat in 1786, Paccard being the moving spirit of the enterprise and surrendering the monetary prize to Balmat. De Saussure climbed Mont Blanc two years later and spent four hours on the summit making his observations.

For 40 years Paccard's route was always used by Mont Blanc aspirants, and the mountain was climbed on an average once a year. The accident to Dr. Hamel's party called attention to the dangerous nature of the route and the present 'ordinary way' became increasingly used. In good conditions it is safe and easy, little more than a very arduous snow slog. The routes on the Brenva Face and by the Péteret and Innominata ridges, however, call for climbing of a very high standard, and such climbs as the Central Pillar of Frèney are recent examples of the modern taste for verticality and exposure.

Monte Rosa (15,203) is on the Italo-Swiss frontier, in the Pennine Alps. It is really a great massif with two distinct summits and several lower but equally distinct peaks. The lowest of these, the Signalkuppe (14,965) was climbed as early as 1842 by Giovanni Gnifetti, the parish priest of Alagna. The second highest summit, called the Grenzgipfel, was reached by the brothers Schlagintweit in 1851. The highest peak is named Dufourspitze after the Swiss General Dufour, and has two rocky horns, the lower first climbed by the three Smyth brothers with Ulrich Lauener in 1854 and the higher by Charles Hudson and party the following year. It is the second highest summit in the Alps. The Margherita Hut, perched on a pedestal of rock on the summit ridge of the mountain, is the highest hut in the Alps—higher than the top of the Matterhorn.

Mount Cook (12,349) named after Captain James Cook, is the culminating peak of the Southern Alps of New Zealand and the highest mountain in that country. Its Maori name is

ONE HUNDRED NOTABLE MOUNTAINS

Aorangi—'big white cloud'. In form it is a long narrow ridge with three summits, steep on all sides, the couloirs falling to tributary glaciers which discharge to the Hooker Glacier on the west and the great Tasman Glacier, 18 miles long, on the east. The bad weather in the Southern Alps is proverbial and Mount Cook receives the worst of it. It was a terrific storm that halted the Rev. William Spotswood Green and his two guides 50 feet below the summit when they climbed the mountain in 1882. They did not actually stand on the top, and the credit for the first ascent of Mount Cook goes to three New Zealanders, Fyfe, Graham and Clark, who reached the summit on Christmas Day 1894.

Mount Etna (10,750) has the distinction of having the earliest recorded ascent of any peak over 10,000 feet. Empedocles, the Greek philosopher, undoubtedly climbed it about 450 B.C., though historians say he did not throw himself into the crater as legend afterwards reported. Etna is the highest active volcano in Europe, and rises 18 miles to the north of Catania in eastern Sicily. Over 260 eruptions have been recorded, two of them in 1928 and 1947; but in spite of this ascents are frequently made. A motor-road has been constructed to the observatory at 9,652 feet, and this is the usual starting point for the uncomfortable scramble up to the edge of the crater.

Mount Kenya (17,040) is the second highest mountain in Africa, Kilimanjaro being 2,500 feet higher. Not until 1849 was it even seen by European travellers, and the report of 'snow on the Equator' was not at first believed. Another fifty years passed before Sir Harold Mackinder climbed to the highest summit, Batian, with his two Swiss guides. Nelion, the lower summit, was reached from Batian by Eric Shipton and Wyn Harris in 1929, an exceptionally fine piece of mountaineering. A feat more remarkable still was performed by three Italian prisoners of war who escaped from a prison camp in 1943 with the sole purpose of climbing the mountain. With only prison-made equipment and very little food they failed to climb Batian, but reached the third summit, Lenana (16,300) before descending and 'breaking into' their prison camp to give themselves up. Felice Benuzzi, the leader of the party, describes the adventure in his book *No Picnic on Mount Kenya*.

Mount Logan (19,850) the second highest peak in North America, is the culminating point of a 20-mile-long range, heavily glaciated, in the Yukon near the Alaskan border. The summit was first reached by Captain A. H. MacCarthy, a noted Canadian climber, in 1925, after 44 days of climbing on snow and ice in sub-zero temperatures. 'For endurance and courage', wrote Arnold Lunn, 'their achievement has rarely been surpassed.' With the famous sourdough Andy Taylor, MacCarthy spent more than two months laying food dumps up the glaciers and on the mountain, during the winter of 1924, ready for the ascent of May and June in the succeeding year. Since that time there have been only two ascents of the highest peak, though five American mountaineers reached the slightly lower eastern peak in 1957.

Mount McKinley (20,270) is the highest mountain in North America. Dr. Frederick Cook claimed to have climbed it in 1906; but though he undoubtedly made an attempt his claim was proved to be as unfounded as his claim to have reached the North Pole. The famous 'Sourdough Ascent' of 1910, made by four miners for a wager, solved the problem of the mountain but ended on the lower of McKinley's two summits. The south summit, only 300 feet higher, was first reached by Hudson Stuck, Archdeacon of the Yukon, in 1913. Ricardo Cassin, the famous Italian climber, made in 1961 the first ascent of the sheer south face of Mount McKinley, known as 'the impossible wall'.

Mount Rainier (14,408) is in the Cascade Range of Washington, U.S.A., and dominates a vast glacier system. It forms the centre of a National Park containing 26 glaciers, now a favourite resort of climbers and skiers. First climbed in 1870 by General Hazard Stevens, Mount Rainier is a dormant volcano and emits steam and hot sulphur springs far above the snowline.

Mount Robson (12,972) was first climbed in 1913 by Captain A. H. MacCarthy, who made the first ascent of Mount Logan. It is the highest peak in the Canadian Rockies and completely dominates the surrounding country with its impressive shape, great height, and isolated position. It is one of the most difficult peaks in North America, and the ascent, which is rendered dangerous by frequent avalanches, is made only rarely.

Mount Tasman (11,475) is a very beautiful mountain clad in snow and ice from base to summit, the second highest peak in New Zealand. It rises above the Tasman Glacier only two miles north of Mount Cook, and sends down many glaciers, one of them—the Fox Glacier—flowing to within 700 feet of sea-level. E. A. Fitzgerald, with the Alpine guide Mathias Zurbriggen and the New Zealander Jack Clark, made the first ascent in 1895. It is a popular mountain nowadays, with several very fine routes up it. The original route over the Silberhorn, which includes a long and sensational ice arête, is one of the best climbs in the New Zealand Alps.

Mount Whitney (14,495) ranks as the highest peak in the United States outside Alaska. It is in the Sierra Nevada of eastern California, only 86 miles from the lowest point in the United States—Death Valley, 276 feet below sea-level. The American geologist Josiah Whitney discovered the mountain, which was named after him. Eleven years later it was first climbed by Lucas, Johnson, and Begole.

Mulhacen (11,411) is the highest summit in Spain, in the Sierra Nevada of the province of Granada. Snow lies on it permanently above 10,000 feet. Like the rest of the southern Sierra, it offers poor climbing compared with the northern ranges such as the Picos de Europa.

THE MOUNTAINS WAIT

Muztagh Tower (23,660) is in the Central Karakoram range of Kashmir. Martin Conway saw it in 1892 and described it as the finest peak in the district. Vittorio Sella photographed it in 1909 from the Baltoro Glacier, whence it appears as a stupendous monolith, 'a rocky mass of single formation—no other of any comparable size is known to exist on the globe'. Though Conway had remarked that the precipitous appearance of the Muztagh Tower was deceptive, it was regarded for 40 years as the epitome of inaccessibility. R. L. G. Irving in 1935 said that it was 'probably the most inaccessible of all the great peaks'. Yet in 1956 the huge Tower became the only Himalayan peak to be climbed by two expeditions, using different routes, in the same week. A British party led by J. M. Hartog (and including Joe Brown, Ian McNaught-Davis, and Tom Patey) climbed the north-west ridge, and a French party led by Guido Magnone climbed from the opposite side. All the members of both parties reached the summit. All were first-class experts of the modern school of mountaineering, and the ascent was probably the most difficult yet achieved in the Karakoram.

Namcha Barwa (25,445) whose name means 'Lightning burning in the sky' is in the Assam Himalaya, the highest of that group of mountains. It has always been a mountain of mystery. It stands in wild and still largely unsurveyed territory which is administered neither by Tibet nor by India but its approaches are commanded by the Chinese in occupation of Tibet. Captain H. T. Morshead, later a member of the first two expeditions to Everest, fixed its height and position in 1912. It rises above the stupendous Tsangpo gorge, on the opposite side of which stands the peak of Gyala Peri (23,460), and the two together must constitute one of the most wonderful mountain features in the world. So far as is known, Nancha Barwa had never been reconnoitred, and remains unclimbed, as does its great neighbour.

ONE HUNDRED NOTABLE MOUNTAINS

Nanda Devi (25,645), pronounced 'Nunda Davey', stands in the heart of a circular wall of mountains 70 miles in circumference and averaging 20,000 feet in height, in the Kumaun Himalaya. The only break in this wall is a narrow and steep-sided gorge many miles long, cut by the torrent of the Rishi Ganga. Dr. Longstaff reached the rim of the wall in 1905 and looked down into the Sanctuary, as the inner enclosure at the feet of the mountain is called, but not until 1934 did anyone succeed in climbing the gorge and entering the Sanctuary. Eric Shipton's book *Nanda Devi* described this adventure. Shipton led that first reconnaissance, but was unable to join the expedition which set out to repeat the journey and climb the mountain; but H. W. Tilman, who had accompanied Shipton, reached the summit with N. E. Odell when an Anglo-American party climbed Nanda Devi by the south ridge in 1936. The lower east peak was first climbed in 1939 by a Polish party led by A. Karpinski.

Nanga Parbat (26,629) is an '*achttausender*' and the tenth highest summit in the world. It was first attempted by A. F. Mummery's party on their 1895 visit to the western Himalaya; but at that time the scale and difficulty of Himalayan peaks were not realized and the attempt was foredoomed to failure. Mummery died during the crossing of one of Nanga Parbat's lower ridges. A German-American expedition in 1932 was the next to try and fail, and from then onwards the Germans regarded the great peak as their own preserve—so much so that a British party who proposed to attempt it met with angry protests and retired in the interests of international friendship. The German climbers in 1934 and 1937 pressed the attack to extreme limits in the face of danger with the result that eleven Germans and fifteen porters lost their lives. Another German attempt in 1938 failed, after the climbers had had the unnerving experience of discovering some of the bodies. The final German attempt, in 1953, was regarded by the leader as 'a sacred trust and a memorial to the dead'. It was a regimented party, directed by a dictatorial leader from base camp, and the members of it were not a happy team. Hermann Buhl and Otto Kempter shared a tent at 22,640 feet on the night of 2nd July. Next day Buhl started out just after midnight, deserting his companion, and reached the summit alone after eighteen hours of climbing. He was forced to spend the night out on the mountain only 500 feet below the top but survived.

Nilkanta (21,640) is a peak in the Kumaun Himalaya only 5 miles west of Badrinath, the pilgrimage goal sacred to Hindus. Though lower in height than many hundreds of unclimbed Himalayan peaks, it had been attempted by at least five parties between 1937 and 1952. One reason for this is its challenging shape, giving the impression of complete inaccessibility; another may be its beauty. Frank Smythe, who saw it in 1931 on his way to climb Kamet, wrote: 'It is one of the loveliest mountains in the world; above the broad buttresses from which it springs its graceful lines lead the eye upwards to a perfectly proportioned summit, a sheer spire of gleaming snow and ice.' He returned in 1937 to try and climb it, without success. Wylie in 1947, André Roch's Swiss party in the same year, a New Zealand expedition led by Hillary in 1951, and Tilly's attempt in 1952, all failed to gain the summit. Nilkanta remains unclimbed.

Nun (23,410) is the highest peak of the Nun Kun, a massif in the Punjab Himalaya. Kun and Pinnacle Peak are the second and third highest. Nun was first climbed by a French party led by Bernard Pierre in 1953. The assault party on the mountain included a woman, Claude Kogan, and a Swiss missionary named Vittos; the others were Pierre and a Sherpa, Pemba Nurbu. Madame Kogan and the missionary were the two who reached the summit.

Nuptse (25,700) rises 3 miles W.S.W. of Everest across the long and deep trough of the Western Cwm—the upper basin of the Khumbu Glacier. Its long east ridge connects it, beyond a saddle, with Lhotse, 4 miles away. It is a difficult peak, harder than Lhotse. A British party led by J. Walmsley attacked it in 1961 and Dennis Davis, Brown, Bonington, Swallow, and the Sherpas Tachi and Pemba reached the summit.

Orizaba (18,700) rivals Fuji-yama in the symmetry of its snow cone and is more than 6,000 feet higher. Like Fuji, this mountain—the highest in Mexico—is an inactive volcano. The upper 3,000 feet are covered in eternal snow, contrasting with the hot Mexican plateau from which it rises on the Puebla-Veracruz border. It was first climbed by F. Maynard and G. Reynolds in 1848.

Ortler (12,972) should properly be called the Ortlerspitze, since 'Ortler' is a mountain group including many peaks and sixty glaciers, in the mountains of Tirol. The Ortlerspitze is the highest peak of the Eastern Alps. At present the mountain is on the Italian side of the frontier, the treaty-makers after the Second World War having left the German-speaking peoples of South Tirol under Italian rule. In 1804 it was the highest peak in the Austrian Empire, and the Emperor Leopold's son ordered it to be ascended. Joseph Pichler, a local chamois hunter, led the Emperor's representatives to the summit after they had made six unsuccessful attempts.

Pik Kommunisma (24,590) was known as Pik Stalina until 1961. The 'de-Stalinization' of the U.S.S.R., of which this great mountain is the highest summit, included a decree changing its name. It rises in the Pamirs of Tadzhikistan, on the southern fringe of the Soviet Union, and looks across the Molotov Glacier to a range of beautiful peaks whose names suggest that in these parts beauty lies in the politics of the beholder; German Communist Party Peak and OGPU Peak are two of them. Kommunisma is a very difficult peak. The All-Union-

THE MOUNTAINS WAIT

Alpine-Section-Of-The-Ministry-Of-Culture-And-Sport Expedition which climbed it in 1933 used eight camps on the mountain. The first men to reach its summit were Abalakov and Gorbunov. In 1962 the British Soviet Expedition of 1962, of which Sir John Hunt was joint leader, climbed Pik Kommunisma; Joe Brown, Ian McNaught-Davis, Graeme Nicol and Malcom Slesser reached the summit with four Russian climbers.

Pik Lenin (23,382) was until 1932 thought to be the highest mountain in the U.S.S.R. Pik Stalin (now renamed Pik Kommunisma) was then discovered to be more than a thousand feet higher. The mountain was originally named Mount Kaufmann and it is thought in certain circles that it may in time revert to this name. It is in the Trans-Alai range on the borders of the Kirghik and Tadzhik Socialist Soviet Republics. W. W. Rickmers, who did much of the pioneer exploration and surveying in this region, made the first ascent in 1928 with members of his Russo-German Alai Pamir Expedition. In the past forty years Pik Lenin has been climbed six times by Soviet mountaineers.

Piz Badile (10,853) is a rock peak above the lovely Bondasca valley of the Ticino, on the frontier between Italy and Switzerland. The summit is not difficult to reach by the ordinary way, and it is the peak's north-east face that has made it famous among climbers. This face is one unbroken wall of smooth granite, 3,000 feet high. It was first climbed by Ricardo Cassin and two companions in 1937, after they had spent two days and nights on the face. Two other young Italians, Valsecchi and Molteni, were attempting the ascent at the same time, and the parties joined forces to defeat the bad weather that had set in. They all reached the top on the third day, in a fierce blizzard. On the way down by the easy route both Valsecchi and Molteni died of exhaution and exposure. For twelve years the north-east face was not climbed again. Then, in 1950,

Gaston Rébuffat and Bernard Pierre made the second ascent. *Piz Bernina* (13,304) is the highest summit of the Bernina Alps, the easternmost section of the Central Alps. Piz Roseg, the next peak of the range, is perhaps more beautiful, but the Biancograt of Piz Bernina is a fine and popular climb. The peak was first ascended by the Swiss climber Coaz in 1850.

Piz Palu (12,835), perhaps better known by name than the other Bernina mountains, is a peak with three summits, beautiful by reason of its snowy outline and translucent glaciers. Its ascent is not difficult by the ordinary route but it has long had a reputation as a 'killer peak'. The sudden and violent storms common in this part of the Alps have been responsible for a number of tragedies, and the snow cornice on the ridge of Palu, which is often overhanging and treacherous, has led to others. Piz Palu became world-famous when the early silent film called 'The White Hell of Pitz Palu' was made by Leni Riefenstahl, the German skier and mountain guide who became a film director.

Popocatapetl (17,887) is the second highest peak in Mexico. The famous view from Mexico City is of the two twin summits Popocatapetl and Ixtacihuatl (17,340) both brilliantly snow-capped against a vivid blue sky. Both are dormant volcanoes. If the record of Fra Lopez de Gomara is to be believed, Popocatapetl remained for 300 years the highest mountain climbed by man. 'Cortez sent ten Spaniards with many Indians to carry their victuals,' wrote Fra Lopez of the 1595 adventure. 'The ground did tremble and shake, and great quantity of ashes disturbed the way; but two of them, who seemed to be most hardy, and desirous to see strange things, went up to the top, because they would not return with a sleeveless answer, and that they might not be accounted cowards. . . .' Cortez was then on his way to meet the Emperor Montezuma, and his soldiers collected sulphur from Popocatapetl to make gunpowder.

THE MOUNTAINS WAIT

Rakaposhi (25,550) is a peak—also a range—of the Karakoram, in Kashmir. There are 31 known summits higher than Rakaposhi but few peaks so impressively beautiful, especially when seen from the northern approach up the Hunza Valley. The legend of its inaccessibility clung to Dumani ('Mother of Mists') as the Hunza natives call it, until 1958, when the first ascent was made by a British-Pakistani Forces expedition. It was the third attempt on the mountain, and the party included the well-known British climbers Mike Banks and Tom Patey—Captain M. E. B. Banks and Surgeon-Lieutenant T. W. Patey.

Roche Melon (11,605) stands above Susa, the little town of north Italy at the southern end of the Mont Cenis tunnel, and is distinguished by being the first Alpine peak to be either attempted or climbed. In 1358 Bonifacius Rotarius, a rich man of Asti who had experienced a narrow escape from death at the hands of the Moors, fulfilled as best he could the vow he had made in gratitude, which was to build a chapel to the glory of Our Lady on the highest summit of the Alps. Since the days of antiquity Mons Romulus, as the Roche Melon was then called, had been considered the highest Alpine peak. Rotarius climbed it and built the chapel, which stands there to this day. Each year a pilgrimage is made to it on 5th August, the festival of Our Lady of the Snows.

Ruwenzori (16,795) is a mountain mass 70 miles long and 40 miles wide, on the Congo-Uganda border in equatorial Africa. The height quoted is that of Margherita, the summit peak of Mount Stanley. The 'Mountains of the Moon' were known by rumour to the ancients as the source of the Nile, but Ruwenzori was not seen by a white man until Stanley, the explorer, viewed it in 1888. In 1906 the Duke of the Abruzzi took a large expedition there, and climbed the three major summits. In 1932 a Belgian expedition explored the many glaciers and ridges of the region. But though all the major peaks have now been climbed there are many minor summits still virgin, and the region surrounding them is one of the most fantastically beautiful in the world.

Saltoro Kangri (25,400), in the Karakoram, is a remote peak and very difficult of access, discovered by Dr. Longstaff in 1909. The area north of the Bilafond Glacier was then completely unknown and none of the peaks had been triangulated; it had been suggested to Longstaff that it was a likely region to find a peak of the first magnitude, and his small surveying and exploring party, having penetrated 7 miles up a glacier whose presence had not been suspected before, were the first men to see the splendid group of peaks now named Teram Kangri, of which Saltoro Kangri is the highest. Longstaff estimated its height at 25,000 feet, but tried to get closer to its true height by taking what observations he could with the aid of compass, clinometer, and a short base-line. When his calculations were worked out at Dehra Dun they produced a height of nearly 30,000 feet—higher than Everest! The error was natural in the circumstances and soon corrected. In 1935 four army officers on leave attempted the ascent of Saltoro Kangri, with two 'Tiger' Sherpas, and came within a thousand feet of the top. It was climbed by a Japanese Pakistani Expedition in 1962.

Scafell Pike (3,210) is the highest mountain in England, 350 feet lower than Snowdon in North Wales. It is a rugged, rather lumpish mountain. Separated from Scafell (3,162) by the narrow ridge of Mickledore, to pass across which the tricky step of Broad Stand has to be made, it is the less interesting of the two. Scafell sends down on its northern side what has been described as 'the most savage barrier of naked rock and scree in England'. On this face are many fine rock climbs, from the classic route up Scafell Pinnacle to the Central Buttress climb—'C.B.'—which for a considerable period ranked as the hardest climb in Britain. Though nowadays far down in the list of hard routes, 'C.B.' still has a *cachet* of its own.

Schreckhorn (13,390) rises on the ridge that separates the Upper and Lower Grindelwald Glaciers in Switzerland, and appears almost surrounded by ice. It is chiefly a rock peak, however, and one peculiarly subject to storms; its name—Terror Peak—is for this reason not unsuitable. The first ascent was made by Leslie Stephen with the guide Christian Michel in 1861.

Sgurr Alasdair (3,251) is the highest summit of the Coolin —often spelled 'Cuillin'—on the Isle of Skye. It is named after Alexander Nicolson, who made the first ascent in 1873 by way of the Great Stone Shoot. Professor Collie later made a more adventurous route; but nowadays it is the spur of Alasdair called Sron na Ciche that provides the main attraction for rock climbers.

Siniolchu (22,600) has been declared by many experienced mountaineers to be the most beautiful peak in the world. It is in the Sikkim Himalaya and difficult of access. The twin peaks soaring above their incredibly steep ridges glittering with fluted ice appear at first sight totally inaccessible, but the appearance is deceptive. A practicable, if steep and difficult, route to the top was found when a German party attempted the peak in 1936, led by Paul Bauer. With three companions and six Sherpas Bauer established a camp at 20,340 feet and next day Wien and Gottner reached the summit. Five of this party of ten were killed on Nanga Parbat nine months later.

Skagastolstind (7,885)—or 'Store Skagastolstind'—is a striking peak of the Horungtinder in Norway. The account of W. C. Slingsby's efforts to make the first ascent (in which he succeeded) makes some of the most exciting reading in his classic book *Norway, the Northern Playground*. The ascent, says a recent Norwegian climbers' guidebook, made climbing history in Norway; and the book adds that it is 'a real "must" for the rock climbers'. Today there are at least eight routes to the summit, and many variations.

ONE HUNDRED NOTABLE MOUNTAINS

Snowdon (3,560) is the name usually given to Y Wyddfa Fawr, the highest summit of the Snowdon massif and the highest point in England and Wales. Strictly speaking, the English name 'Snowdon' applies to the whole group of mountains in North Wales north of the Glaslyn river, and was given to them by English-speaking seamen who saw them, snow-capped, from their passing ships; but usage has made the highest point, with its summit hotel and convenient rack railway, known to everyone as Snowdon. It is not known who first gained the summit, but in 1639 it was climbed by a botanist, Thomas Johnson. To the Welsh it is almost a sacred mountain, subject of many poems. By the middle of the nineteenth century it was a very popular ascent, with as many as 300 tourists reaching the top in one day; local guides charged from seven to ten shillings for the climb, which was often made on pony-back from Llanberis. Y Wyddfa itself has little or no rock climbing on it though in winter the gullies give good snow climbing. The outlying peak of Lliwedd has many long 'mountaineering' routes, and the modern climber finds his needs provided for on the verticalities of Clogwyn du'r Arddu, affectionately known to the monoglot English as 'Cloggy'.

Tirich Mir (25,263) is the highest peak of the Hindu Kush mountains, in the state of Chitral (Pakistan). It is a difficult mountain and as late as 1928 was thought to be inaccessible. A German expedition in 1935 reached about 19,500 feet but afterwards claimed that they were not making a serious attempt to climb Tirich Mir. A small English expedition tried in 1939 by the Germans' route and reached 22,000 feet. A Norwegian expedition led by Professor Arne Naess climbed the mountain in 1953. With them as liaison officer was Captain Tony Streather of the Chitral Scouts; he was co-opted into the climbing party and was one of the three who reached the summit.

Trisul (23,360) in the central Himalaya of Garhwal was first climbed in 1907 by Dr. T. G. Longstaff, with his Alpine guides Alexis and Henri Brocherel and the Gurkha Karbir. From a camp 6,000 feet below the summit they made the assault by what Longstaff called 'rush tactics', getting to the top in 10½ hours of hard climbing and descending the same evening to their camp on the moraine at 16,000 feet—a performance that has never been equalled. It was the first Himalayan ascent to reveal what a small and resolute party could do on peaks more than 8,000 feet higher than the highest of the Alps.

Ushba (15,410) is in the Caucasus, the fifth highest mountain of that range. It has two peaks of almost equal height, the south summit being only about 12 feet higher than the north summit. J. G. Cockin and Ulrich Almer climbed the north peak in 1888, and in 1903 the south summit was reached by a strong German party. The Oxford University Mountaineering Club carried out an expedition to the Caucasus in 1937 and made a new route up the south peak.

Ventoux, Mont (6,273) was to the ancients 'Mons Ventosus', the Windy Mountain. It is a western outlier of the Alps, standing isolated above the Rhone Valley, and though the naked limestone of its upper part might be called ugly it changes, like the Dolomites, with atmospheric conditions and can be a very beautiful mountain. The poet and scholar Francesco Petrarch satisfied his boyhood's desire by climbing to the summit in 1336, and felt (as most climbers have felt) the consciousness of self drop away from him as he gazed round him. Then he took out the copy of St. Augustine's *Confessions* he had carried up with him, opened the book at random, and read: 'There are men who go to admire the high places of the mountains . . . and forget themselves.' He descended in a chastened mood, feeling (as most climbers do not) that he had sinned by neglecting his soul in the admiration of earthly things.

ONE HUNDRED NOTABLE MOUNTAINS

Vignemale (10,820) is the highest summit of the French Pyrenees. Count Henry Russell, an Irish Catholic with a Papal title, made the Pyrenees his special climbing ground and in the mid-nineteenth century made no less than nineteen first ascents in the range, including that of the Vignemale, his favourite mountain. It has been said that Russell fell in love with the mountain. It is a precipitous peak, but the Count climbed it 33 times, making the thirty-third ascent at the age of 70. He spent a night on the summit buried to the neck in a 'grave' and covered with stones; he constructed a grotto in the rock wall at the head of the Ossoue Glacier, 10,500 feet above the sea, and lived there for weeks at a time. When ice and snow rose above it he retreated to another grotto lower down. This was too low for him. In 1893 he had a grotto—blasted out with dynamite—constructed on the summit itself. By that time the surrounding communes had rewarded his devotion by presenting him with the mountain.

Weisshorn (14,792) was thought by John Ball, first President of the Alpine Club, to be the most beautiful of all the Alpine peaks. It is pyramidal in shape, with formidably steep faces between its superbly mounting ridges. Professor Tyndall made the first ascent with his guide Bennen in 1861. In the course of time all the faces and ridges were climbed, and other routes invented. Geoffrey Winthrop Young in *On High Hills* writes that he had attained the summit of the Weisshorn eight times, 'reaching it by six different lines, four of them new, and leaving it again by four different lines, three of them first descents'.

Wetterhorn (12,153) rises above the Grindelwald valley in the Bernese Oberland. The peak which features in nearly all picture-postcards of Grindelwald is not the highest summit but the second highest, the Hasli Jungfrau, and two other summits—Mittelhorn the highest, and Rosenhorn—stand out of sight beyond the impressive mountain known to tourists as the Wetterhorn. In fact, little more than forty feet of height differentiates the three tops. Desor, the geologist, climbed the Rosenhorn in 1844 and his three guides climbed the Hasli Jungfrau. In 1845, finding the highest point still virgin, a young Englishman, S. T. Spear, climbed it. When Alfred Wills arrived in Grindelwald nine years later he was told that the Hasli Jungfrau was as yet unclimbed, and made the historic ascent with Balmat whereon Christian Almer made his first appearance in Alpine history. Thus, although the development of mountaineering as a sport is usually dated from this 'first' ascent of the Wetterhorn, it was actually the second ascent of the second highest summit.

Yerupaja (21,758) in the Andes of Peru is probably the most difficult mountain under 25,000 feet ever climbed. Its Spanish name is 'El Carnicero', The Butcher, and it resembles in shape a gigantic axe-blade threatening the sky. For many years it was the highest peak still unclimbed on the American continents. A strong party of expert German climbers tackled the ascent in 1936 but were unable to get within 2,000 feet of the highest point, which is on a long knife-edge with tremendous ice precipices on either side and approachable only up an ice *arête* of formidable steepness. The Harvard Andean Expedition of 1950 finally climbed Yerupaja, Dave Harrah and G. Maxwell being the only pair fit enough to make the attempt on the knife-edge. Just after they had started the descent the edge gave way and Harrah fell straight down the ice wall. Maxwell just managed to hold him on the rope, and by an incredible effort he regained the crest. Before they could reach their bivouac they were overtaken by darkness and had to spend twelve hours clinging to the ice; but though Harrah lost all his toes from frostbite both men survived their terrible ordeal.

Zuckerhütl (11,503) the highest peak in the Stubai range of the Austrian Alps, makes a nice contrast to the foregoing, being a popular tourist peak described by Baedeker as 'not difficult for adepts and those with steady heads'. Its name means 'Sugarloaf', and from the Pfaffensattel, whence the short but very steep east *arête* is climbed to the summit, it presents the appearance of a narrow white dome. It is especially remarkable for a view 'of the greatest magnificence', and—perhaps not less —for the number of comfortable Austrian Alpine Club huts to which the descent can be made and where the abundance of the food is as satisfying as the excellence of the beer.

BIBLIOGRAPHY

Annapurna, Maurice Herzog, Jonathan Cape, 1952.
Alpine Tragedy, Charles Gos, Allen & Unwin, 1948.
The White Spider, Heinrich Harrer, Hart-Davis, 1960.
Rock Climbing in North Wales, G. and A. Abraham, G. P. Abraham, 1906.
This My Voyage, Tom Longstaff, John Murray, 1960.
The Playground of Europe, Leslie Stephen, Longmans, 1894.
Kamet Conquered, F. S. Smythe, Hodder & Stoughton, 1930.
Abode of Snow, Kenneth Mason, Hart-Davis, 1955.
Brenva, T. Graham Brown, J. M. Dent, 1944.
Red Peak, Malcolm Slesser, Hodder & Stoughton, 1964.
No Picnic on Mount Kenya, Felice Benuzzi, William Kimber, 1952.
K2, The Savage Mountain, Charles Houston and Robert Bates, Collins, 1955.
Tirich Mir, Members of the Expedition, Hodder & Stoughton, 1952.
Everest 1938, H. W. Tilman, Cambridge University Press, 1948.
The Ascent of Everest, John Hunt, Hodder & Stoughton, 1953.
Americans on Everest, J. R. Ullman, Michael Joseph, 1965.
The Epic of Mount Everest, Sir Francis Younghusband, Arnold, 1926.
Mountains of Britain, E. C. Pyatt, Batsford, 1966.
The Early Alpine Guides, Ronald Clark, Phoenix, 1949.
The Victorian Mountaineers, Ronald Clark, Batsford, 1966.

BIBLIOGRAPHY

The Mountaineer's Weekend Book, Showell Styles, Seeley Service, 1951
Scrambles Amongst the Alps, Edward Whymper, Nelson, 1900.
My Climbs in the Alps and Caucasus, A. F. Mummery, Nelson, 1900.
Peaks, Passes and Glaciers, Alpine Club members, Everyman.
The Alps, R. L. G. Irving, Batsford, 1939.
Tiger in the Snow, Walter Unsworth, Gollancz, 1967.
Mountains of the Midnight Sun, Showell Styles, Hurst & Blackett, 1954.
The West Face, Guido Magnone, Museum Press, 1955.
Standard Encyclopaedia of the World's Mountains, Anthony Huxley, Weidenfeld & Nicolson, 1962.

INDEX

Abalakov, E., 240
Abominable Snowman, 101-4
Abraham, Ashley, 61-7, 130
Abraham, George P., 61-7, 130
Abruzzi, Duke of the, 111, 227, 242
Aconcagua, 154, 217
Aiguille Verte, 112
Ailefroide, 117
Aletschhorn, 116, 218
Almer, Christian, 83, 112, 145, 248
Almer, Ulrich, 246
Alpine Club, 54, 114, 136, 138, 142, 148
Alpine Distress Signal, 125
Anderegg, Melchior, 113, 135, 148
Anderson, Pete, 73-9
Andes, 120, 150, 220, 227, 248
Ang Nyima, 209
Angerer, Willy, 178-88
Annapurna, 70, 218
Ararat, Mount, 129
Arctic Norway, 68-72, 105-8, 132, 142
Assiniboine, Mount, 218
Aufdenblatten, Alfred, 192
Auten, Al, 41-6

Ball, John, 114, 136
Balmat, Auguste, 83, 155
Balmat, Jacques, 114, 140, 232
Band, George, 229
Banks, M. E. B., 242
Barrington, Charles, 223
Batian, 233
Baudha, 103
Bauer, Paul, 244
Belloc, Hilaire, 81
Ben Macdhui, 87-91
Ben Nevis, 142, 219
Bennen, J. J., 115, 147, 247
Benuzzi, Felice, 55, 234
Berardini, Lucien, 197-203
Bishop, Barry, 41-6
Bogdo Ola, 219

Bonifacius Rotarius, 242
Bonington, C., 224, 239
Borthwick, Alistair, 89
Boss, Emil, 127
Bourdillon, Tom, 213
Bourrit, M. T., 140
Brenva Face, of Mont Blanc, 137, 191-6
Brenva Glacier, 191
Brenva Ridge, 113, 137, 191
Brevoort, Marguerite, 116, 122, 145, 231
Bristow, Lily, 226
Brocherel, A. and H., 246
Brown, Joe, 36, 37, 228, 236, 239
Brown, T. Graham, 143, 191-6
Browne, Dr. G. F., 150
Bruce, C. G., 117, 153
Buchaille Etive, 121
Buhl, Hermann, 118, 238
Burdsall, Richard, 231
Burgener, Alexander, 92-6, 119, 124, 137, 226

Cader Idris, 61-7, 130, 135
Cairngorms, 86
Carrantuohill, 219
Carrel, J.-A., 13, 119
Cassin, R., 226, 234, 240
Castelnau, Boileau de, 231
Caucasus, 126, 133, 222, 224, 238-9
Central Buttress ('C.B.'), 243
Changabang, 219
Charlet, Jean, 144
Chimborazo, 150, 220
Cho Oyu, 220
Chogolisa, 118
Chomolungma, 220
Clark, Jack, 233, 235
Clinch, Nicholas, 225
Clogwyn du'r Arddu, 245
Clough, Ian, 224, 225
Cockin, J. G., 246
Col du Géant, 163, 192

INDEX

Col Moore, 194
Collie, J. N., 87–91, 120, 244
Compagnoni, A., 228
Conway, W. M., 117, 121, 153, 227, 236
Cook, Mount, 127, 232
Cook, Dr. Frederick, 234
Cooke, C. R., 228
Coolidge, W. A. B., 112, 116, 123, 145, 150, 231
Coolin, 120, 142
Cortez, 241
Cotopaxi, 220
Crib Goch, 204–8
Croz, Michel, 17, 123, 128, 231

Da Namgyal, 210
Dagory, Adrien, 197–203
David, T. W. E., 224
Davies, Rev. Lloyd, 222
Davis, Dennis, 239
De la Motte, 227
Dent Blanche, 131, 220
Dent, Clinton, 119, 124
Dent du Géant, 163–9
Desio, Ardito, 75, 228
Devil's Kitchen, 97–100
Devil's Thumb, 134
Devil's Tower, 221
Dhaulagiri, 221
Disteghil Sar, 222
Dom, 222
Donkin, W. F., 126
Douglas, Lord Francis, 17, 124
Dru, Aiguille du, 124, 163, 197–201, 217
Dufourspitze, 232
Durnford, Joseph, 159, 160
Dyhrenfurth, Norman, 41, 224
Dykhtau, 222

E 61, 222
Écrins, 117, 123, 137, 223
Edwards, J. M., 139
Eiger, 112, 223
Eigerwand, 24–30, 178–88, 223
Eiselin, Max, 222
Elbruz, 126, 137, 224
Empedocles, 233
Etna, Mount, 233
Evans, Charles, 213, 229
Everest, 41–6, 117, 129–30, 133, 134, 139, 143, 152, 209–13, 220, 224

Ferlas Mor, 87–91

Finsteraarhorn, 136, 147, 225
Fitzgerald, E., 154, 235
Floyd, Charles, 51
Forbes, J. D., 125, 147
Franco, Jean, 230
Freshfield, Douglas, 125, 224
Fuji-yama, 225
Furggen Ridge, 92–5

Galdhöppiggen, 225
Galton, Francis, 14
Garmo Peak, 139
Gasherbrum, 225
Gauri Sankar, 225
George, Rev. H. B., 126, 145
German Communist Party Peak, 239
Gilkey, Arthur, 228
Glittertind, 225
Gnifetti, G., 232
Gorbonov, 240
Gosainthan, 226
Graham, W. W., 219
Grands Charmoz, Aiguilles de, 226
Grandes Jorasses, 112, 226
Grands Mulets, 31–5, 52, 140, 159
Graven, Alexander, 192
Great Gully (Craig y Cae), 61–7
Green, Rev. W. S., 127, 233
Gregory, Alfred, 209
Grépon, 226
Grossglockner, 226
Gyala Peri, 236

Hadow, D., 17, 124, 128, 231
Hamel, Dr., 52, 157–62, 232
Hardy, Rev. J. F., 19
Harlin, John, 223
Harrah, Dave, 248
Harrer, Heinrich, 24–30, 223
Harris, Wyn, 233
Hartog, J. M., 236
Hasli Jungfrau, 247
Hastings, G., 142
Haston, Dougal, 223
Hawkins, Vaughan, 115
Heckmair, Andreas, 24–30, 223
Henderson, Gilbert, 159
Henniker, Captain, 102
Herzog, Maurice, 170–7, 218
Hillary, Edmund, 209–13, 224, 230, 238
Hinchliff, T., 113
Hinterstoisser, A., 178–88
Holdsworth, R. L., 228
Hornbein, Tom, 41–6

INDEX

Hort, Rev. F. J. A., 136, 146
Howard-Bury, Colonel C. K., 101
Huascaran, 227
Hudson, Rev. Charles, 17, 124, 129, 231, 232
Hunt, Sir John, 36, 139, 209, 224
Huxley, Julian, 103

Illimani, 122, 227
Imboden, Joseph, 132
Irvine, A. C., 129, 224
Irving, R. L. G., 236
Izzard, Ralph, 104

Jackson, John, 104
Jegervand, 105
Jenni, 19
Jerrold, Douglas, 49
Johnson, Thomas, 245
Johnson, W. H., 222
Jones, Owen Glynne, 61–7, 130, 221
Jungfrau, 117, 127, 145, 227

Kabru, 228
K 2, 111, 227
Kailas, 228
Kamet, 228
Kangchenjunga, 143, 228
Karakoram, 117, 151
Karpinski, A., 237
Kasparek, Fritz, 24–30, 223
Kaufmann, Mount, 240
Kaufmann, U., 127
Kazbek, 126, 137
Kempter, O., 238
Kennedy, E. S., 18–23, 131
Kibo, 229
Kilimanjaro, 229
Kogan, Claude, 238
Kosciusko, Mount, 229
Kun, 238
Kurz, Toni, 178–88

Lacedelli, L., 228
Lachenal, Louis, 170–7
Ladies' Alpine Club, 132
Lainé, Marcel, 197–203
Lambert, Raymond, 209, 224
Lauener, Ulrich, 82, 232
Le Blond, Mrs. Aubrey, 132
Lenana, 234
Lhotse, 230
Lliwedd, 134, 245
Lloyd, Tom, 73–9
Lloyd-Lewis, Emmeline, 144

Llyn Cae, 61
Longland, J. L., 5
Longstaff, T. G., 129, 133, 237, 243, 246
Lopez de Gomara, 241
Lowe, George, 209
Lyngen, 68–72, 105–8, 132

MacCarthy, A. H., 234, 235
Mackinder, Sir Harold, 233
Magnone, Guido, 197–203, 236
Main, Elizabeth, 132
Makalu, 230
Maladetta, 230
Mallory, G. H. L., 130, 134, 224
Manaslu, 230
Maquignaz, J.-J., 163
Margherita Hut, 232
Matterhorn, 13–17, 92–6, 113, 116, 117, 119, 123, 128, 137, 148, 149, 230
Matthews, C. E., 135
Matthews, W., 113, 136
Mauna Kea, 231
Maxwell, G., 248
Maynard, F., 239
McGonagall, Charlie, 73–9
McKinley, Mount, 73–9, 234
McNaught-Davis, Ian, 36–40, 236, 239
McPhee, Billy, 75, 79
Mehringer, Karl, 178, 223
Meije, 112, 117, 231
Meyer Brothers, 227
Meyer, Hans, 229
Meynet, Luc, 16
Minya Konka, 231
Mischabelhorner, 222
Mittelhorn, 247
Mönch, 227
Mont Blanc, 31–5, 114, 129, 139, 140, 143, 157–62, 191–6, 231
Mont Blanc de Courmayeur, 191
Monte Pelmo, 114
Monte Rosa, 129, 147, 232
Monte Viso, 123
Moore, A. W., 112, 113, 136, 191
Morshead, H. T., 236
Moss Ghyll, 88, 121
Mount Everest (*see under* 'Everest')
Mount Everest Committee, 153
Mount Kenya, 55–60, 233
Mount Logan, 234
Mount Rainier, 234
Mount Robson, 235

INDEX

Mount Tasman, 235
Mount Terrier, 133
Mount Whitney, 235
Mulhacen, 235
Mummery, A. F., 92–6, 119, 126, 137, 163, 222, 226, 237
Murray, W. H., 82
Muztagh Tower, 236

Naess, Arne, 245
Namcha Barwa, 236
Nanda Devi, 237
Nanga Parbat, 118, 138, 237
Naples Needle, 130
Nelion, 233
Newman, Henry, 101
Nicol, Graeme, 36–40, 239
Nicolson, Alexander, 244
Nilkanta, 238
Noel, J. B. L., 153
Noyce, Wilfred, 37, 138
Nun Kun, 238
Nuptse, 238

Odell, N. E., 237
OGPU Peak, 239
Orizaba, 239
Ortler, 239
Oudot, Jacques, 172–7
Outram, Sir James, 219

Paccard, Dr. M. G., 115, 139, 232
Patey, Tom, 236, 242
Pauhunri, 139
Peck, Annie S., 227
Peel, Sir Robert, 51, 53
Penhall, William, 137
Pelvoux, Mont, 13
Péteret Ridge, 191
Peterkin, Grant, 152
Petrarch, Francesco, 246
Petree, Dave, 75
Philips, Francis, 51
Pichler, Joseph, 239
Pierre, Bernard, 238, 241
Pik Kommunizma, 36–40, 239
Pik Lenin, 240
Pik Stalin (purged), 239
Pillar Rock, 142
Pinnacle Peak, 152, 238
Pioneer Peak, 122
Piz Badile, 240
Piz Bernina, 19, 241
Piz Palu, 241
Plan, Aiguille du, 31

Popocatapetl, 241
Pronin, Professor, 104
Pyrenees, 145, 246

Rainer, Edi, 178–88
Rakaposhi, 242
Rébuffat, Gaston, 170–7, 241
Reiss, Dr., 220
Requin, Dent du, 120, 142
Rey, Emile, 163–9
Reynolds, G., 239
Rickmers, W. W., 240
Riefenstahl, Leni, 241
Roberts, Carson, 163–9
Roch, André, 238
Roche Melon, 242
Rosenhorn, 247
Rum Doodle, 204
Russell, Count Henry, 247
Ruttledge, Hugh, 14, 143
Ruwenzori, 111, 242

Sackville-West, Hon. W., 51
Saltoro Kangri, 152, 243
Saussure, H. B. de, 115, 140, 231
Scafell, 142, 243
Scafell Pike, 243
Schatz, Marcel, 173
Schoberth, G., 228
Schlagintweit, A. and R., 228, 232
Schmidt, Franz and Toni, 231
Schreckhorn, 131, 144, 244
Sedlmayer, Max, 178, 223
Sella, Vittorio, 111, 236
Sgurr Alasdair, 244
Shipton, Eric, 5, 143, 224, 233, 237
Signalkuppe, 232
Siniolchu, 244
Siri, William, 230
Skagastolstind, 244
Skye, 120
Slesser, Malcolm, 36–40, 239
Slingsby, W. C., 141, 244
Smith, Albert, 49–54
Smith, Robin, 37, 139
Smyth Brothers, 232
Smythe, F. S., 82, 142, 195, 228, 238
Snellgrove, Dr. D., 104
Snowdon, 113, 204–8, 244
Spissthorn, 68–72
Stanley, H. M., 242
Straton, Miss, 144
Stephen, Leslie, 80, 82, 126, 143, 244
Stevens, General H., 235
Stortind, 105

INDEX

Streather, Captain Tony, 245
Strzelecki, Sir Paul, 229
Stuck, Hudson, 79, 234

Taugwalder, Peter, 17, 93, 95
Taylor, Andy, 234
Taylor, Billy, 73–9
Tenzing Norkhay Sherpa, 209–213, 224
Terray, Lionel, 170–7
Terror, Mount, 224
Thackeray, W. M., 143
Tichy, Dr. Herbert, 220
Tilman, H. W., 102, 103, 219, 237
Tirich Mir, 245
Torino Hut, 167, 192
Toubkal, Djebel, 222
Trisul, 133, 245
Tryfan, 97, 98, 131, 139, 204
Tschingel, 144
Tucker, C. C., 145
Tuckett, F. F., 145, 218, 223
Tyndall, John, 116, 147, 157, 247

Ullman, J. R., 46
Unsoeld, Willi, 41–6
Ushba, 246

Venetz, 92
Ventoux, Mont, 246

Vignemale, 247
Vörg, Ludvig, 24–30, 223

Walker, Horace, 137, 226
Walker, Lucy, 148
Walker Spur, 226
Walmsley, J., 239
Watzmann, 118
Weisshorn, 148, 247
Wetterhorn, 83–4, 112, 151, 247
Whillans, Don, 225
Whymper, Edward, 13–17, 120, 124, 128, 129, 137, 149, 220, 223, 230
Wills, Alfred, 83, 112, 150, 248
Woolf, Virginia, 143
Workman, Dr. and Mrs., 151
Wylie, C., 238

Y Garn, 204
Yerupaja, 248
Yeti, 101–4
Young, G. W., 88, 134, 247
Younghusband, F. E., 152

Zemu Gap, 102
Zinal Rothhorn, 132, 144
Zmutt Ridge, 113, 137
Zuckerhütl, 248
Zurbriggen, Matthias, 153, 235